Communion, Covenant, and Creativity

Communion, Covenant, and Creativity

*An Approach to the Communion
of Saints through the Arts*

by

Paul S. Fiddes, Brian Haymes,
AND Richard L. Kidd

CASCADE *Books* · Eugene, Oregon

COMMUNION, COVENANT, AND CREATIVITY
An Approach to the Communion of Saints through the Arts

Copyright © 2020 Paul S. Fiddes, Brian Haymes, and Richard Kidd. All rights reserved. Except for brief quotations in critical publications or reviews, no part of this book may be reproduced in any manner without prior written permission from the publisher. Write: Permissions, Wipf and Stock Publishers, 199 W. 8th Ave., Suite 3, Eugene, OR 97401.

Cascade Books
An Imprint of Wipf and Stock Publishers
199 W. 8th Ave., Suite 3
Eugene, OR 97401

www.wipfandstock.com

PAPERBACK ISBN: 978-1-5326-6863-0
HARDCOVER ISBN: 978-1-5326-6864-7
EBOOK ISBN: 978-1-5326-6865-4

Cataloguing-in-Publication data:

Names: Fiddes, Paul S., author and editor. | Haymes, Brian, author. | Kidd, Richard L., author.

Title: Communion, covenant, and creativity : an approach to the communion of saints through the arts. / by Paul S. Fiddes, Brian Haymes, and Richard L. Kidd.

Description: Eugene, OR: Cascade Books, 2020. | Includes bibliographical references and index.

Identifiers: ISBN 978-1-5326-6863-0 (paperback) | ISBN 978-1-5326-6864-7 (hardcover) | ISBN 978-1-5326-6865-4 (ebook)

Subjects: LCSH: Aesthetics—Religious aspects—Christianity. | Christianity and the arts. | Communion of saints in art. | Communion of saints in literature.

Classification: BR115.A8 2020 (print) | BR115.A8 (ebook)

Extracts from "The Waste Land" and "Little Gidding" from FOUR QUARTETS in *The Poems of T. S. Eliot, Volume 1*, edited by Christopher Ricks and Jim McCue ©Set Copyrights Limited 2015 are reprinted by kind permission of Faber & Faber Ltd.

Excerpt from "Little Gidding" from FOUR QUARTETS by T. S. Eliot. Copyright© 1942 by T. S. Eliot, renewed 1970 by Esmé Valerie Eliot. Reprinted by permission of Houghton Mifflin Harcourt Publishing Company. All rights reserved.

Extracts from "Via Negative" and "The Absence" in R. S. Thomas: Collected Poems 1945–1990 ©1993 R. S. Thomas are reprinted by kind permission of The Orion Publishing Group, London.

Extracts from *Story of a Soul*, translated by John Clarke, O.C.D. are copyright ©1975, 1976, 1996 by Washington Province of Discalced Carmelites, ICS Publications, 2131 Lincoln Road, N.E.Washington, DC 20002-1199, U.S.A. www.icspublications.org, and are used by permission.

Extracts from *St. Therese of Lisieux: Her Last Conversations* translated by John Clarke, O.C.D. are copyright ©1977 Washington Province of Discalced Carmelites, ICS Publications, 2131 Lincoln Road, N.E.Washington, DC 20002-1199, U.S.A. www.icspublications.org, and are used by permission.

Extracts from St Therese, *General Correspondence Volume Two* translated by John Clarke, O.C.D. are copyright © 1988 by Washington Province of Discalced Carmelites ICS Publication, 2131 Lincoln Road, N.E.Washington, DC 20002, U.S.A. www.icspublications.org, and are used by permission.

Extracts from *Thérèse*, Music by John Tavener, Text by Gerard McLarnon are © Copyright 1973 Chester Music Limited, all Rights Reserved, International Copyright Secured, and are used by permission of Hal Leonard Europe Limited.

The image "We are Making a New World" by Paul Nash ©The Imperial War Museum The Image (IWM) is reproduced by kind permission of the IWM, London.

The image "*Landscape of the Vernal Equinox*" by Paul Nash is reproduced by kind permission of Royal Collection Trust/All Rights Reserved.

The cover image "Black on Maroon. Sketch for Mural No. 6", 1958, by Mark Rothko (1903–1970) © 1998 Kate Rothko Prizel & Christopher Rothko ARS, NY and DACS, London is reproduced by permission. The photo of this image is copright ©Tate, London 2019, and reproduced by permission.

Manufactured in the U.S.A.   03/12/20

Contents

Introduction: Communion, Covenant and Creativity | ix

I. The Communion of Saints: Indications

1. Three Literary Versions of Communion with the Dead: Thomas Hardy, James Joyce, and T. S. Eliot | 1
   —Paul S. Fiddes

2. Perceiving an Absent Presence: The Visual World of Paul Nash | 23
   —Richard L. Kidd

3. Telling Little, Revealing Much: Transcendence through the Art of Mark Rothko | 51
   —Richard L. Kidd

4. A Death Observed: St. Thérèse of Lisieux and the Music of John Tavener | 77
   —Brian Haymes

5. The Journey and the Dwelling: After Death in the Musical Images of Elgar and Brahms | 103
   —Paul S. Fiddes

II. The Communion of Saints: Reflections

6. One World | 122
   —Brian Haymes

7. Hiddenness | 140
   —RICHARD L. KIDD

8. Participation | 157
   —PAUL S. FIDDES

Bibliography | 181
Index | 189

Introduction

Communion, Covenant, and Creativity

ANY VISITOR TO THE "Painted Monasteries" of the Bucovina region in Romania will immediately perceive—through all the senses— how central the doctrine of the communion of the saints is to Orthodox worship.[1] Through the painted walls, both outside and inside the churches, worshipers and tourists alike are immersed into a fellowship of the living and the dead. In their setting among the forests, mountains, and rivers of the area, the icons which are open to the sky and exposed to wind and rain also seem to extend the communion they represent into the wider, natural world and to make connections with all living things. Confronted by this witness to the communion of saints, the tradition of nonconformist or "Free" Protestant churches seems poor in comparison, an aesthetic barrenness broken here and there only by stained-glass windows of a mainly Victorian piety.

However, Christians whose roots lie in the more radical wing of the Reformation—especially Baptists, Congregationalists, and Mennonites— do have a substantial theological contribution to make to the doctrine of the communion of saints. This is the idea of "covenant," a biblical theme about the relation of God to people, and people to each other, which some Christians have made basic to the nature of the church. Indeed, we may even claim that there was an overlooked "fourth strand" of the Reformation (alongside the Lutheran, Reformed, and Anglican forms of reformation) that may be called "covenant ecclesiology."[2] The conviction that God has made a new covenant with humankind through Christ, as a fulfillment of the "old" covenant with Israel, has of course been pervasive in Christian

---

1. Sinigalia and Boldura, *Medieval Monuments of Bukovina*, 9–22, 195–97. One of the authors made such a visit in November 2018.
2. See Fiddes, *Fourth Strand of the Reformation*, 1–14.

theology since the time of the New Testament. But it was a minority group of Christians at the time of the Reformation who applied this belief to the very structure of the church, to a way of gathering a congregation.

Readers of this book in North America and the UK may find unexpected common ground here in their heritages. A definitive expression of the "covenant ecclesiology" approach can be found in a record of a group of early seventeenth-century English believers, "Separatists" from the recently established Church of England, who met in two congregations in nearby villages in Lincolnshire—Gainsborough and Scrooby. One of their number, William Bradford, was later to become Governor of the Plymouth Bay Colony in the New World, and in his memoir recalled many years later an occasion of covenanting together in 1606 or 1607:

> They joyned them selves (by a covenant of the Lord) into a Church estate, in the fellowship of the gospell, to walke in all his wayes, made known, or to be made known unto them, according to their best endeavours, whatsoever it should cost them, the Lord assisting them.[3]

Brief though it is, this account contains the essence of a covenant ecclesiology, conceiving covenant in two dimensions at once, vertical and horizontal; that is, the church was gathered by the members' making a covenant or solemn agreement *both* with God *and* with each other. There is the characteristic pledge "to walk in the Lord's ways," which reaches back to the earlier congregational covenants in a Separatist heritage, and forward to the many covenants of local Congregationalist (or Independent) and Baptist churches from the late seventeenth century onwards.

Within a year of the covenant-making in England the part of the congregation that gathered in Gainsborough would be in exile in Amsterdam with their pastor, John Smyth, and within two years would have adopted the practice of believers' baptism. Some members of that church would return to England in 1611 with Thomas Helwys as their pastor to found the first General Baptist church on English soil. The other part of the original covenanting group, who worshiped in Scrooby, were to follow their fellow believers to Holland, though not into Baptist convictions. From their church in Leiden, served by John Robinson as its pastor, many of them would sail for America on the *Mayflower*—including William Bradford—and would contribute to the story of Congregationalism in New England. North America was also gradually to become a place of refuge for other Baptists and Congregationalists from England and Wales, as well as for Anabaptists—including

---

3. Bradford, *History of Plymouth Plantation*, 1:20–22.

Mennonites and Amish—from the European continent, who had a separate history of gathering their churches by covenant.[4]

We, the authors of this volume, have cowritten an earlier one in which we set out to integrate this kind of covenant ecclesiology with the traditional doctrine of the communion of saints as inherited within the Orthodox tradition in the East, and in the Roman Catholic tradition in the West.[5] In that book we suggested that a covenantal perspective could assist in developing the idea of an ongoing communion of prayer with the saints, alive and dead, which did not depend on the dualism of a disembodied soul existing after death but which strongly affirmed the Christian tradition of the resurrection of the body. We proposed there that "dwelling in" the triune God after death, and God's maintaining of the identity of human persons, were illuminated by convictions about an ecclesiology of covenant. We placed this doctrinal proposal in the context of such typical human phenomena as the gifts of memory, the persistence of hope, and the experience of mysterious interconnections between events and people.

In this new volume, which may be read on its own and does not require the reader to be familiar with the first, we continue to explore the idea of the communion of saints against the background of such human experiences. This time we weave a third strand of "creativity" into the braiding together of "covenant" and "communion," giving special attention to the arts of painting, music, poetry, story-writing, and liturgy. We explore the various ways that artists express the sense of what we can discern, from a Christian theological perspective, to be a "communion of saints." Without imposing religious intentions on artists when they do not own them, we suggest that the idea of the communion of saints can contribute to our appreciation of art even when reference is not being explicitly made to any doctrinal idea, and that our understanding of this communion will be deepened by reflection on the arts. Without distorting the works being reviewed, we can find "indications," "rumors," or "hints" of a communion—especially prayer—between all those living and dead whom God is making holy, or is leading to a life of personal well-being and self-giving love for others.

In this project the importance of a non-dualistic approach to the world is further stressed, with attention to encounter with God through the materials and bodies of creation. On the one hand we think that this approach contributes to a distinctively Christian approach to aesthetics. On the other hand we aim to show that Christian churches have been hampered by a dualistic understanding of existence, and that their life and

---

4. See Yarnell, "Covenant Theology of the Early Anabaptists," 15–62.
5. Fiddes et al., *Baptists and the Communion of Saints*.

mission would be transformed through a proper concern for bodies in the human and the natural world, and by giving a central place to the doctrine of the communion of saints.

The book is not a mere series of essays but, as with our earlier book, presents a sustained argument on which we, as authors, have worked together for a number of years. Five chapters which follow this introduction relate the idea of the communion of saints to the work of various artists—two painters, two poets, a prose writer, a devotional writer, a librettist, and three composers of music. Confidence in the doctrine is built, and credibility is increased, through the accumulation of imaginative forms. Through this exegesis a collection of creative work is also being put together which can be the object of further analysis in the second section of the book, where each of the authors comments on the work of his fellow-authors, and highlights a particular emphasis that has run throughout the chapters—non-dualism in one world, hiddenness and participation.

We hope that this account of the communion of saints, interwoven with a theology of the covenant and reflection on human creativity, will be of interest beyond those who already hold to an ecclesiology of covenant. We would like both volumes to contribute to an ecumenical theology, and in particular to a convergence between covenant and the ecclesiology of *communio* or *koinonia*. Both these latter terms, indicating "fellowship" between churches and also wider human relationships with the triune God, have emerged in ecumenical conversations initiated by the World Council of Churches, and in the Roman Catholic Church following the Second Vatican Council.[6] Conversations between the Baptist World Alliance and the Pontifical Council for Christian Unity of the Catholic Church have identified a fruitful overlap between covenant and *communio* or *koinonia*: all these terms, it has been agreed, seek to link local congregations with the universal church, and integrate a "horizontal" vector of fellowship between members of Christian communities with a "vertical" vector of fellowship with a triune God whose life is characterized by relationships. An agreed statement between Baptists and Roman Catholics runs:

> The *koinonia* of the church may also be understood as a "covenant community" although this language is less familiar to Catholics than to Baptists. "Covenant" expresses at once both the initiative and prior activity of God in making relationship with his people through Christ, and the willing commitment of people to each other and to God. The church is a "gift" in the sense that it is "gathered" by Christ, and it "gathers" in response

---

6. Kasper, *Harvesting the Fruits*, 72–78.

to the call of Christ. The term *ekklesia* indicates an "assembly" that is "called out" by God. Calling the church a "fellowship of believers" does not mean that the church is constituted only by faith: faith is always a response to the initiating grace of God.[7]

Supplementing the comment that covenant language is less familiar to Catholics than Baptists, the report goes on to note that "'covenant ecclesiology' is parallel to *'communion* ecclesiology', and will be more familiar language to Baptists."[8] Baptists and Catholics agreed this communion, *koinonia,* or covenant relationship means that "the local fellowship does not derive from the universal church, nor is the universal a mere sum of various local forms, but that there is mutual existence and coinherence between the local and universal church of Christ."[9] The report, if briefly, extends this convergence on the language of covenant and communion to the communion of saints. Urging that "Local churches must be in visible and not only spiritual communion with each other, or else communion will lack fullness," it goes on to assert that "Both Baptists and Catholics hold that they are in communion with the blessed in heaven in the communion of saints."[10] Understanding prayer to be "to the Father through the Son and in the Holy Spirit" the report affirms that "We pray like this in the company of all the saints who are praying with Christ, those who are alive and those who have gone before us. So the church prays *with* Mary (Acts 1:14) and learns to pray *like* Mary in the communion of saints."[11]

Despite this agreement, however, Roman Catholic conversation-partners do not generally show themselves aware of "covenant" as shaping the very structure of the church itself. The authors of this book hope that ecumenical convergence might deepen through exploring the reality of the communion of saints from a different direction than is normally to be found in ecumenical reports. This is a book about communion, covenant, and *creativity.* Through artifacts of the imagination, and through the embodiment in art of human relations across even the divide of death, we aim to explore that commitment of the triune God to the material world to which the painted monasteries of Bucovina bear witness. The image of the communion of saints makes clear that this divine commitment never comes to an end.

---

7. *Word of God in the Life of the Church,* 40.

8. *Word of God in the Life of the Church.* The link between communion and covenant has been made in Roman Catholic theology by Ratzinger, *Called to Communion,* 32.

9. Ratzinger, *Called to Communion,* 37. For the idea of coinherence or *perichoresis* in ecclesiology see Fiddes, "Church Local and Universal," 108–15.

10. *Word of God in the Life of the Church,* 25.

11. *Word of God in the Life of the Church,* 88.

1

Three Literary Versions of Communion with the Dead

Thomas Hardy, James Joyce, and T. S. Eliot

PAUL S. FIDDES

Who is the third who walks always beside you?
When I count, there are only you and I together
But when I look ahead up the white road
There is always another one walking beside you
Gliding wrapt in a brown mantle, hooded
I do not know whether it is a man or a woman
—But who is that on the other side of you?[1]

IN THIS PASSAGE FROM his poem *The Waste Land,* T. S. Eliot evokes a common human experience, that those who have died can in some moments seem close to us, joining our company in a mysterious way, unexpectedly making their presence felt. In his own notes to his poem Eliot recalls one such instance of which he has read and which—he says—stimulated his lines here: on an Arctic expedition, "it was related that the party of explorers, at the extremity of their strength, had the constant delusion that there was one more member than could actually be counted." At an earlier point in the notes to the poem he also recalls the Gospel story of the disciples journeying on the road to Emmaus, joined by the unrecognized figure of the Christ who had been crucified, and associates him with the one "who

---

1. Eliot, *Poems,* 69.

walks beside you."[2] Later we shall return to the Emmaus narrative as giving a significant clue to the nature of this phenomenon of the company of the dead, but it certainly happens more widely than on either occasion to which Eliot alludes.

The question is how we should understand such experiences, in the light of the kind of theology of the communion of saints we are developing in this book. I and my fellow-authors intend to warn against the supposition that the dead are present with us *in the same way* as the living, since this does not take account of the decisive breach in life made by death. We want to contest a dualistic account of the human person, whereby an individual soul might leave an "outer shell" of the body behind at the point of death, and so be able under some circumstances to appear to the living as if they were still essentially the same as before. Such a concept, we argue, owes more to Platonism than to Jewish-Christian concepts. If we think of the communion of saints from the perspective of a covenanted community that transcends the boundaries of the living and the dead—such as held in the Baptist tradition—it cannot be a gathering of disembodied souls. We have already tackled this issue extensively in the first book on the communion of saints that we wrote together (although it is certainly not necessary to have read that former volume to make sense of the present one).[3] Now I want to approach it from a different direction, by exploring three presentations in creative literature of communion with those who have died, to see how imagination might shape a theology.

Thomas Hardy: Communion in Absence

Thomas Hardy may seem a curious witness to call in a book about the communion of saints. His renunciation of the orthodox Christian faith of his early years is well-known, and integral to his mature viewpoint was a firmly-held and bleakly-expressed conviction that death is the total end to life. His poems (we shall not be concerned here with his novels) look mortality unflinchingly in the face, as the destiny towards which life and remorseless fate steer every living being. The places which he celebrates testify to the *absence* of those who were once loved and have passed into oblivion. They are no longer here, and yet the very place with which they were associated will not—it

---

2. Eliot notes: "I associate [the Hanged God] with the hooded figure in the passage of the disciples to Emmaus in Part V." *Poems*, 72.

3. Fiddes et al., *Baptists and the Communion of Saints*, esp. 18–24, 46–53, 81–101, 131–42.

seems—let them go; the place preserves their presence, and the more their absence is dwelt upon, the stronger their presence is felt.

Given Hardy's theoretical belief in an unconscious, immanent Will operative through laws of nature,[4] one might be inclined to call this a poeticizing of memory—that all that is really meant is that the person is still present in the mind and emotions of the poet, especially in a guilty conscience, and that the place triggers the recollection. But it is not easy to reduce the poetry to this rational statement: the poetry itself constantly says more. Nor can it be reduced to a belief in animism, the sense of a literal spirit inhabiting physical place, though Hardy was interested in the studies made of such primitive beliefs by the Oxford anthropologist Max Müller.[5] What his poetry is telling us is that there is presence in absence, indeed communion in absence, an experience that defies rationalization.

This is true preeminently of poems about his dead first wife, Emma, who is memorialized in some hundred and fifty poems, among which the small collection entitled *Poems 1912-1913* form what has been rightly called "the most intense elegiac writing in English."[6] The poems owe their effect to Hardy's expression of his feelings in terms of place, and a mysterious oscillation there between a sense of absence and presence in the operation of memory. Here I want to comment in detail on only one example, "The Voice,"[7] which begins in a paradoxical sense of loss—the woman missing and yet also speaking:

> Woman much missed,[8] how you call to me, call to me,
>
> Saying that now you are not as you were
>
> When you had changed from the one who was all to me,
>
> But as at first, when our day was fair.

The experience of hearing the voice of a beloved dead person is common in bereavement, but here the voice seems conveniently to be reinforcing the view of the poet about the tragic, slow disintegration of their marriage over the years. While Emma had become more querulous and censorious of him, especially in her disapproval of his attack on Christian marriage in

---

4. Hardy had developed this view, influenced by Schopenhauer, by the time of *The Dynasts* (1904-1908). See Scott, "Literary Imagination," 273-81; Tomalin, *Thomas Hardy*, 223-25.

5. See Bullen, *Thomas Hardy*, 16. The reference is to Müller, *Physical Religion*.

6. Bullen, *Thomas Hardy*, 214.

7. Hardy, *Complete Poems*, 346.

8. Thus the opening words are published in Hardy, *Satires of Circumstance*. The MS in the Dorset County Museum has "O woman weird": see Hardy, *Complete Poems*, 961.

Jude the Obscure, his attention had wandered to younger women elsewhere. In this opening stanza he has her admitting that *she* was the one who had "changed." The poet seems to be aware of this imbalance, and doubts arise: "Can it be you that I hear?" For reassurance he turns to place, to the locations in Cornwall that had been the scene of their courting and first love, a much-loved landscape which she had desperately wanted to revisit in her last years, and where he had refused to take her. After her death, in grief and guilt, he made an actual pilgrimage to those places of their past happiness, recording the traces of her "voiceless ghost"[9] on the cliffs where she rode, and in the waterfall and cave where once they "haunted here together." In the poem "After a Journey" the poet exclaims, "I see what you are doing: you are leading me on."[10] In "The Voice," however, he is making the journey in imagination, traveling in memory to the town of Boscastle where, in August 1870 he had returned to see the young Emma Gifford whom he had met for the first time the previous March:

> Can it be you that I hear? Let me view you, then,
>
> Standing as when I drew near to the town
>
> Where you would wait for me: yes, as I knew you then,
>
> Even to the original air-blue gown![11]

The place evokes the presence ("yes"), and yet it is an absent-presence. Poignantly, she is wearing an "air-blue" gown,[12] not—as we might expect—a "sky-blue" gown. The critic John Bullen has pointed out that "sky-blue (...) hovers in our minds, producing the sense of a bright summer's day," but the adjective chosen is "air-blue," producing the impression of weightless substance, an evanescence which Bullen suggests "introduces into the poem a single note of sensuous pleasure."[13] It also introduces, I suggest, a curious note of absence into this welcome appearance, just as in the poem "After a Journey" the poet ends:[14]

> Soon you will have, Dear, to vanish from me,
>
> For the stars close their shutters and the dawn whitens hazily.

Yet he asks her, "bring me here again!"

---

9. It is printed thus in Hardy, *Collected Poems*, 349, but MS and *Satires* have "interview a" for "voiceless."

10. "After a Journey," in Hardy, *Complete Poems*, 349.

11. "The Voice," in Hardy, *Complete Poems*, 346.

12. Thus published in *Satires*, but MS has "hat and gown."

13. Bullen, *Thomas Hardy*, 219.

14. Hardy, *Complete Poems*, 349.

In "The Voice" the note of uncertainty introduced by the "air-blue gown" gains force in the next stanza as Hardy is transported back from Boscastle to Max Gate, his house on the water meadows of Fordington Fields where Emma had died:

> Or it is only the breeze, in its listlessness
> Travelling across the wet mead to me here,
> You being ever dissolved to wan wistlessness,[15]
> Heard no more again far or near?

The woman of the "air-blue" gown is dissolving into air, just as "listlessness" breaks down into "wistlessness." Again, the sense of place is strong, this time of "wet mead," and the poet staggers forward into the harsh, unyielding autumnal landscape in his search for his wife:

> Thus I; faltering forward,
> Leaves around me falling,
> Wind oozing thin through the thorn from norward,
> And the woman calling.

In contrast to the second stanza, the prevailing tone of this fourth is that of absence and desolation, and yet it ends with the impact of a presence: "and the woman calling." The same blend of a sense of a communion with a dead loved one with the recognition that she has nevertheless undeniably "vanished" persists through Hardy's many poems about Emma, as in the later "The Figure in the Scene." Here he recalls how, on a craggy slope in the gloom and the rain he had sketched her in pencil on a piece of paper that was stained and blotted by the water. Now the place itself is like the paper, retaining the impression of a figure which is present only in a blurred outline:

> Yet her rainy form is the Genius still of the spot,
> Immutable, yea,
> Though the place knows her no more, and has known her not
> Ever since that day.[16]

These poems are about a single human figure who is absent-present, but Hardy has a similar sense of a vanished-present community located in

---

15. Thus *Collected Poems* (1919). But MS and *Satires* (1914) have "consigned to existlessness." On Hardy's constant revisions see *Complete Poems*, xxxvi. On reflection over time, was Hardy making the voice of the dead more mysterious? "Wistlessness" is a coinage of Hardy's—lack of wistfulness—so perhaps "inattentive," "having no yearning".
16. "The Figure in the Scene," in Hardy, *Complete Poems*, 476.

a particular place, such as the church musicians who haunt the gallery and the graveyard of the parish church in Mellstock.

In his late poems he has the same sense of his own identity as he anticipates death. In "Afterwards" he contemplates his own imminent absence from the world:

> When the Present has latched its postern behind my tremulous stay,
>
> And the May month flaps its glad green leaves like wings,
>
> Delicate-filmed as new-spun silk, will the neighbours say,
>
> 'He was a man who used to notice such things?'[17]

So the poem proceeds, with the neighbors, the community that lives on, remarking on seeing a "dewfall hawk" that "to him this must have been a familiar sight." Or, seeing the hedgehog that "travels furtively over the lawn" in the "nocturnal blackness, mothy and warm," they might reflect:

> (. . .) 'He strove that such innocent creatures should come to no harm,
>
> But he could do little for them; and now he is gone.'

Or, "hearing that I have been stilled at last," and watching the "full-starred heavens that winter sees," they might remember: "He was one who had an eye for such mysteries." The poet Malcolm Guite points out that the statement of mortality in the poem subverts itself: the poem is about the anticipated absence of the poet from the world, and yet "never has the world been more vividly and magically present." Ostensibly the poem laments the destructiveness of death, and yet at the same time the world is being transfigured. He quotes another poet, Seamus Heaney, who says of this poem that "Hardy's ultimate achievement is forever to transform that familiar world into something rich and strange."[18] Nobody, comments Guite, could call this poem "escapist": "It seeks to confront rather than to evade the finality of death. And yet the finality of death is counterbalanced by the almost numinous realisation of beauty in each verse."

To this observation I would add that, in an extraordinary way, the community that continues after his death is recognizing Hardy's own presence at the time they exclaim about him, "he used to notice such things."[19] It is not just the world that is being transformed but—in some way—Hardy himself. The poem ends with another statement that Hardy has departed, vanished, his face no longer to be seen; and yet in recalling him he is

---

17. "Afterwards," in Hardy, *Complete Poems*, 553.

18. Guite, *Faith, Hope and Poetry*, 186–87.

19. Armstrong, *Haunted Hardy*, 10–15, suggests that "poetry is afterlife" for Hardy—imagining himself dead is a defensive way of establishing his "self" through poetry.

inevitably present, his outline—like that of Emma—imprinted on the place. Because he was a person who "noticed", they are noticing him.

> And will any say when my bell of quittance is heard in the gloom,
> And a crossing breeze cuts a pause in its outrollings,
> Till they rise again, as they were a new bell's boom,
> 'He hears it not now, but used to notice such things'?

Perhaps Guite takes one step too far when he writes "We cannot help feeling that the intensity of the poetry . . . hints at a vision of beauty that has been granted to the poet after his death, and not before,"[20] but he may be allowed the insight of a poet himself. My point is that the "neighbours" only find the world transfigured because the poet's eye, though absent from the scene, has become in some way part of their own vision.

James Joyce: Communion as Connection

In Joyce's short story, "The Dead," one Gabriel Conroy is enjoying the hospitality of a supper party at the house of his three spinster aunts, all music teachers who are hospitably entertaining friends and pupils on a snowy winter's evening. Indeed, in the speech which he gives at the table, having carved the goose, Gabriel speaks rather pompously of Irish hospitality, not forgetting to mention loved ones who have died, "absent faces" who are present with them only in memory.[21] This is the kind of mood that Hardy summons up so well in his poems of memorial. But later, one such absent face is to intervene on his emotions with more force than memory.

At the end of the evening Gabriel retires with his wife Gretta to a nearby inn, not wishing to make the journey home at night. Gretta originally came from the West of Ireland, a region that we gather Gabriel regards as primitive and unsophisticated compared with the civilization of Dublin and its environs. He has, however, we learn, been protective of his wife whom his mother had regarded as beneath their social dignity and whose marriage to him she had opposed. Gabriel is portrayed as being proud of Gretta, and still full of desire for her in their middle age, after many years of marriage and childbearing. He is looking forward to satisfying this intense desire that night, but she has been deeply upset by an Irish folk song performed that evening at the party, the *Lass of Aughrim*, of which we hear only three lines:

20. Guite, *Faith, Hope and Poetry*, 187.
21. "The Dead" from *Dubliners* in Levin, *Essential James Joyce*, 159–60.

> O, the rain falls on my heavy locks
> And the dew wets my skin,
> My babe lies cold . . . [22]

The words are peculiarly poignant. She tells Gabriel that it was a favorite song of a seventeen-year-old lad, Michael Furey, whom she knew as a girl, and who for love of her had stood out, shivering, in the rain in her garden looking up at her window the night before she was leaving home for school in Dublin. He was already suffering from a wasting disease (presumably tuberculosis), and she recalls that "I implored of him to go home at once, and told him he would get his death in the rain. But he said he did not want to live." She heard later of his death, and now she recalls, sobbing bitterly, that "I think he died for me."[23]

Gabriel feels the presence of Michael as a hostile force: "A vague terror seized Gabriel at this answer ["he died for me"], as if, at that hour when he had hoped to triumph, some impalpable and vindictive being was coming against him, gathering forces against him in its vague world." This is a more direct presence than memory, and yet still indirect, as is flagged up by the word "vague." Later, when she has cried herself to sleep, Gabriel reflects, in a more generous mood, while lying beside her in bed, that this dead young man had loved Gretta when he—he now has to admit to himself—had felt tenderness and desire for her but not really love. "He had never felt that himself towards any woman, but he knew that such a feeling must be love." As Florence Walzl observes, this discovery means that "hence to his wife he is less real than Michael Furey, this shade of her youth."[24] Again he feels an indirect presence of the dead man:

> The tears gathered more thickly in his eyes and in the partial darkness he imagined he saw the form of a young man standing under a dripping tree. Other forms were near. His soul had approached that region where dwell the vast hosts of the dead. He was conscious of, but could not apprehend, their wayward and flickering existence. His own identity was fading out into a grey impalpable world . . . [25]

There is here a half-articulated awareness of communion with the dead in their "flickering existence." Reading the story we feel the need for a more complete, a more satisfying, connection, something to bring the

---

22. Levin, *Essential James Joyce*, 165.
23. Levin, *Essential James Joyce*, 172.
24. Walzl, "Gabriel and Michael," 436.
25. Levin, *Essential James Joyce*, 174.

living and the dead closer together, and we are given it in the last line: "His soul swooned slowly as he heard the snow falling faintly through the universe and faintly falling, like the descent of their last end, upon all the living and the dead."

What connects the living (Gabriel) with the dead is the snow—an element of nature itself. There is some medium in which communion happens. There must be some means of mutual relation and interaction to join the emotions of Gabriel with Michael, so that Michael is not felt as a hostile force intervening between husband and wife but can be simply accepted as one who loves. The snow has featured constantly throughout the story of this musical evening in Dublin, continually invoked as having something fresh and life-giving about it, compared to the stuffiness of the house. Now, lying in bed, Gabriel decides that "the time had come for him to set out on his journey westwards. Yes, the newspapers were right: snow was general all over Ireland."[26] We recall that earlier in the story, a nationalistic woman friend had challenged Gabriel to make a trip to the western parts of Ireland, to recover a familiarity with his country, and he had refused, citing his preference to travel on the continent. At least part of the meaning of "his journey westwards" is a decision to get to know his country better by visiting the home region of Gretta.

But we feel a deeper symbolism—Gabriel needs also to enter more deeply in sympathy into the realm of the dead, for the snow (we read) "was falling, too, upon every part of the lonely churchyard on the hill where Michael Furey lay buried. It lay thickly drifted on the crooked crosses and headstones . . ." The story acknowledges a mutual dependency of the living and the dead, and nature itself—focused in the element of snow—is, mysteriously, the connection or mediation between them. "Snow was general all over Ireland."

In a moment I intend to reflect theologically on the medium in which interdependency and mutual communication happens, but for the moment we should notice that the story is strongly autobiographical. Joyce is writing a series of stories, *Dubliners*, of which this is the last, to recapture his memories of life in Dublin and to rekindle his affection for his home city and country. One critic, Richard Ellmann, aptly comments that this story, written in Rome in 1907–1908, is "his first song of exile."[27] Having left Ireland to find artistic freedom, he is now learning to be a Dubliner. From the continent, he is challenging himself, in the person of Gabriel, to rediscover the "western" isle. Woven into the story are many reminiscences—supper

26. Levin, *Essential James Joyce*, 174.
27. Ellmann, "Backgrounds," 28.

parties at the Dublin house of his three great-aunts where his father carved the goose and gave the after-dinner speech, several friends of his family who turn up in disguised form, and his mother's disapproval of his marriage with his wife from a country area. But above all, this is a retelling of an incident in the west of Ireland, Galway, where a young man, Michael Bodkin, had courted the girl who was to be Joyce's wife, Nora Barnacle. Just as in the short story, Michael contracted tuberculosis and then stood out in the rain under an apple tree to sing to her on the evening she was to leave for Dublin. Nora learned in Dublin that Michael was dead, and was buried—as in the story—in the churchyard in Oughterard. In fact, when she met Joyce she was first attracted to him because—as she told her sister—he resembled Michael.[28] Joyce, we know, was deeply jealous of those who had enjoyed his wife's affections before he had known her, and resented Nora's regarding him as similar to other men she had known.

This biographical detail was obviously one trigger for the story, and another was Joyce's fascination—one might say obsession—with an old Irish song called "O, Ye Dead," which was about the jealousy of the dead for the living, and their complaint to those alive that they no longer had the bodily existence they once enjoyed. At the time of writing *Dubliners*, Joyce asked his brother to send him the words, and learned to sing it himself. Richard Ellmann comments that "His feelings about his wife's dead lover found a dramatic counterpart in the jealousy of the dead for the living in [the] song."[29] It is this counterpart that plays out like counterpoint in the short story, as Gabriel feels the force of a "vindictive being" to match his own frustration at the story his wife tells him.

It is, then, the more remarkable that in Joyce's short story this explosive conflict of emotions is defused, and a more peaceful interaction of living and dead is evoked as Gabriel comes to a greater self-awareness (though a disillusioned one), recognizing that his own feelings are less in some ways than the love of Michael. The only explanation for this in the story—and it is not a rational explanation—is the creative power of the symbol of the snow. There is, of course, no reason to think that this is an account of Joyce's own process of self-realization. James is not simply Gabriel; this is a piece of fiction, however much shaped by biographical detail. The "implied author" of the narrative is not exactly the same as the historical James Joyce, any more than he is the same as the third-person narrator.[30] But the craft of the story is in leading us, as readers, to sense that there is some larger context, some

---

28. Ellmann, "Backgrounds," 18.
29. Ellmann, "Backgrounds," 19.
30. See Lothe, "Authority, Reliability and the Challenge of Reading," 104–9.

greater environment, in which both Gabriel and Michael are held and embraced. For this, the snow which covers and wraps everything is a symbol pointing beyond itself.

The critic Jakob Lothe has pointed out that the snow is continually associated with Gabriel, from the moment when "a light fringe of snow lay like a cape on the shoulders of his overcoat" as he arrives at his aunts' house,[31] to the final paragraph in which, in nearly every sentence, he is the observer of the snow's falling. Lothe suggests that "the gradual development of the snow symbol is linked to the characterization of Gabriel," and to his perspective on the world.[32] But at the same time he also underlines that Michael is strongly associated with the snow, along with rain and water generally (especially given the circumstances of his death); indeed, he suggests that the polarity between Michael and Gabriel echoes the relation between the two archangels of the same names, Michael being symbolically represented in tradition by water—"the snow prince"—and Gabriel by fire.[33] Although Lothe himself does not explicitly draw the conclusion that it is therefore the snow that imaginatively relates the two protagonists and holds them together, the way that the third-person narrator uses the symbol to describe the two leads us, as readers, to feel that this is the case. Nor can the symbol be confined to the two protagonists: they are included within some more universal reality.

T. S. Eliot: Communion in Prayer

For our third literary example we return to T. S. Eliot with whom we began, but this time with an Eliot converted to Anglo-Catholic Christianity whose *Four Quartets* offer a recapitulation, rewriting, and transmutation of his earlier poem *The Waste Land*. Like Joyce's scene, Eliot's fourth "Quartet" begins its first movement in snow, though it is a light drift in a winter landscape of ice, the hedgerow "blanched for an hour with transitory blossom/ of snow."[34] He calls the season "midwinter Spring," since the sun is "flaming the ice" as a "pentecostal fire/ In the dark time of the year." It is a kind of spring which is out of the sequence of time, "not in time's covenant," not part of the "scheme of generation." The white blossom of snow in the brief sunlight neither buds nor fades like the "voluptuary sweetness" of the whiteness of the hedges in May, but it is foretaste of spring and summer. Here then is sounded the first

31. Levin, *Essential James Joyce*, 140.
32. Lothe, *Narrative in Fiction and Film*, 132, 150.
33. Lothe, *Narrative in Fiction and Film*, 147.
34. "Little Gidding," in Eliot, *Poems*, 201.

great theme of this poem, that in the midst of life there is an "intense, blinding promise of life"[35] to come, like sun blazing on the ice of winter, though this can be reached only through purging, Pentecostal fire. There is a human destiny, which Eliot hints (without directly stating) is life beyond death, when "all shall be well and all manner of thing shall be well,"[36] and yet this eternal state can be realized here and now in the midst of time, since—as he puts it later in the poem—"history is a pattern/ Of timeless moments."[37]

A second theme is now introduced, for this "midwinter Spring" landscape is a road on the way, not to Emmaus but to Little Gidding, the location of an Anglican chapel that had been the center of a small religious community in the seventeenth century, established for prayer and contemplation, and which had been restored for worship in the nineteenth century. This destination gives its name to this fourth Quartet. Eliot had visited the chapel in the spring of 1936, and had for some while been interested in the life of the pre-Cromwellian community there and its leader, Nicholas Ferrar, friend and literary executor of the poet George Herbert.[38] The continuity of prayer through the years in this church makes it one of those places which are "at the world's end," where people who are anchored in time and space can serve the purposes and live by the values of a realm which is greater than their own place and time. There are many places like this, but this is "the nearest, now and in England." This second theme now modulates into a third, taking up phrases from the first two, but which is more elusive, though closest to the concerns of this chapter. We can find our way into it through the passage that ends the first movement of the poem.

> You are not here to verify,
> Instruct yourself, or inform curiosity
> Or carry report. You are here to kneel
> Where prayer has been valid. And prayer is more
> Than an order of words, the conscious occupation
> Of the praying mind, or the sound of the voice praying.
> And what the dead had no speech for, when living,
> They can tell you, being dead: the communication
> Of the dead is tongued with fire beyond the language of the living.
> Here, the intersection of the timeless moment
> Is England and nowhere. Never and always.[39]

---

35. So Harding, "Little Gidding," 125.
36. Eliot, *Poems*, 209, citing the Lady Julian of Norwich.
37. "Little Gidding," in Eliot, *Poems*, 208.
38. For details see Eliot, *Poems*, 989.
39. "Little Gidding," in Eliot, *Poems*, 202.

The third theme, full of ambiguity, is "the communication of the dead." In the first place, this is a vivid way of expressing a constant concern of Eliot's—how to use the tradition from the past in the present, taking up past values to transform contemporary art and society. Like other modernist poets, Eliot is using verbal forms in a way that challenges former conventions, overthrowing formal structures that inhibit expression. At the same time, these poets are disturbing the surface of language, dislocating, reassorting and overlaying images in sometimes shocking ways, and rejecting mere imitation of nature, with the hope of finding the underlying values that will remake both aesthetics and politics. Eliot differs from humanist modernists (and is in agreement with other Christian poets like David Jones) in understanding true values to be preserved and celebrated within the Christian tradition, decadent though it has become at times in its course. Hearing "what the dead had no speech for when living" means searching the "dead" past to find the values which were inadequately expressed at the time, or to which new meaning can be given in the present.

The second and third movements of the poem support *this* understanding of "the communication of the dead." The second movement puts the poet in conversation with his other self, his former humanist self, who was searching for exact use of words and clear thought but without any sense of spiritual values to enliven them. The picture that emerges is one of futility, of a dreary literary culture from which the poet believes he has been delivered. The third movement reflects on the way that history can be used and misused in the cultivation of spiritual values: "History may be servitude / History may be freedom."[40] The poet distinguishes between indifference, where the past is neglected, and "detachment."[41] The latter, as put by one of the earliest critical readers of the poem, D. W. Harding, "allows us to use both our own past and the historical past in such a way as to draw on their present spiritual significance for us without entangling us in regressive yearning for a pattern which no longer is."[42] In this way we can celebrate "dead men" and "those who opposed them/And those whom they opposed / folded in a single party." Aptly Harding quotes:

> See, now they vanish,
> The faces and places, with the self which, as it could, loved them,
> To become renewed, transfigured, in another pattern.[43]

---

40. "Little Gidding," in Eliot, *Poems*, 206.
41. "Little Gidding," in Eliot, *Poems*, 205.
42. Harding, "Little Gidding," 126.
43. "Little Gidding," in Eliot, *Poems*, 206.

Whether intended or not, we catch an echo of the seeming absent-present in Hardy's experience. And this leads us to a second sense of the "communication of the dead" which surely cannot be suppressed, given the context of Little Gidding and Eliot's orthodox Anglican faith. Somehow we need to fit into this Christian modernist concern the reality of a community of prayer.

It is in a passage about prayer, which is "more than order of words" that Eliot reflects on the communication of the dead which is "tongued with fire beyond the language of the living." In the fourth movement of the poem Eliot is going to celebrate the descent of the Holy Spirit as a dove, in Pentecostal fire, and to reflect that "Love is the unfamiliar name" behind the terrible purgatorial fire that "redeems from fire," discharging from sin and error. If we were to read these lines in the first movement together with the fourth, the implication would be that the communication of the dead is in words that have been redeemed along with the speakers. We cannot exclude the idea that Eliot is talking about *the praying of those who are dead, and so redeemed, for those who are still alive*. In this way their communication is "tongued with fire beyond the language of the living." Prayer is more than our words; it is a participation in a community of prayer which transgresses the boundary between the living and the dead. In the fifth movement of the poem we have the declaration:

> We die with the dying:
> See, they depart, and we go with them.
> We are born with the dead:
> See, they return, and bring us with them.

T. S. Eliot himself, reflecting on his passage about "the communication of the dead" some twenty years later, is reported as to have offered yet a third meaning. He is recorded as saying, "I had chiefly in mind that we cannot fully understand a person, grasp the totality of his being, until he is dead. Once he is dead, the acts of his life fall into their proper perspective and we can see what he was tending toward."[44] We are bound to remark that this seems a prosaic interpretation of the lines "the communication/ Of the dead is tongued with fire beyond the language of the living," but perhaps this is what one deserves if one asks a poet to explain himself. There is no reason, of course, to take Eliot's gloss as excluding any other meaning. Recovering values from the past, understanding a person fully after his death, and sharing in prayer in a way which includes the activity of the dead are

---

44. So William Turner Levy reports a conversation with Eliot on January 2, 1962; cited in Eliot, *Poems*, 1001.

not incompatible with each other. The ambiguity *does* prevent us, I suggest, from understanding "communication" as any simple *message* from the dead. "What the dead . . . can tell us" cannot mean direct speech, but what we can learn from them. We are not so very far from the experience of absence-presence in Hardy, or the need for some kind of mediation to achieve mutuality of relation in Joyce.

In fact, positively, all three meanings of the passage I have identified find their place within some kind of community of prayer such as Little Gidding represents. Within the communion of prayer there is a vast and unlimited network of communication, linking not only persons but values and meanings in past and present. What may be more difficult for envisaging such an interaction is an understanding of eternity as strict timelessness in contrast to the moving time of history, such as Eliot seems to espouse, influenced no doubt by the Platonic-Christian tradition stemming from Augustine. If eternity, or life beyond death, is entirely without time it is impossible to conceive of the dead as praying, or of their prayer as somehow containing and enabling a recovery of the values of the past for the present. Some kind of sequence or duration is necessary, some becoming as opposed to pure being.

Elsewhere I have argued, however, that Eliot's poetry itself keeps undermining any absolute metaphysical view of a timeless eternity.[45] The fifth movement of this poem exemplifies this subversion, with its paradoxical concept of history as a "pattern" of timeless moments. Timelessness ought not to make a pattern, but Eliot has taken up the theme of the journey from the first movement, now not with a graphic visual depiction of the hedgerows by the side of the road leading to Little Gidding, but allowing us to share in a mind which is working things out. If indeed "what we call the beginning is often the end" and "the end is where we *start* from," then there is no simple simultaneity of beginning and end. "We shall not cease from exploration," declares Eliot gnomically, and when we arrive "where we started" it will not be the same: we shall "know the place for the first time."[46] Eternal values are not static, but require a process of exploration.

This is not a condition of complete simultaneity, such as Augustine envisioned, but "a condition of complete simplicity / (costing not less than everything)." As an instance of aesthetic value, Eliot offers the example of a poem where every phrase and sentence is in the right place, every word supporting another, "an easy commerce of the old and the new." This could be a manifesto for modernist poetry, but not for unchanging truths.

---

45. Fiddes, *Promised End*, 119–40.
46. "Little Gidding," in Eliot, *Poems*, 208.

Rather, as Harding puts it, "the final section develops the idea that every experience is integrated with all the others" and, in this way, the detachment celebrated in the third movement "is seen to give liberation from the future as well as the past."[47]

We should, perhaps then, understand the word "timeless" as "freed from the limits and constraints of the time we know," or "liberated from the tyranny of a successiveness where the past cannot be redeemed." In such a redemption, "communication of the dead" plays its part in all three of the senses we have identified, including a communion of prayer, in which we can experience "the drawing of this Love and the voice of this Calling."

Literature and Christian Doctrine

I am aiming in this chapter to bring three artists who have written about communion with the dead into conversation with the Christian doctrine of the communion of saints. Immediately we should observe that there is a fundamental difference between the nature of literature and doctrine. Poetic metaphor and novelistic narrative rejoices in ambiguity and the opening up of multiple meaning, as we have seen in our exploration of Hardy, Joyce, and Eliot—the voice, the snow, the tongues of fire, none of these have a conceptual precision and all are quite open-ended. Doctrine, however, will always seek to reduce to concepts the images and stories upon which it draws, including those within its own Scripture. In our previous book on the subject of the communion of saints, my fellow-authors and I were engaged in that kind of exercise, in formulating and exploring ideas in a rigorous way. While we should recognize that some creative writers deliberately use Christian images and ideas—Eliot here is an obvious example—while others do not, the way they employ them is vastly different from the theologian, whether or not the writer has a personal faith. Literature always emphasizes the playful freedom of imagination, while doctrine aims to create a consistent and coherent system of thought, putting into concepts the wholeness of reality that imagination is feeling after.[48]

Of course, doctrinal statements are bound to go on using symbol and metaphor since it is not possible to do without them in speaking of the mystery of God as infinite and transcendent reality. The very idea of a "communion" and of "relations" in God that we have been using to develop a doctrine of the communion of saints are analogies. I certainly do not mean

---

47. Harding, "Little Gidding," 127.

48. For further detail on this approach, see Fiddes, *Freedom and Limit*, 16–21; Fiddes, "Concept, Image and Story," 3–23.

to suggest that doctrine is literal speech about God in contrast to the images of poetry. But doctrine uses metaphor in an attempt to *fix* meaning, to define and limit a spectrum of possible interpretations. In short, literature tends to openness and doctrine to closure.

What, I suggest, we should be looking for is a mutual influence between literature and theology which is without separation and without confusion, where the images and narratives of literature can help the theologian to make doctrinal statements, while at the same time doctrinal concepts can provide a perspective for the critical reading of literary texts. In short, we are seeking a dialogue in which full respect is given to both partners. But, as Christian thinkers, we do have a reason for supposing, as we embark upon the venture, that the dialogue will be illuminating. Whether we are concerned with doctrinal concept, poetic image, or story, these can all be understood as human response to a self-revelation of God.

In poetry, drama, and novel the imagination reaches out towards mystery, towards a reality for which the writer feels an ultimate concern, but which eludes empirical investigation. A Christian thinker will regard this Other as the mystery of God, and think that our very capacity for self-transcendence is being prompted by the self-opening of the mystery to us. As Paul Tillich expresses it, we have ultimate concerns because what is ultimate—God as Being itself—is already participating in our existence.[49] Symbols thus open up a way into a final reality which is already present in our experience, though in a hidden way.[50] Similarly, Karl Rahner observes that the human spirit appears to have a natural openness to the infinite,[51] and maintains that this openness to mystery can never be separated from God's own openness to us in gracious self-communication. The movements of grace and nature are always bound up together, so that God's offer of God's self to us is prior to all human freedom and self-understanding.[52] There is a theological perspective here upon the sense of mystery which is articulated in image and story: the work of the creative imagination is one kind of response to revelation.

All creative writing, since it is concerned with human experience, will be occupied with themes that also occupy Christian faith and theology. The movement of the human spirit towards self-transcendence is bound to overlap with the theological understanding of the human spirit as being grasped by transcendent reality. As long as we do not pretend that the secular writer

---

49. Tillich, *Systematic Theology*, 1:88–93, 181–84; 2:203–4; 3:235–37.
50. Tillich, *Theology of Culture*, 54, 72–73.
51. Rahner, *Foundations of Christian Faith*, 32.
52. Rahner, *Foundations of Christian Faith*, 127.

is actually making the jump from one dimension to the other, then the Christian perspective upon revelation allows the systematic theologian to set any writer's use of metaphor, symbol, and story side by side with those from the Christian tradition, together with the Christian concepts which (as we have seen) are used to organize and limit them. In our present study, the tradition is that of "the communion of saints," and as a group of authors we have been particularly interested to ask what happens when the Baptist tradition of "covenant" is brought as an interpretive lens to that communion. The question now is how the symbols, images, and narrative of Hardy, Joyce, and Eliot on the theme of communion with the dead might assist the theologian in *making* doctrine, not just *illustrating* it. The latter approach would both trivialize literature and fail to take seriously the universal self-revelation of God that I have briefly sketched out.

Communion as Absence, Connectedness, and Prayer: a Doctrinal Reflection

Thomas Hardy's subtle sense of an absent presence (imaged, for instance, in a voiceless voice), to which he gives no dogmatic explanation, should surely alert the theologian to the complexity of relations within the covenant made between human beings and between humans and God. In our earlier book on the communion of saints I and my fellow-authors drew on the covenant tradition of Dissenting churches (and especially Baptists) to affirm that this covenant bond is not broken by death. Through baptism into the resurrection of Christ, the covenant community of the church includes the living and the dead.[53] This does not mean that the boundary of death is insignificant, putting an end as it does to the wholeness of psychosomatic life. Rejecting a dualistic account of the survival of disembodied souls, we developed a theology in which the identity of the dead was assured solely by participation in God rather than by any element of survival in themselves. God, as it were, "stands in" for persons who have died, "representing" their distinct natures, until their re-creation with a transformed embodiment in the resurrection; yet their life and love within the triune God is so maintained by the living God that they can be conceived as praying for the world, and those who are still alive may at times recognize aspects of their personality which is held in God.[54] Though

---

53. Fiddes et al., *Baptists and the Communion of Saints*, 127–42.

54. This proposal is thus different from surviving simply in the memory of God (Tillich, *Systematic Theology*, 3:400–409), or from a merely "subjective immortality" (Hartshorne, *Logic of Perfection*, 245–62). See Fiddes et al., *Baptists and the Communion of Saints*, 84–95.

we did not underline the fact, this must imply that covenant relations between the living and the dead are not exactly the same as in life.

If we accept that all created beings are in some kind of covenant relation with God, though this may be different from the particular covenant made with the church,[55] then the experience to which Hardy witnesses in his poems should enable us to think more clearly about a relation with the saints that is characterized by both absence and presence. It should help the theologian to develop a vocabulary and a set of metaphors for the phenomenon of absent presence, and to explore the way that this is inseparable from places that both recall relationships made in the past and which offer new opportunities to remake them in the present. The theologian learns from Hardy that absent presence needs to be embodied in physical place, and will be enabled to think in new ways about the Christian tradition of pilgrimage and sacred space. The theologian will also be alerted to the way that a sense of guilt and an uneasy conscience can shape and perhaps distort such experiences. It does not matter that Hardy is not deliberately thinking of life beyond death; what matters is the truth of the emotions that he is recording, which the theologian may legitimately interpret in a different way from him.

Joyce expresses in his story the need for some reality to connect the feelings and thoughts of the living and the dead, which his narrative makes clear cannot be connected *directly* in a healthy way. He can only offer the symbolism of the snow, falling on all, to point to the possibility of this connectedness. In Christian theology, as we have established previously,[56] this connectedness is nothing less than participation in the triune God, a dwelling within the movements of relation that have traditionally been called "persons." The ancient formula of the Trinity, created by the Church Fathers, refers to "three persons (*hypostases*) in one essence." They did not intend to speak of three "persons" in the modern sense of three self-conscious individuals, but aimed to speak of a divine life which was rich in relationships and which escaped literal description. By *hypostasis* the Fathers meant a "distinct reality" which has being, and the hypostases were entirely characterized by being in relation with each other and the world that God had created. Thus Augustine says, in an experimental (even playful) way, that "the names, Father and Son, do not refer to the substance but to the relation, and the relation is no accident."[57] Thomas Aquinas later gave formality to the notion by creating the term "subsistent relation," stating that "'divine person' signifies

---

55. This idea is worked out further in chapter 8, below, 159–62.

56. See Fiddes et al., *Baptists and the Communion of Saints*, 79–81. For a fuller explanation, see Fiddes, *Participating in God*, 34–50.

57. Augustine, *De Trinitate* 5.6; translation by McKenna in *Trinity*, 180.

relation as something subsisting . . . 'person' signifies relation . . . "[58] These relations are like a father sending out a son on mission into the world, a son responding in love and obedience to a father, and a spirit of hope opening up these relations to new depths and a new future. These relations of giving and receiving in love can also be gendered in different ways; in different situations of life it may be more appropriate to express our experience of them as being like the love of a mother and a daughter. They are metaphors for the mystery of God, not literal descriptions, and so the test is whether the language is appropriate to both revelation and experience.

There is a communion of saints, of the living and the dead, because all are embraced and held within this relational life of God. There is a particular kind of dependence on God on the part of those who have died, as I have just suggested, but the identity of all created beings is maintained by their engagement in God and their connection to each other in God. Those alive do not connect directly with the dead, as the phenomenon of absent presence makes apparent, but only through God. If we accept this theological vision, it does not mean that Joyce's symbol of the all-embracing and all-covering snow is simply being replaced by the theological symbol of the Trinity, as if this is simply superior. Rather, the experience of sharing a cloak of gently falling snow, and knowing that this is being experienced by many others, can be one moment in which the reality of engaging in God is disclosed and comes alive for us. We can only experience God through the physical world which indwells and is indwelt by the Creator; it is not that nature is God, but that it is a sacrament of the presence of God. Joyce's story alerts us to look for other moments in which we experience the connectedness of communion, other physical sacraments.

Joyce's story also makes us aware that there are emotions such as jealousy of others which persist through their death, and may even be prompted by it. This is a theme that Joyce himself explores elsewhere. In *Ulysses*, for example, Stephen Dedalus recalls a dream where his dead mother appears, "Her glazing eyes, staring out of death, to shake and bend my soul . . . her eyes on me to strike me down." He can only cry out, "No Mother, let me be and let me live."[59] Finnegan in *Finnegan's Wake* rises from his death-fall as a dangerous presence. Theology knows that it would be destructive for us were we to connect directly with each other rather than through the medium of God's love. Imaginative literature can enable the theologian to explore these emotions and build a theology of participation in God which can deal with the turmoil.

58. Aquinas, *Summa Theologiae* 1a.29.4.
59. Joyce, *Ulysses*, 10–11.

Here the passage from *The Waste Land* with which we began gives us an important clue. We notice that when Eliot thinks of the experience of feeling the companionship of the dead he turns immediately to the Gospel story of Jesus, who comes as a companion to the disciples on the road to Emmaus. This is at a stage in his life when his earlier Christian faith, fallen into abeyance, has not yet been renewed in a conversion to Anglican Christianity. For him, the dead Christ is merely an exemplification of the "hanged God" whom the anthropologist Frazer traces in patterns of myth, and who is evoked earlier in the poem through the image of the "hanged man" on the Tarot cards of the clairvoyant. Eliot writes in his notes that "I associate [the Hanged God] with the hooded figure in the passage of the disciples to Emmaus."[60] There is nothing here of the surprise of the resurrection which is central to the gospel narrative. Yet Eliot evidently feels that two fragments of experience (expressed in literary texts) belong together—the phenomenon of the closeness of the dead and the disciples meeting Christ on the road. It is imaginative witness, I suggest, to the fact that we cannot know communion with the dead in any other way than through Christ. There is no direct connection. We enter the communion of saints only through the relation of Christ to the God whom he called Father, a relation declared to be eternal through the resurrection, and we relate to the dead through the prayer that is continuously going on between the Father and the Son in the love of the Spirit.

This is the only way that the theologian can think of what Eliot calls, in the fourth Quartet, the "communication of the dead." Eliot's poem points to the community of prayer as the context in which the communion of saints becomes actual, in which we can hear what Hardy evokes in his poetry as the voiceless voices of the dead, and which Eliot knows are tongued with the fire of love. Through Eliot's poem the theologian becomes aware of the part that this communication plays in our experience of time and its healing. The theologian works with Eliot through the problems of the relation of the past to present and future. How can the best of the past be appreciated and taken up into the making of the present, without getting stuck in nostalgia for the past or being paralyzed by guilt about the past or simply rejecting the values of the past in the name of modernity? Eliot's poetry exemplifies the complaint of Augustine that the self is broken by the flow of time.[61] His tantalizing phrase about the "communication of the dead . . . tongued with fire beyond the language of the living" opens for the theologian the possibility that the relation between past, present, and future can be experienced in a new and liberating

60. See note 2 above.
61. Augustine, *Confessions*, XI.29.

way through prayer in the communion of saints. The saints who come from the past, even our recent past, may help us to untangle our confusions about the past. Their prayer for us may redeem the past.

I am not suggesting that Eliot intentionally proposes this idea, when he writes that "we are born with the dead;/ See they return and bring us with them." The point is that his imaginative exploration of the relation between stages of time, in the context of prayer, enables the theologian to find new depths in the doctrine of the communion of saints. At the same time the dialogue works the other way: though I have been less concerned to analyze this, from the perspective of theology we can detect that there are tensions in the way that all three writers use their images of communion with the dead. We can discern marks of a self-deconstruction: Eliot puts the concept of "timelessness" under strain; at times the symbol of the snow in Joyce cannot bear all the weight that is put on it; and Hardy's preoccupation with mortality is subverted by a kind of hope that cannot be suppressed. But the writers all know the limits of their imagery, not least Hardy who ends a poem about the "dregs" of the winter, the death-lament of the wind and the "corpse"-like features of the land, by celebrating the "evensong" of the thrush:[62]

> That I could think there trembled through
>
>   His happy good-night air
>
> Some blessed Hope, whereof he knew
>
>   And I was unaware.

---

62. "The Darkling Thrush," in Hardy, *Complete Poems*, 150.

2

Perceiving an Absent Presence

The Visual World of Paul Nash

Richard Kidd

In this chapter my aim is to develop themes that I first began to explore in my contribution to the earlier work of myself and my fellow authors on the communion of saints. There I offered several critical reflections, gathered around a variety of personal experiences that had contributed to my growing confidence in what I like to describe as "deep connectedness," spanning the vastness of the universe we inhabit. This, I suggested, draws our attention towards identifiable patterns that can also serve to strengthen our confidence in an equally vast interconnected communion of saints. In one chapter,[1] I highlighted the peculiar place played by memory in shaping the way that our lives unfold within a complex network of human and other interconnections, strengthening our sense of life's coherence by providing bridges linking past, present, and future. In another chapter,[2] I focused on what I chose to call the "strangeness" of much human experience: a strangeness that, if given due credence, can also build our courage to speak more boldly about hidden depths of meaning, in contrast with, and largely inaccessible to, merely empirical analysis. Three core concepts, then—connectedness, memory, and strangeness—provided a broad foundation around which more explicit work on the communion of saints could be built.

Here and in a complementary chapter, I want to call fresh witnesses, who can offer additional weight to the heavily self-referential testimony in my earlier work. Each of these chapters will revolve around the work of a widely acclaimed visual artist. In this chapter, I will be interrogating the

---

1. Fiddes et al., *Baptists and the Communion of Saints*, 31–53.
2. Fiddes et al., *Baptists and the Communion of Saints*, 55–72.

work of the graphic artist and painter, Paul Nash (1889–1946), who over a long period of years has played no small part in inspiring and shaping my reflections on connectedness, memory, and strangeness. I will, however, be calling other witnesses too, particularly scientists and philosophers, who can corroborate and enhance the insights I glean from Nash. I am keen to understand more about the ways in which visual artists, including many not especially known for their religious convictions,[3] can contribute to our confidence in what I am calling deep connectedness and provide a rich metaphorical resource out of which a wider discourse concerning the communion of saints can continue to grow.

Paul Nash: Seer of Hidden Depths

Just occasionally, often at a formative moment on our spiritual journeying, we come upon a fellow traveler with whom we find an immediate rapport, someone whose vision of the world immediately connects with our own intuitions, and opens fresh pathways for further exploration and the development of our unfolding ideas. It is now more than thirty years since I first came upon a copy of the then newly-published, still definitive, monograph on Paul Nash by Andrew Causey,[4] and I immediately realized that I had discovered in Nash a significant soul-friend. Over the years I have collected a substantial library of primary and secondary literature concerned with his *oeuvre*, and I have seen his work exhibited in galleries in many parts of the world. Coming upon individual etchings and pictures by Nash has increasingly become like meeting up with old friends, and I never cease to marvel at the way that one person's artistic output can have such enormous significance on the life of another human companion.

Nearly eighty years after his death, Paul Nash has finally become recognized as one of Britain's most significant twentieth-century artists, the subject of an ever-increasing proliferation of monographs and retrospective exhibitions.[5] My argument in this chapter is that visual artists like Nash are uniquely placed to build on our experience of memory, and—for some viewers—to

---

3. A similar interest was at the heart of my earlier work. See Kidd and Sparkes, *God and the Art of Seeing*.

4. Causey, *Paul Nash*.

5. See, for example, Jenkins, *Paul Nash*. This was the catalogue of a substantial retrospective at the Dulwich Picture Gallery, February 10 to May 9 2010; also, eighty years after Nash's death, there was a major exhibition at the Tate Britain from October 26 2016 to March 5 2017, which was accompanied by a substantial catalogue (Chambers, *Paul Nash*).

enhance our awareness of an interconnectedness that is fundamental to our appreciation of the world's provocative strangeness.

Causey's monograph had introduced me not only to Nash's drawings and paintings but also to Nash's brief, but hugely engaging, autobiography entitled *Outline*,[6] comprising reflections based on selective episodes from a relatively short life. *Outline* was the end result of prolonged editing and re-editing, and largely deals with the period only up to 1913, viewed from the perspective of later life around the age of fifty years. It is, therefore, amongst many other things, a fascinating case-study in the exercise of human memory.

My own intuitive resonance with Nash's "way of seeing"[7] initially revolved around his deep sensitivity to the specialness of "place," the *genius loci* as he often chose to call it. This "spirit of a place" was something that Nash had recognized as important from early life, and one of the features that first drew me to his work is that I too experience being strongly drawn to the specialness of certain places. Often, they are places where I feel uniquely "at home," as life's secure harbors and anchorages, although sometimes they double as places that challenge and disturb. When such places gain special recognition by large numbers of people, some Christian writers have chosen to call them "thin" places,[8] and many of them have become famous places of pilgrimage; but I am also interested in special places that remain uniquely my own. In my experience, these become the substantive symbols around which a whole way of seeing ourselves and our world comes to be built, and I am keen to understand more about how they take shape in a human mind.

Nash appeals to me because he does not rush to dualistic models for interpreting the world that, over the centuries, have proved so beguiling to religious philosophers of many persuasions. In our earlier work on the communion of saints, all three of its authors were clear about their resistance to easy dualisms. As a visual artist, Nash wanted his art to uncover and express significant levels of meaning, not by importing them from a remote or abstracted world of ideas, but by focusing with great intensity on the real and actual materiality of the cosmos out of which his experience of a paintable world gained shape.

---

6. First published under the title *Outline: an Autobiography and Other Writings* in 1949. A new edition, published in 2016, also incorporates Margaret Nash's "Memoirs of Paul Nash, 1913–1946" (Nash, *Outline*). This adds an important additional perspective on Paul's life and work.

7. This is a phrase which, in the minds of a whole generation, remains associated with an influential book by John Berger (Berger, *Ways of Seeing*).

8. A term George MacLeod liked to use of the Island of Iona.

Nash was understandably resistant to overly hasty "religious" interpretations of his work; so, as a person deeply embedded in a religious tradition and with strong religious convictions of my own, I will need to tread cautiously lest I do him injustice. In his original "Preface" to *Outline*, Nash wrote:

> [*Outline*] aims at telling the story of the development of an artist's life, a development which, on looking back, appears to have a curious "inevitable" quality, like a line of fate in the palm of the hand. I do not wish to exaggerate the significance of this impression, or to suggest anything mystical.[9]

Later, in her own "Memoire," Margaret Nash provides an interesting comment on the implicit role of religion in their life together. She writes:

> We never talked about religion, but we understood about that spiritual protection to which one is forced to turn when everything else failed. The experience of all this separation, anxiety, privation, sometimes unavoidable wild apprehension, developed in both of us an early reliance on that spiritual understanding. I do not mean that the conventional religious practices meant much to us, nor do I mean that we talked about our religious beliefs, although both of us were the children of deeply religious fathers and mothers, who openly practised their faith in the simple accustomed manner of their generation. Both Paul and I had a revulsion from formal religion, and this was curious since we both of us had a disciplined pattern of life.[10]

This short extract is a reminder of two strong forces shaping their attitudes to religion: their upbringing in traditionally religious families, and the distressing impact of massive uncertainties generated through two extended periods of war.

On balance, I venture to suggest that the word mystical is not entirely inappropriate in a description of Nash's artistic vision. My guess is that his reluctance to speak directly the language of mystery is rooted in his assumption that to do so would imply an "additional" religious sense, dualism again, something which somehow bypasses the "normal" senses, most pertinently his highly-prized sense of seeing. This is a conviction I readily share, even given my religious commitments and, in fact, is crucial for my own mapping of so-called religious experience. Nash's view of the world attracts me greatly, and I want to understand what it is he finds in particular visual forms that open for him this deeper account of lived experience, this

---

9. Nash, *Outline*, 10.
10. Nash, *Outline*, 196.

radical strangeness of life as we know it—enough indeed, against strong odds, to sustain evident hopefulness for the world and its people. Recalling early memories, Nash puts it like this:

> There are places, just as there are people and objects and works of art, whose relationship of parts creates a mystery, an enchantment, which cannot be analysed. This place of mine [a childhood memory of the Round Pond in Kensington Gardens] was not remarkable for any unusual features that stood out. Yet there was a peculiar spacing in the disposal of the trees, or it was their height in relation to these intervals, which suggested some inner design of very subtle purpose . . .[11]

Here again my own life intersects with that of Nash in a strong love of trees, for me readily traceable to happy years in the company of my father, a carpenter and great lover of everything wood. Nash wrote:

> (. . .) as I grew up and discovered new places and later began to record them in drawings and paintings, it was always the inner life of the subject rather than its characteristic lineaments which appealed to me, though that life, of course, is inseparable, actually, from its physical features. So that the secret of a place lies there for everyone to find, though not, perhaps, to understand.[12]

That is right. Many people do "see" it, and maybe even feel it, at least in part, but few are able to make adequate use of it in their quest to plumb the meanings in a human life.

As I noted in our earlier book, one of the most tragic features of contemporary western cultures is that so many people have become reluctant to embrace this deeper "seeing," believing (falsely, I would say) that rigorous empirical analysis has exposed such seeing as a "mere" fiction or emotional indulgence. My argument is that we need to find new confidence to embrace genuine mystery at the very heart of this universe, to expose its strangeness to critical analysis, and to allow it to shape our unfolding views of the world. Nash, I am convinced, has so much to offer in helping us to do just that.

A Phenomenological Approach to Perception

Here I want to call another witness, the philosopher, Maurice Merleau-Ponty (1908–1961), whose contribution to the so-called phenomenological strand

---

11. Nash, *Outline*, 35.
12. Nash, *Outline*, 36.

in western philosophy is being quoted with ever increasing frequency by contemporary writers on Christian spirituality.[13] Phenomenologists, in a tradition most strongly associated with the pioneering work of Edmund Husserl (1859–1938),[14] are concerned to take seriously both the subjective and the objective dimensions that they identify in all epistemological processes. If we imagine a spectrum, towards one end of which empiricists put an almost exclusive emphasis on objectivity and, towards the other end, existentialists and various other modernists putting enormous emphasis on subjectivity, phenomenologists seek to describe an indissoluble dialectical relationship between the subject and the object in every occasion of human perception. As Merleau-Ponty puts it:

> Phenomenology's most important accomplishment is, it would seem, to have joined an extreme subjectivism with an extreme objectivism through its concept of the world or of rationality.[15]

It is not at all surprising, then, that Merleau-Ponty should have become such a strong point of reference for so many of today's Christian writers, because he offers a way of understanding the world and our place within it that sharply challenges two popular outlooks in our time: religious dualism and scientific reductionism, both of which have taken such a strong hold on western cultures.

Scientific reductionism has become hugely influential and is seriously challenging to most inherited "religious" interpretations of the world. Writers like Richard Dawkins have captured the public imagination with enormous effect, his appeal fueled by the seemingly successful impact that the scientific method has had on almost every aspect of life in the modern world.[16] The leap, however, from engineering and technological success to near exclusion of all talk of transcendence and religious mystery is a huge one, and something that phenomenologists have challenged since the early twentieth century,[17] and Merleau-Ponty's *Phenomenology of Perception* challenges the absurdity of this leap with remarkable force.

---

13. For example, Williams, *Edge of Words* and McGilchrist, *Master and His Emissary*.

14. The key text was Edmund Husserl's *The Idea of Phenomenology*.

15. Merleau-Ponty, *Phenomenology of Perception*, lxxxiv.

16. A continual focus for much discussion about Dawkins and his robust engagement with Christian theology has been his book, *The God Delusion*.

17. An important mediator of these ideas into the world of theoretical science was the chemist, Michael Polanyi, whose book, *Personal Knowledge: Towards a Post-Critical Philosophy* (first published 1958), used the concept of "tacit knowledge" to argue against an assumed objectivity for the scientific method, and enabled a whole generation of scientists to revise the way they thought about their work (Polanyi, *Personal Knowledge*).

I also find here resonances with Kurt Gödel's "Incompleteness Theorems" that have been so influential across the disciplines of modern mathematical physics and beyond.[18] Gödel's theorems establish the inherent limitations in all systematic mathematical and logically related models of reality. Simply put, they remind us that we humans are not able to pick ourselves up in the baskets in which we are already standing;[19] or, in this instance, that analytical logic alone will never enable us to argue for the exclusive priority of logical reasoning. One might not like religion or the concepts of mystery and transcendence but, if Gödel is right, none of these ideas are accessible for reductionist extermination.

With special relevance to this chapter, Merleau-Ponty has much to say about memory and the way that human perceptions of time become the focus for the way we understand interconnections between past, present, and future. Here I merely focus on four motifs in Merleau-Ponty's wide-ranging interests, motifs I have already begun to identify in the creative vision of Paul Nash. First, Merleau-Ponty helps us challenge a frequently assumed dichotomy between the arts and the sciences, and a prevalent presumption that a "scientific" view of the world somehow eliminates the need for such categories as transcendence or inherent strangeness. Affirming a properly reflective approach to human perception, he writes:

> Reflection does not withdraw from the world toward the unity of consciousness as the foundation of the world; rather, it steps back in order to see transcendences spring forth and it loosens the intentional threads that connect us to the world in order to make them appear; it alone is conscious of the world because it reveals the world as strange and paradoxical.[20]

It is easy picking, of course, to mock a view of this kind. From within the straitjacket of empiricism, mystery always has the appearance of "cop-out," and an appeal to the intrinsic inscrutability of the universe needs skill and confidence to defend. Merleau-Ponty writes:

> The unfinished nature of phenomenology and the inchoate style in which it proceeds are not the sign of failure; they were inevitable because phenomenology's task was to reveal the mystery of the world and the mystery of reason.[21]

---

18. There is a usefully accessible account of Gödel's work and its potential significance across a range of intellectual disciplines in Casti and DePauli, *Gödel*.

19. See also my comment concerning a motif in the work of Paul Tillich in Fiddes et al., *Baptists and the Communion of Saints*, 68–69.

20. Merleau-Ponty, *Phenomenology of Perception*, lxxvii.

21. Merleau-Ponty, *Phenomenology of Perception*, xxxv.

I want to suggest that a visual artist like Paul Nash has a skill-set uniquely designed to expose "the mystery of the world and the mystery of reason."

It would be foolish to pretend that it is easy to interrogate the work of an artist; the work of a painter will always be opaque to the scrutiny of merely mechanical probing. Dissect it on the laboratory bench and all we will find is ink on paper and oil on canvas. As the infant Nash testified, however, it was the "inner life of the subject rather than its characteristic lineaments which appealed to me, though that life, of course, is inseparable, actually, from its physical features."[22] So, difficult as it might be, I will continue to look for ways to articulate how intimations of transcendence surface in Nash's work, and a phenomenological approach commends itself as a promising point of entry.

Second, Merleau-Ponty can help us as we think further about the theme of connectedness, gathered around his emphasis on embodiment, and humans as body-subjects. "We are mixed up with the world and with others in an inextricable confusion,"[23] he wrote, highlighting ways in which the viewer and the viewed cannot be artificially separated from each other; this we know for certain, we are in this together. He writes:

> Rationality is not a problem; there is no unknown behind it that we would have to determine deductively or prove inductively beginning from it. We witness, at each moment, this marvel that is the connection of experiences, and no one knows how it is accomplished better than we do, since we are this very knot of relations. The world and reason are not problems; and though we might call them mysterious, this mystery is essential to them, there can be no question of dissolving it through some "solution", it is beneath the level of solutions.[24]

I like his confidence in the power and trustworthiness of human perception. We do this well, he suggests, because we are "this very knot of relations"; our intrinsic embodiment is a sufficient basis on which the reliability of human perception can be founded. This reminds me of Albert Einstein's now famous epithet: "The most incomprehensible thing about the universe is that it is comprehensible."[25] There is such an extraordinary level of connectedness between human persons and the entirety of the given universe. For Merleau-Ponty, it is only because we are simultaneously

---

22. See Note 8 above.
23. Merleau-Ponty, *Phenomenology of Perception*, 481.
24. Merleau-Ponty, *Phenomenology of Perception*, xxxv.
25. Einstein, *Ideas and Opinions*, 292.

body *and* subject that we find ourselves able to map with such surprising intelligibility the universe around us.

When, therefore, a body-subject like Paul Nash commits to canvas an image, perhaps a landscape, it becomes possible for fresh dimensions of the universe to be exposed and "transcendence springs forth," as Merleau-Ponty puts it so well. The following words are especially relevant to an artist with a color palette as his primary tool of communication:

> Myself as the one contemplating the blue of the sky is not an acosmic subject standing before it, I do not possess it in thought, I do not lay out in front of it an idea of blue that would give me its secret. Rather, I abandon myself to it, I plunge into this mystery, and it "thinks itself in me."[26]

This notion, that the universe is in some sense thinking itself through us, must be one of the largest-scale webs of interconnection we can possibly imagine.

Third, Merleau-Ponty explores the workings of memory and how this relates to our immediate experience of the world around us. He writes:

> To perceive is not to experience a multitude of impressions that bring along with them some memories capable of completing them, it is to see an imminent sense bursting forth from a constellation of givens without which no call to memory is possible. To remember is not to bring back before the gaze of consciousness a self-subsistent picture of the past, it is to plunge into the horizon of the past and gradually to unfold tightly packed perspectives until the experiences that it summarizes are as if lived anew in their own temporal place. To perceive is not to remember.[27]

Two "plunges" in rapid succession! In our earlier book, I reflected on the way that the retrieval of a memory always entails its unavoidable modification.[28] In many of Nash's pictures, memories from the past intersect with the present as these are brought together in new configurations, and this process of intersection opens fresh layers of insight not only into the present moment, but also into possibilities for futures yet unformed.

Before we return to Nash's paintings, a fourth theme in Merleau-Ponty's work pulls together many of the points I have made so far, and it concerns our perception of time. This is, I think, one of the most penetrating

---

26. Merleau-Ponty, *Phenomenology of Perception*, 222.
27. Merleau-Ponty, *Phenomenology of Perception*, 23.
28. Fiddes et al., *Baptists and the Communion of Saints*, 50–51.

pieces of analysis in his seminal book.²⁹ We have long been familiar, at least since the time of Emmanuel Kant, with thinking of time as a category with an essentially regulative function, primarily offering a way of negotiating our life in the world. With the late-modern development of deconstruction in the twentieth century, however, we have learned to be critical of the forms this category is encouraged to take. At the heart of Merleau-Ponty's deconstruction is his challenge to the notion of time as "flowing" as our primary metaphor of choice. It tends to give to time, and with it to the transmission of memories, the same kind of solidity that we associate with water moving down a stream, something flowing by as we stand and watch at a distance from the riverbank; what it fails to embrace is the complementary notion that time only takes shape as "we" move in it and it moves or flows through "us." Merleau-Ponty writes:

> Time presupposes a view upon time. Thus, time is not like a stream; time is not a fluid substance . . . Time is neither a real process nor an actual succession that I could limit myself simply to recording. It is born of my relationship with things. In the things themselves, the future and the past are a sort of eternal pre-existence or afterlife . . . Whatever is past or future for me is present in the world.³⁰

In a distinction made possible by two words for time in the Greek language of the New Testament, Merleau-Ponty is putting the major emphasis on *kairos* rather than *chronos*. He continues:

> It is often said that in the things themselves the future is not yet, the past is no longer, and the present is strictly speaking merely a limit, the result being that time collapses. This is why . . . Saint Augustine could demand, for the constitution of time, beyond the presence of the present, a presence of the past and a presence of the future.³¹

This reference to Augustine cries out for further exploration. Merleau-Ponty is here alluding to Book XI of Augustine's *Confessions*,³² where there is indeed much that supports his own view of time, as well as some things that do not. Augustine's parallel to Merleau-Ponty's description of humans

---

29. There is a long section on the perception of time, under the sub-heading of "Temporality," in Merleau-Ponty, *Phenomenology of Perception*, 432–57.
30. Merleau-Ponty, *Phenomenology of Perception*, 433–34.
31. Merleau-Ponty, *Phenomenology of Perception*, 434.
32. Augustine, *Confessions*, 252–53.

as "this very knot of relations" comes out in his response to his own question, "What, then, is time?":

> I know well enough what it is, provided that nobody asks me; but if I am asked what it is and try to explain, I am baffled. All the same I can confidently say that I know that if nothing passed, there would be no past time; if nothing were going to happen, there would be no future time; and if nothing *were*, there would be no present time.[33]

In other words, time takes shape within the process of human perception; we perceive time as participants and not as external observers.

After a long and detailed exploration, Augustine's now well-known conclusion is the following summary:

> [N]either the future nor the past exist, and therefore it is not strictly correct to say that there are three times, past, present, and future. It might be correct to say that there are three times, a present of past things, a present of present things, and a present of future things. Some such different times do exist in the mind, but nowhere else that I can see.[34]

It is, however, the particular issue of memory that concerns us most in this chapter, and Augustine here concisely expresses what I think we see worked out in a typical Nash painting:

> When we describe the past correctly, it is not past facts which are drawn out of our memories but only words based on our memory-pictures of those facts, because when they happened they left an impression on our minds by means of our sense-perception.[35]

This analysis, I will argue, provides a fertile lens through which to view the work of a visual artist like Paul Nash, to which we will soon return.

Before that, one further comment on Merleau-Ponty. I mentioned the existence of elements in Augustine's view of the world that do not rest easy with Merleau-Ponty's wider philosophical convictions. Augustine and Merleau-Ponty meet around their insistence that time is something we know about only because we ourselves are caught up as participants in its passing. Fortunately for us, Augustine's ability to express this so clearly was not compromised by his otherwise profoundly dualistic view of the world. For

---

33. Augustine, *Confessions*, 263.
34. Augustine, *Confessions*, 269.
35. Augustine, *Confessions*, 267.

Augustine there is a deep gulf between the temporal and the eternal, the created and the uncreated, with which neither Merleau-Ponty nor I can identify. In my own view, shared by most exponents of the "process" models that I explored in our earlier book, it can make sense to speak of some kind of temporality in God and of God in some way connected into the temporal process.[36] Augustine's usefulness for this conversation is the extraordinary quality and honesty of his analysis of human experience. This is what we now put to work as we examine some of the paintings of Paul Nash, bringing with us a hermeneutic that enables us to understand why certain ways of reporting the past from the context of the present can be so potent in developing and sustaining our hopefulness as we look to the future.

Paul Nash: Sensor of the *Genius Loci*

As I have already noted, a primary focus for the art of Paul Nash was always special places, and there are several passages in *Outline* that reveal where the seeds of his "sense of place" were sown. Recalling another incident as a very young child in a Kensington Park, he writes:

> Then, as I turn to follow the others, I have a strange impression. Away to the left, perhaps a hundred yards distant, there seems to be a part of the Gardens I have never seen before. I feel an almost cold thrill stir me, as may a traveler in the desert who beholds a mirage, or a sailor in the archipelago who, just as the sun dips below the horizon, thinks he sees an island standing to the west. "Harriet, Harriet, wait for me! [Harriet was his nanny] I want to look at something over there." "What is it?" "Only a place." "No, come along, it's getting late, it will be there tomorrow." "No, no." "Nonsense, come along, you can find it another day."[37]

I feel the weight of tragedy in his cry of "No." It was an early encounter with an adult world that did not understand the intensity of his visual experience. Many adults never seem to understand. Again, looking back, this time on an early experience also in London, he writes:

> It [the Bird Garden] was undoubtedly the first place which expressed for me something more than its natural features seemed to contain, something which the ancients spoke of a *genius loci*—the spirit of a place, but something which did not

---

36. See the section entitled: "The Making of the Present" in Fiddes et al., *Baptists and the Communion of Saints*, 40–44.

37. Nash, *Outline*, 37.

suggest that the place was haunted or inhabited by a genie in a psychic sense. Like the territory in Kensington Gardens which I found as a child, its magic lay within itself, implicated in its own design and its relationship to its surroundings. In addition, it seemed to respond in a dramatic way to the influence of light. There were moments when, through this agency, the place took on a startling beauty, a beauty to my eyes wholly unreal. It was this "unreality", or rather this reality of another aspect of the accepted world, this mystery of clarity which was at once elusive and so positive, that I now began to pursue and which from that moment drew me into myself and absorbed my life.[38]

The phrase that catches my attention is "this reality of another aspect of the accepted world." This "other aspect" is fundamental to understanding Nash's work, and rests well with a heightened awareness of the subjective dimension in perception as described by Merleau-Ponty's phenomenological dialectic. This other aspect, something discerned and represented in an artist's work, also has much in common with my own critical reflection on the strangeness of human experience; both are fueled by engagements with significant memories, connecting ours and others' pasts to present and future dimensions of perception. This is something familiar to all of us who allow ourselves to be immersed in ancient narratives of Scripture so as to gain a lens through which to view the world of the present day, a process that in turn shapes the way we feel about yet unformed futures.

As Nash reflected in *Outline* from the perspective of mature experience, he continued to identify peculiarly formative memories, primarily associated with places, and to consider how they provided him with a solid symbolic foundation on which to build a vision for his continuing life in the world. It is often remarked how few human figures appear in Nash's pictures and, in purely representational terms, this is undoubtedly true. That does not exhaust, however, all that needs to be said about human presence in his pictures. There is another real sense in which multitudes of humans are also profoundly present, and it is the intimation of their absent-presence that resonates most compellingly with our reflections on the communion of saints. A Christian understanding of this communion, a vast and largely hidden community of companions, past, present and future, does not rely on their visible presence in the field of daily experience. We may learn from Nash that their absence from visbility is not necessarily a barrier to providing a meaningful account of their real presence.[39]

38. Nash, *Outline*, 106–7.

39. It was particularly noticeable and, in my own view, short-sighted, that the 2016 Nash retrospective in Tate Britain made no reference at all to an implicit human presence

Many of the places that caught Nash's attention and feature in his most celebrated pictures are sites where human populations have played a very significant role in shaping the landscape that he presents, and have an implicit presence almost stronger than if they were to appear on a photographic plate. Indeed, it is deeply ironic that despite their explicit absence, his vision is one of a profoundly human world in which populations past, present, and future are deeply interconnected. This is precisely the kind of world we are attempting to describe when we speak of living our lives in the context of an immense communion of saints, and Nash can help us explore this conviction more fully, without necessarily sharing the same belief himself.

By the time he became an official War Artist in the trenches of the 1914–1918 conflict, Nash had already accumulated a significant inventory of "special places." Many of them were ancient sites of human community: stone circles, barrows, iron age forts, their glories now long past, but according to Nash in some way still very much speaking into his present. A recurrent motif in Nash's pictures was the iron-age site at Wittenham Clumps, not far from Oxford, a place that was also readily accessible to me at the time I first read the Causey monograph, a place to which I soon began to develop my own attachment. Before long, I found myself going in search of Nash's other special places too: Dymchurch on the coast of Kent, and Avebury Ring in Wiltshire, a stunning but less over-worked variation on the theme of Stonehenge. Having adopted these places, images of them appear, sometimes quite obliquely, in the most unlikely of paintings right throughout the span of Nash's career. Always when he represents them they seem to carry a weight of mystery, holy mystery even: something slightly foreboding, but simultaneously strangely comforting and inviting. I am reminded of the phrase Rudolph Otto used so powerfully to expound the concept of the holy, *mysterium tremendum et fascinans*, something both disturbing and strangely inviting at one and the same time.[40]

Nash's images of Wittenham Clumps[41] utilize recurrent symbols that connect us with narratives we have imbibed from childhood on, telling us to think "mystery," with just a tinge of foreboding. There are ominous birds circling over the trees; there is something strangely secretive about the tight-packed copses (reminiscences of Tolkien's legends, or maybe Kenneth Graham's *Wind in the Willows*, abound), and there is something in the implied message of "ancientness" which belongs with any iron-age site connecting us

---

in Nash's later work. A consistent assumption throughout the exhibition was that the presence of humans entirely loses its importance after the earliest period of his work.

40. Otto, *Idea of the Holy*.
41. See, for example, his "The Wood on the Hill" (1912).

with ancestors from the dawn of human time. These images quietly signal to us a message that we somehow belong here, deeply belong, in this very human landscape. In the language of the communion of saints, we find ourselves strangely connected with many who have been in these places before us, and their elusive presence strengthens our own courage to explore more fully our own place in a vast web of cosmic interconnections.

I have selected just two of Nash's pictures to discuss in detail in this chapter, and the reader will need to use computer searches to find other similar and related images, as well as to see the images chosen in their original colors. My choice is designed to maximize our focus on life and death, central to the themes of this book. It is also determined by my desire to show how, despite his deeply troubled and often traumatic life, Nash successfully used visual images to express and sustain a hopeful vision in a broken world. These are pictures that have for many viewers, like myself, radiated a power to inspire hope and build courage for the future.

At this point, then, I focus on an image from that period when Nash newly rose to the challenge of working as a war artist. From the outbreak of war some years earlier Nash had been keen to do his part for the war effort. Having offered himself for training, his first tour of duty took him to Ypres Salient in March 1917. Immediately he was confronted with the gruesome reality of trench warfare. At this time, he had no formal role as an artist but, of his own volition, he worked tirelessly at sketches, mainly using brown paper and chalks, gathering a store of images ready to rework them on return to Britain. It was a period when, thankfully, the conflict was less intense than it had been before and would be again soon after and, although he was exposed visually to the devastating impact of weaponry on people and landscape, he remained relatively unscathed until, accidentally slipping and falling into a trench, he broke a rib and found himself transported back to England only months after his arrival.

Undeterred, however, on recovery, and following a successful exhibition of some of his now reworked sketches at the Goupil Gallery in June, he was anxious to return to the front line, and sought the support of colleagues to acquire an appointment as official war artist, returning in October 1917. Now much closer to the action, he gathered large numbers of further preparatory sketches, developing as he did so his distinctive style. In a fashion uniquely his own, Nash brought together his already developed skills in landscape painting with a range of modern styles and techniques, including contemporary "symbolist" and "vorticist" influences now widespread across the European art world. It was only on his final return, health now permanently damaged, not least by exposure to chemicals and harsh conditions in the trenches, that he began to use oils to construct what have become some of the most memorable images of those years. Many of his pictures were place-specific, charting the locations of shifting conflicts in the region of Ypres Salient and Passchendaele. Paul Gough[42] compares the names of these paintings to "a litany of the moving focus": Ridge Wood, Hill 60, Gheluvelt, Lake Zillebeke, Vimy Ridge. Few of these pictures include more than a scattering of human figures, but his unique way of representing a devastated landscape, with its degraded natural forms, never fails to generate a strong sense of human presence: humans as perpetrators of violence, as victims of aggression, and as destroyers of nature.

There is, however, one picture that stands with quite singular qualities amongst his prolific output from this period. It has no figures whatsoever, is charged with symbolist passion, and carries the deeply ironic title, "We Are Building a New World."

Much has been written about this picture: about its style, the techniques it engages, and the meanings it generates. It was developed from an earlier sketch, entitled "Sunrise: Inverness Copse," which acts as a useful point of reference to highlight some of the distinctive features of this later oil. Not least, it helpfully confirms that the moment captured in "We are Making a New World" is indeed a sunrise, and not a sunset, both being

---

42. Gough, *Brothers in Arms*, 55.

recognized as very significant moments in the day for those conscripted to the trenches, times when it was particularly easy for irrational fears to rise to the surface. The title of the sketch also roughly locates the place, although on balance the oil offers an imaginative scene, bringing together elements gleaned from a number of locations associated with his sketches and memories of Flanders.

Few viewers will remain unmoved by its intense evocation of desolation. There is no escaping the all-pervading expanse of mud, once the site of lush farmland reaching across the Flanders region. Only the machinery of war, engineered and managed by human hands, could have wrought such devastation. We feel the debilitating, life-sapping, effects of water and mud on the lives of combatants, and we are left in little doubt that many, some their body-parts now scattered far and wide, are already entombed in these coagulating mounds. It is the trees, however, or the remains of them, that appear to cry out with peculiar agony. Remember, Nash had been a passionate lover of trees from infancy, and had drawn and painted them, strong and healthy, in every imaginable season of the year. These skeletal forms, all that now remains, remind me of the words of the prophet Ezekiel, as the cry goes up "Can these bones live?"[43] An uprooted log in the foreground might easily transmute into the body of a fallen soldier, perched precariously where his dismembered body has fallen. The boles of the trees that still remain upright seem to reach for the heavens, calling out their torment in chorus. All their vital organs, branches, leaves, flowers, and seeds stripped away, it is not hard to imagine a familiar wail of lament, "How long, O Lord?"[44]

What, however, is happening in the further distance? We see a long line of clouds reaching down to the horizon; but their colors, striking earth-reds, reinforce as in an echo the barrenness of the foreground scene. The comparison with "Sunrise: Inverness Copse" is telling once again. The clouds, their profile not dissimilar to a distant range of hills, have now acquired two localized summits, a little to the left of center, that were not in the original sketch. I cannot look at them without sensing just a suggestion of Wittenham Clumps, that ancient symbol so dear to Nash, representing a now long-vanished human presence that has nonetheless lastingly shaped the landscape. If such a resonance with an iron-age site has any validity at all, perhaps we are once again being presented with an instance of Nash's imaginative engagement with the idea of absent-presences—both the presence of human ancestors in memories of an Oxfordshire landscape, and the presence of fallen soldiers in the devastated landscape of the trenches

43. Ezek 37:3.
44. Ps 13:1.

in Flanders. It is this symbolic use of seemingly empty landscapes charged with an absent-presence, echoing earlier human activity, that I am suggesting we might deploy in the elusive task of imagining a world that includes hidden depths of the kind implied by a communion of saints.

The rising orb in the earlier sketch is also more ambiguous in identity, its color interchangeably suggestive of either moon or sun, a synthesis of primal forces: the gentle but chilling caress of the moon and the strong life-energizing warmth of the sun. Here in this oil, the clouds, white and grey in the original sketch, are shot through with the colors of dried blood, the remnants of life that has been poured out and now, it seems, about to engulf the earth.

It is, however, a sunrise. The sun has once again emerged from the horizon, as it has from time immemorial, and all the devastating powers of the human destructive machine have not been able to hold it down. Nash had sometimes mused in letters home during his first visit to Ypres Salient on the extraordinary resilience of nature: even the most brutally wounded trees offering out new shoots, slurries of mud becoming once again home to elegant flowers. He wrote home to Margaret:

> Flowers bloom everywhere and we have just come up to the trenches for a time and where I sit now in the reserve line the place is just joyous, the dandelions are bright gold over the parapet and nearby a lilac bush is breaking into bloom; in a wood I passed through on our way up, a place with an evil name, pitted and pocked with shells, the trees torn to shreds, often reeking with poison gas—a most desolate ruinous place two months back, to-day it was vivid green; the most broken trees even had sprouted somewhere in the midst, from the depth of the wood's bruised heart poured out the throbbing song of a nightingale. Ridiculous, mad incongruity![45]

Incongruous indeed, but an expression of that same hopefulness coded perhaps in the rising sun. In "We are making a New World" we find the convergence of two archetypal motifs. The first, an image of total devastation, reported by others also recently returned from the trenches to be instantly recognizable, one of the most convincing representations of the experience ever painted, some said. The second, this image of the rising sun, a fragile intimation of hope for the rebuilding of another future.

I find in this picture extraordinary continuity with the visionary world of the infant Nash, and the barely formed testimony from his young years to being caught up in a vision of strange beauty and transcendent hope. I also

---

45. Causey, *Paul Nash*, 67.

find in this picture a striking illustration of those key motifs in Merleau-Ponty's phenomenological account of perception. Nash gives us access to an unparalleled moment when stark materiality and hopeful humanity intersect. Here is an artist, already shaped by memories of a better world, finding his vision synthesizing into fresh realizations of possibility, and of hopefulness not entirely overwhelmed.

A Phenomenology of Belonging

Before we explore a second image in detail, I want to tease out further this phenomenon of "special places," and also other forms, that in some way exercise a strange power to grasp us and fuel our hope. How does this work? Are there common themes at play that it might help us to explore? I think there are.

As a baseline, I suggest that much of our resonance with certain places and with natural forms more generally, trees for example, is a clear indicator of the degree to which our human "being" is somehow rooted, interconnected, with every other manifestation of "being" in this gloriously diverse universe. There is, we might say, a fundamental communion of all "beings", a broad and deep communion of universal proportions, that underpins our more focused attention on a communion of "saints." There is, as many theologians and philosophers have told us, a deep "analogy of being." There are, as it were, themes at play in the inner choreography of the material universe, which can surface anywhere, and which we recognize, even if unconsciously, when from time to time something triggers a link that comes alive within us. Familiar patterns recur at every level of the cosmos: from the wheel-like formations of nebulae, through the orbital arrays of planetary systems, the swirling of spirals of tidal currents and tropical storms, the radial and web-like configurations of fauna and flora, through to the very structure of the atoms and the sub-atomic particles that comprise them: wheels within wheels, nested like layers of a Russian doll.

One very well-documented dimension of this ubiquitous patterning concerns the pervasive occurrence of a number, known since ancient Greece, and usually represented by the Greek letter *phi*. Its extraordinary prevalence seems to suggest that it signals something of the deep connectedness I am struggling to describe, and it has played no small part in the history of art. It is a number with uniquely connective properties. Strangely, and seemingly without our deliberate choosing, we humans often experience a profound sense of comfort, an at-homeness, when our eye is drawn to a point in a picture that is situated such that its distance from the edges is in the proportions of *phi*, and we intuitively warm to things that are shaped by these proportions too. It is no coincidence, for example, that the millions of credit and other valuable cards that now fill the wallets all have the same dimensions (85.60mm x 53.98mm) in the proportion of *phi*, being approximately 1.618. Even artists who have become otherwise famous for their subtlety of composition have exploited this ratio with shameless repetition.

Phi is a number that arises across a range of mathematical processes. Mathematicians associate it with the Fibonacci Series, generated by a mathematical formula characterized by simplicity and symmetrical beauty. Biologists have mapped its recurrence across the natural world: in the patterns of seeds in sunflower heads, in the shape of the nautilus shell, and so on. It seems that this same mathematical motif, growing out of fundamentally simple symmetries, pervades the world, including our own physiological and psychological structures, both our bodies and our minds. Of itself, of course, this does not *prove* anything at all of much empirical significance; but approached phenomenologically, it could be thought deeply important that humans, embodied-subjects fully sharing the materiality of this universe, unselfconsciously delight in shapes and patterns that relate to this number, shells and leaves, and that we find such a heart-warming consolation in their presence.

I am attracted to the idea that our being in the presence of forms that have such deep-rooted levels of correlation with elements in our own form—formal connections you might say—are hugely significant, especially in their power to generate feelings of beauty, and our sense of belonging and well-being in the world. It seems that a "fundamental communion of beings," to which I have already drawn attention, makes itself known as a human experience of interconnectedness with the whole gamut of the non-human as well as human world. On such a model, our interest in a "communion of saints" becomes a particular outworking of a much larger communion spanning the whole created order.

My own experience suggests that by living in certain natural environments for sustained periods of time, our sensory memory enables us to "make friends" with the forms and basic lineaments of the underlying structure. Almost without our knowing it, unrecognized elements of geology, speciation, and overall landscape formation become normatively beautiful for us. After twenty years in the vicinity of Derbyshire's White Peak, for example, I find myself profoundly at-home in its limestone configurations; much more, I hasten to add, than simply because it offers an abundance of images that as artist I like to paint. That said, in the skilled hands of Paul Nash, it is precisely landscapes like these that he framed so as to capture just those defining-structures that make us feel at home in our own land, part of what gained him a reputation for being so quintessentially English.

This, however, is only a point of entry into a much wider exploration of forms that move and challenge us. Why is it, I ask myself, that so many people are attracted by the movement of breaking waves, such that they can sit on the shore transfixed for hours, finding the experience strangely therapeutic? Why are we drawn to see beauty in the seemingly random patterns of leaves that fall with autumn winds on a lonely landscape, and the finely sculpted configurations of sand that gather into dunes, anchored by wild grasses on an otherwise desert scene? What these examples have in common, and I venture to suggest significantly so, is the fact that all these forms are generated by a wild and dramatic interplay between chaotic and ordering factors.

Using as an example the way that autumn leaves fall, shaping such attractive patterns as they land on the ground, the factors are easy to name. On the one hand, there are wild and unpredictable forces: wind and assorted weather, and the unpredictable chemical changes in individual leaf stems leading to the potential of leaf-fall. On the other hand, there are the utterly reliable contours of gravity that give order to the downward movement of each and every leaf, and there is the steady beat of an underlying genetic time-clock, naturally synchronized across the tree. The result of this meeting of chaotic and ordering principles is a pattern of extraordinary beauty, a perfection some would say, a fine-graded distribution of shapes and colors. Perhaps most surprising of all is that we humans can detect even the slightest intrusion by "abnormal" factors. Should a human intervene, making the smallest rearrangement, our suspicions are instantly roused; we immediately recognize when what we think of as "natural" beauty has been compromised. Why should this be? On reflection, it is not at all obvious that it should be so. Again, I want to point to a deep correlation between the ordering of the world around us and the ordering of our own embodied lives. I wonder if when we recognize, perhaps unconsciously, the comfortably reliable outcomes of a collision between chaotic and ordering forces, we warm to them because, at some level, they also give us courage about something not dissimilar at work in our own lives, supporting a small but significant promise that all is not lost; when an artist like Nash captures a moment in which, despite all the chaos of trench warfare, order and security are still manifest, we are heartened and inspired. Is this not a vital clue to something that Nash did for his fellow combatants and countrymen in his reporting of the battle for the trenches?

Finally here, I want to connect this exploration of belonging and its attendant hopefulness to the work of the pioneering sociobiologist, Edward

O Wilson.[46] In 1984, late in a life rich in experience, Wilson published a remarkable book under the title *Biophilia*,[47] its argument suggesting a further cluster of metaphorical resources with which to explore the way that humans are predisposed to respond to the natural world and the forms of its landscape. A major theme in his earlier work in the emergent field of sociobiology had been to show that previously unexplained elements of altruistic behavior make perfectly good sense when viewed as part of the elaborate outworking of biological evolution. In *Biophilia*, this approach is extended to consider how our active, caring responses to certain environments and to species other than our own might also be deeply rooted in evolutionary processes. We emerge from millions of years in the making, he suggests, hard-wired for *biophilia*, a "love of life." Because, as various eco-sciences have now demonstrated with such clarity, all life-forms are to some degree mutually interdependent for survival—there is an intrinsic interconnectedness in life itself—evolutionary processes have naturally selected for those creatures that will also care for the survival of their interdependent neighbors. This is the same interconnectedness of life and loves that we are here exploring through the image of the communion of saints. Wilson's description of another level of interconnectedness across the world might not, of course, *prove* anything of itself about either the past or the future; as I have written elsewhere, I myself am not at all interested in "explaining away."[48] I am, however, interested in offering explanatory models that by their very articulation further shape the ways in which we perceive and actualize our presence in the world.

In a chapter entitled, "The Right Place,"[49] Wilson offers a proposal with strong resonances to Nash's and my own love of "special places." He directs us to consider the preferred environments in which *homo sapiens* first evolved on this planet and to ask whether these in any way still inform the preferences we favor today, expressed in aesthetic choices that influence our judgments concerning habitat, architecture, and decoration. Wilson has no hesitation in identifying the terrain we know as "savanna," intermediate between forest and desert, as the primary location of human origins. More tentatively, he then identifies three key features that might constitute a bridge between ancient and modern times:

---

46. His prize-winning research, published under the titles *On Human Nature* (1978) and *The Ants* (1990), and his monumental text *Sociobiology: The New Synthesis* (1980) have been an inspiration for scientists working in a wide range of human sciences.

47. Wilson, *Biophilia*.

48. For example, Fiddes et al., *Baptists and the Communion of Saints*, 46.

49. Wilson, *Biophilia*, 103–18.

First, the savanna by itself, with nothing more added, offered an abundance of animal and plant food to which the omnivorous hominids were well adapted, as well as the clear view needed to detect animals and rival bands at long distances. Second, some topographical relief was desirable. Cliffs, hillocks, and ridges were the vantage points from which to make still more distant surveillance, while their overhangs and caves served as shelters at night. During longer marches, the scattered clumps of trees provided auxiliary retreats sheltering bodies of drinking water. Finally, lakes and rivers offered fish, mollusks and new kinds of edible plants. Because few natural enemies of man can cross deep water, the shorelines became natural perimeters of defense.

Put these three elements together: it seems that whenever people are given a free choice, they move to tree-studded land on prominences overlooking water.[50]

The White Peak scores at least two out of three here, as also Wittenham Clumps. Again, however, I emphasize that my aim is not explanation, but merely intimations of possible factors burrowing away, deep in the human psyche. I do emerge thinking that Nash is, at some level, an artist who manages to connect with many of these things, and these are some of the dimensions that give his work such wide appeal.

Returning just once more to the vision that Nash explored in "We are Making a New World," a devastated scene shot through with intimations of potential rebirth, I begin to recognize in Wilson's use of the term *biophilia* something that adds to my understanding of why such a picture is able to generate hopefulness in me, a passionate longing for the survival of an environment and its accompanying species. Nash has made explicit in his image something to which we are intrinsically committed, a special kind of beauty, the beauty of a secure home and of hopeful interconnectedness, and we warm instinctively to the cause.

Nash: Ever Tenacious in Hope

For my second choice of picture, we come to an image from the final months of Nash's life when, with lengthy retrospect, he pulled many of his most important symbolic forms into a single picture, "Landscape of the Vernal Equinox."

---

50. Wilson, *Biophilia*, 110.

This is just one of a series of highly acclaimed oils painted in the last phase of Nash's troubled life. Three images from this period draw on similar themes, and all three can easily be viewed online in their original color. "Landscape of the Vernal Equinox," "Landscape of the Summer Solstice," and "Landscape of the Moon's Last Phase" were all painted in 1943–1944 when Nash was in little doubt that his life was drawing to an imminent end. Endless coughing, not least originating from damage to his lungs years before in the trenches of Passhendaele, increasingly limited his movements. Often he remained indoors, needing to paint seated rather than standing (as he would have preferred), his heart now showing the medical signs of significant strain.

All these images originate from visits to the home of a friend on Boars Hill, not far from Oxford. Although the groundwork for his pictures all began on location, the paintings were only completed on return to his own home. None of these pictures offers a literal representation of the view from the balcony on Boars Hill that looked out across the countryside. We know more detail of the actual view from a work by Stanley Spencer, who also stayed at this house, than ever we will from Nash.[51] Nash has constructed imaginative variations on a basic theme. "Landscape of the Vernal Equinox" was completed in three versions, each with its own minor distinctives. I have

51. Stanley Spencer, "Oxfordshire Landscape" (1939).

chosen this version, now belonging to the Royal Collection, to discuss because of striking symbols in the foreground, absent from the other two.

Nash was by this time highly dependent on his use of binoculars with which to survey the scene from his window. Seen through binoculars, his old favorite, Wittenham Clumps, appears greatly enlarged, a deliberate effect that makes its own significant contribution to his composition. The near and the far, foreground plants and distant hills are brought into focus in a single picture plane, a fusion of horizons you might say,[52] suggesting near equal significance to all of its several parts. This is not an effect that is natural for the naked human eye. Our eyes have to choose, tending to focus either on the foreground or, relaxing, on the distance and infinity. It was only with the invention of the camera that it became possible for us to see the near and the far in simultaneous focus, especially when a photograph is taken in strong light with a small aperture, increasing what photographers call the "depth of field."[53] A photographic print enables our eyes to focus on the single plane of the paper, and we are able to take in the entire image at a single viewing. This effect is extremely significant for artistic composition, and it opens a way to talk at more length about the impact of this particular picture. Seeing the near and the far in single focus undoubtedly contributes to our largely unconscious sense of strangeness when we view a picture of this kind. It becomes one of the ways that, in these late works, Nash succeeds in making visible an extraordinary range of interconnections, bringing together in a new unity elements that had remained in unresolved tensions in so much of his earlier work. Here again we find Nash encouraging us to imagine a world rich with interconnected absent-presences—not just the human presences that help us to conceive a communion of saints, but nonhuman presences that prompt us to see this human life deeply embedded in the entirety of the world.

As indicated earlier, I selected this image from amongst the three possible versions of "Landscape of the Vernal Equinox," because it is the only one to include the snake, to the left, and the crudely hand-built frame, to the right, in an extended foreground. These, at first sight incongruous additions, develop a theme similarly at work further back in the picture; namely, the act of bringing together in one connected composition symbolic opposing forces. The significance of the vernal equinox is that it is the day (March 21 or 22) each year when day and night are of equal length; or, putting that another way, both moon and sun take precedence for equal periods. As in

---

52. A term associated with the hermeneutical method of Hans-Georg Gadamer.

53. My co-writer Graham Sparkes developed this concept in relation to a picture by Georgia O'Keeffe entitled "From the Faraway Nearby" in Kidd and Sparkes, *God and the Art of Seeing*.

the sketch "Sunrise: Inverness Copse," we find again a meeting of polarities symbolized by the moon and sun. This picture, the left lit by the cool light of the white moon, the right illuminated by the golden warmth of a reddened sun, finds new harmony in the equivalence of the equinox. The snake, ancient symbol of primitive energy and volatility, here associated with the moon, stands in counterpoint to the alien frame-structure, the product of rational human intervention, associated with the light of the sun. Some writers have made much of the fact that Nash had recently been reading with evident enthusiasm James Frazer's *Golden Bough*; they make much of the legendary association between the "golden" branches of dying mistletoe and hopes for rebirth and new life.[54] All his critics have been keen to explore ways in which so much of Nash's tortured life finds expression through the lens of binary conflicts in this picture, dating back to traumatic experiences in childhood: the early loss of his mother that he felt so sharply; his ongoing struggle to relate comfortably to women; a long-standing inner conflict around issues of life and death; and, most obviously, the horrors to which he found himself exposed on the battlefields of two wars.

I myself find in this late picture, as Nash wrestles with the certainty of approaching death, signs of a massive achievement of inner reconciliation. To use the phenomenological categories that we explored in the work of Merleau-Ponty, it suggests an authentic dialectic between subjective vision, the creative imagination of the artist, and objective realities gathered from long exposure to the material reality of the visible world. It also suggests a gathering of moments connecting across long lengths of time: the artist's time, from birth to death; and the landscape's time, from ancient days when earthworks were thrown up on the Oxfordshire hills up to and including Nash's own present. Causey writes of this picture:

> Just as in 1912 Wittenham had offered a link between himself and the remote past—in Macleod's phrase 'ancestral nearness'—so now in 1943 Nash was trying to draw upon his own past some thirty years distant, and as far from him in time as the Clumps were from Boars Hill in space, and link it with his present and possibly future.[55]

This is a creative vision suggesting inner and outer reconciliation, genuine connectedness, without loss of distinctions—and all achieved in a very human way without the explicit appearance of a single human figure. Here we see Nash pushing to the limit his ability through the painted image

---

54. This is especially strong in the biography by James King (King, *Interior Landscapes*, 209).

55. Causey, *Paul Nash*, 330.

to evoke a wide network of absent human presences, and this project is a potentially fertile gift for us as as theologians as we aim to create imaginative metaphors through which to articulate a communion of saints.

As we have noted earlier, Nash wrestled all his life with the challenge to express matters of profound human importance using only non-figurative, landscape forms. As a young man he sometimes filled his skies with mystical figures, godlike or angelic in form: most famously in his "Vision at Evening" (1911), where a ghostly female form stretches across the sky over a rural landscape; and again his "Angel and Devil" (1910), where a mythical angel and demon bird fight their battles against a starlit sky over a dense patch of woodland. These pictures belonged to days when Nash was still strongly influenced by the forms and techniques we associate with the pre-Raphaelites, especially Dante Gabriel Rossetti. Gradually, with the passing of years, these mythical figures disappeared from his images; without, however, losing an overwhelming sense of human presence, strangely present by their very absence in the actual form of the landscape. It is fascinating to find Merleau-Ponty describing, and commending, just this same development in a reflection on the work of Cézanne—almost every word fitting the work of Nash equally well:

> The thing and the world, we said, are presented to perceptual communication like a familiar face whose expression is immediately understood. But a face in fact only expresses something through the arrangement of colors and lights that compose it; the sense of this facial expression is not behind the eyes, but upon them, and a touch of color more or less is enough for the painter to transform the facial expression of a portrait. In the works of his youth, Cézanne sought to paint the expression first, and this is why he missed it. He gradually learned that expression is the language of the thing itself, and is born of its configuration. His painting is an attempt to connect with the physiognomy things and faces through the complete restitution of their sensible configuration. That is what nature effortlessly accomplishes every moment. And this is why Cézanne's landscapes are "those of a pre-world where there are still no men."[56]

In "Landscape of the Vernal Equinox," this is achieved with extraordinary success and the effect is beguiling. Here is an artist at the height of his powers, handling a wide color palette with delicacy and beauty, giving voice to profound insights accumulated over a lifetime of inner and outer struggles, all pointing towards a holistic vision. It gives strong testimony to

---

56. Merleau-Ponty, *Phenomenology of Perception*, 336–37.

the deep interconnectedness of all things, human and non-human, paving the way for a relatively reconciled engagement with death—which came to him in his sleep in the night on July 10, 1946.

The "Landscape of the Vernal Equinox" is a treasure-trove of symbols culled from a lifetime of insightful observation. Most of Nash's oils from this period include a dark tunnel-like entrance into the forest, a narrow entrance at the meeting point of many converging lines, an entry into the secure place where, still hopeful, he will make his lasting home. The route is lined with trees, some moon-lit, others lit by the sun, a path guarded by upright fir trees, standing as markers and guardians on the pilgrim's way. Grateful for his hopeful vision, I was moved to read these words towards the end of Margaret Nash's very personal "Memoire":

> I am thankful to say that almost his last words to me on the evening before he died in the early hours of the morning, assured me that life had been good for him in the last few years, and that he had been able to extract what he needed from it to feed his imagination and to carry on the unceasing creation which had been his goal from boyhood.[57]

It is not easy to give an adequate account of the impact this and others of Nash's pictures have had on my own life. At some deep level he inspires confidence in my own spirit that there is a profound interconnected coherence in the universe. He provides me with visual assurance that there is indeed sense in the midst of all this strangeness, a transcendent mystery that is secure and available to be embraced at the end of a lifetime's endeavor. He also provides me with a much-needed reminder that hope for the future is primarily energized by reflection on the past. As a Christian pilgrim, I live my life out of the shared memory of a vast communion of fellow travelers, many of whom would summarize their future hope for "life after life" in words that go something like this: given my experience of God's goodness formed and sustained throughout the days of life, I cannot easily believe that such goodness and sustaining love will simply cease in the single moment of death. Nash, then, joins other witnesses in strengthening for us a broad and hopeful vision of interconnectedness that can helpfully add to our confidence in the mystery we call the communion of saints, where seeming absence becomes a characteristic of presence.

---

57. Margaret Nash in Nash, *Outline*, 253.

3

Telling Little, Revealing Much

*Transcendence Through the Art
of Mark Rothko*

RICHARD KIDD

> *Some artists want to tell all like at a confessional.
> I as a craftsman prefer to tell little.*[1]

I AM DRAWN TO Rothko's carefully crafted minimal style because, as a theologian, I have long found Rothko's "little" unusually potent in its ability for "revealing much" and, in so doing, it has helpfully informed my spiritual journey. The quotation chosen to start this chapter, from Mark Rothko's 1958 address to the Pratt Institute, is a statement that will ring true for all who admire Rothko's later work—almost anything belonging to what is now termed his "classic" period, running from approximately the mid-1940s through to his death in 1970. We will, of course, need to exercise caution when we meet contradictions between what the artist says concerning his own work and what over-enthusiastic commentators try to project upon it; Rothko never encouraged strongly religious readings of his canvases, and this chapter will aim to respect his own understanding of spiritual significance in his work.

I am in no doubt, however, that Rothko's "classics" will make excellent conversation partners as we continue to explore some of the wider themes that have caught our attention whilst exploring the topic of the communion

---

1. Rothko, *Writings on Art,* 126. This is part of a transcription of a recorded conference that Rothko gave at the Pratt Institute, accompanied by questions from the audience and Rothko's answers. According to the author of the original published article, Rothko did not read from notes during the conference.

of saints. As in my chapter on the work of Paul Nash, I am turning to visual images in the belief that they can further strengthen our confidence in things about which we are compelled to speak but find it desperately hard to express either in word or picture, necessarily remaining invisible to the inquiring eye and ear.

Repeatedly we have found that our attempts to do justice to such an elusive concept as "life beyond life" push us to what Rowan Williams aptly terms "the edge of words," where the search for an appropriate metaphor becomes seriously challenging—if not downright impossible.[2] The conviction underpinning this chapter is that sometimes, especially in the hands of a skilled craftsperson, a seemingly simple configuration of oil on canvas can speak in remarkably revealing ways. In some contexts, especially around the "edge," it seems that visual images can have a unique role, complementing verbal images as we struggle at the boundaries of human understanding.

Mark Rothko—a Brief Introduction to His *Oeuvre*

Rothko resists easy classification. Whilst his paintings show significant continuity of style and technique over the better part of thirty years, there were also significant developments and frequently conflicting accounts of what he understood himself to be doing at the core of his practice as an artist. A recent exhibition at the Royal Academy in London, gathered under the title "Abstract Expressionism," located his work firmly at the center of a large and diverse group of artists, largely North American, whose creative output spanned a couple of decades beginning in the late 1930s.[3] In this Academy exhibition, Rothko's canvases literally took center-stage, out from which it was possible radially to venture forth and visit rooms dedicated to his contemporaries: Jackson Pollock, Willem de Kooning, Barnett Newman, Clifford Still, Frank Klein, Ad Reinhardt, and others. Whether they would all have willingly owned this grouping and the label attached to it is not without question, even though there can be no doubt that they were very much aware of each other's work and that they deeply influenced each other's artistic development. By 1958, addressing the Pratt Institute, Rothko was firmly challenging the assumption that his work should be associated

---

2. This was the title under which Rowan Williams gathered the chapters of a book largely originating with his 2013 Gifford Lectures in the University of Edinburgh (Williams, *Edge of Words*).

3. The exhibition which ran at the Royal Academy of Art in London from September 24, 2016 to January 2, 2017 was accompanied by a substantial catalogue (Anfam, *Abstract Expressionism*).

with the term "expression"—at least, that is, when the focus is on "self-expression." In contrast, it would have been harder to question the presence of self-expression in the work of Jackson Pollock, with his vigorous choreography over the surface of stage-like canvases; but Rothko always maintained a measured critical distance from these friends and colleagues.[4]

In a letter addressed jointly by Adolph Gottlieb and "Marcus" Rothko to the *New York Times* in 1943—a response to reviews of the Federation Show, which included examples of their own work—we find a shortlist of "aesthetic beliefs."[5] These certainly describe the mood of a movement that later would be labeled Abstract Expressionist, but they do much more than that too. They begin to point in some of the quite unique and distinctive directions that Rothko's own art would take over the following two decades. It is an intriguing list, and is reproduced here in full:

> 1. To us art is an adventure into an unknown world, which can be explored only by those willing to take the risks.
>
> 2. This world of the imagination is fancy-free and violently opposed to common sense.
>
> 3. It is our function as artists to make the spectator see the world our way—not his [*sic*] way.
>
> 4. We favour the simple expression of the complex thought. We are for the large shape because it has the impact of the unequivocal. We wish to reassert the picture plane. We are for flat forms because they destroy illusion and reveal truth.
>
> 5. There is a widely accepted notion among painters that it does not matter what one paints as long as it is well painted. This is the essence of academicism. There is no such thing as good painting about nothing. We assert that the subject is crucial and only that subject matter is valid which is tragic and timeless. That is why we profess spiritual kinship with primitive and archaic art.[6]

---

4. The term "abstract" is not that much less ambiguous in its range of possible meanings. Pollock, it would seem, embraced the idea of abstraction to mean a complete break with all intentional content; his work was the product of rapid unpremeditated movements, combined with the consistent and more orderly pull of gravity on his liquid paint. Rothko, however, will want to argue that the content of his canvases is ultimately more tipped towards something intentional; his work is an abstraction "from something," and not merely "from nothing."

5. Rothko, *Writings on Art*, 35–36.

6. Rothko, *Writings on Art*, 36.

Immediately I can identify here key elements of what I have come to think of as an essential Rothko spirit: passionate commitment to strike out in new directions, flying in the face of common sense; commitment to simplicity, typically offered through large flat forms; detailed attention to subject matter, however minimal that subject might at first seem to be.

The first of two classic Rothkos I have chosen for this chapter is one of the so-called Seagram Murals, "Black on Maroon," Mural No. 6 (1958). Rothko's sketch for this painting is reproduced on the cover of our present book.[7] The mural is a big canvas—105 inches by 150 inches—and I single it out here in glad memory of my own earliest encounter with Rothko and his *oeuvre*. The venue was the Liverpool Tate in the late 1980s, and my initial response was far from positive. I was bemused—and not a little angered. Why would the Tate dedicate a whole room, the entirety of one of its much-coveted ground-floor galleries, to seven immense, apparently near-empty canvases, largely comprising wide expanses of somber blacks and maroons? This presented a real shock to my then inexperienced eye. My first inclination was to see them as one enormous "waste of space"—ironic really, as in the end it is their very provision of "space" that has become so very significant for my deeper understanding and increasing pleasure in Rothko's work.

In an introductory article for the brochure that accompanied the 1988 Liverpool exhibition, Michael Compton described in detail the confusion that now surrounds the original commission of these huge murals—just seven out of a possible nine were brought to Liverpool in 1988.[8] The paintings had acquired the Seagram label on the grounds that they were originally commissioned for display in the Seagram Building in New York by Phyllis Lambert and Philip Johnson in 1958—specifically for the Four Seasons Restaurant. As Compton says:

> Rothko had achieved quite suddenly in 1949, a kind of painting whose scale and character could induce viewers to stand before it, committing themselves completely for a while and receiving in return a transcendent experience.[9]

In my reading of this quotation, the really significant words are "for a while," and they go some way to explaining why Rothko might initially have preferred the location of a restaurant to that of a conventional gallery. It is not difficult to imagine how the context of a meal might provide the kind of sustained presence that Rothko desired for his would-be

---

7. It is reproduced in Borchardt-Hume, *Rothko*, 114–15.
8. Compton, *Mark Rothko*, 8–17.
9. Compton, *Mark Rothko*, 10.

viewers. A tendency in most galleries is for people to flit from picture to picture, their minds shifting rapidly between different images, artists, and artistic styles. From early in the process of creating these murals, Rothko began laying down detailed criteria for where and how they should be hung. It was important to him, for example, that the attention of the diners should not be distracted by the work of any artist other than himself. The levels of light and the precise spacing between pictures were all carefully prescribed—designed to engage the fullest possible field of vision and to generate maximum impact.

Other elements in Compton's short quotation, however, are less insightful; he appears to provide an example of the temptation I named earlier; namely, to project an interpretation onto an artist's work that further reflection might encourage us to resist. The idea of "receiving in return a transcendent experience" needs very careful examination. It seems to suggest that something arrives from an undefined transcendent "beyond," into the experience of a receptive viewer. This notion, however, depends on a clear dualism between matter and spirit, the immanent and the transcendent, that I hope I can show is very much alien to Rothko's way of understanding the significant materiality of the world. It also suggests what I will show to be a very non-Rothko way of thinking about human experience, which for Rothko is primarily shaped by a creative interplay between a material of the image (oil on canvas) and what a viewer "brings to" it (their consciousness already developed over time) rather than "receives" from beyond.

After Rothko's death a variety of stories began to circulate concerning the detail of how the Seagram commission finally took shape, and why eventually the restaurant environment was aborted in favor of an alternative location in Tate London. It was never going to be easy to secure a long-term home for these enormous murals, a home that would also guarantee such detailed prescriptions for the long-term environment in which they would be seen. From the start, a venue in the Four Seasons Restaurant had chafed against a number of Rothko's strongly-held convictions. He did not favor rich New Yorkers as the primary, potentially exclusive, viewers of his work; and it soon became evident that the noise of chattering and all the other distractions of a meal-table were unlikely to induce the kind of concentration that Rothko had intended.

All the murals are substantial in size, the largest of them 102 inches in height and 180 inches in width. In 1958 Rothko had rented a large studio, 222 the Bowery, within which he erected scaffolding to replicate the exact dimensions of the dining room in the restaurant. This enabled him to experiment in detail with the relative positioning and the lighting of his canvases. The murals, however, never took up their potential location in the Four Seasons. By 1965 discussions were taking place between Rothko and Sir Norman Reid, then director of Tate London. Negotiations were still continuing in 1969 when Reid visited Rothko, now too ill to travel, in his New York studio. Eventually in relative haste, a detailed agreement was drawn up to accompany the gift of a selection of paintings to the Tate. These words were key in the agreed text:

> (...) there will be no other works of art of any kind except those created by me which are being given this date and the painting which was previously given to you. It may not be that all the paintings will be exhibited in that room at one time.[10]

The paintings arrived in 1970 and have been on display almost continuously ever since. I myself have seen them on several occasions, exhibited in a room carefully configured to Rothko's instructions at what is now London's Tate Modern. Their precise height above the floor, their relative spacing, the color of the walls for mounting and the light levels in the room are all still carefully tuned to Rothko's original wishes. I always find the impact of these paintings, seen in their prescribed context, to be enormously strong and inspiring. The overall effect generates an environment in which my mind and spirit are freed to journey in ways which, for me at least, rightly deserve the label "spiritual"—even if that is a term which Rothko used himself only very sparingly during his own lifetime. This experience of freedom also leads me—as I hope to show—to reflect that this "spirituality" can be best understood within the perspective of the Christian idea of the communion of saints.

"One must go further, one must go further."[11]

I have chosen this quotation from Søren Kierkegaard's *Fear and Trembling* as the title for a short section in which I want to explore my claim to Rothko as a credible "spiritual" companion. It was in the 1958 Pratt Institute Lecture, noted above, that Rothko made enthusiastic mention of "a marvellous book: Kierkegaard's *Fear and Trembling*."[12] It seems that he had spent significant time with this text over an extended period, and the quest to discover just what it was that he found so "marvellous" offers important clues as to how Rothko saw his own work. It was certainly no

---

10. Compton, *Mark Rothko*, 15.

11. Kierkegaard, *Fear and Trembling*, 123. It is quoted at the head of a subsection in James Breslin's major biography of Rothko (Breslin, *Mark Rothko*, 378).

12. Rothko, *Writings on Art*, 126.

simple alignment of religious convictions. Rothko, born into a Jewish family, and Kierkegaard, the Danish Christian philosopher, really only meet in their shared reception and interpretation of the dramatic Abraham story in Gen 22:1–19, where Abraham is taken to the brink in facing what he perceives as God's demand to offer in sacrifice his son Isaac.

Before we follow up the Kierkegaard connections, it will be helpful to have sight of a second list, this time Rothko's own, which he offered as part of the 1958 Pratt Lecture. This is the form in which we now have access to it:

> The recipe of a work of art—its ingredients—how to make it—the formula.
>
> 1. There must be a clear preoccupation with death—intimations of mortality . . . Tragic art, romantic art, etc., deals with the knowledge of death.
>
> 2. Sensuality. Our basis of being concrete about the world. It is a lustful relationship to things that exist.
>
> 3. Tension. Either conflict or curbed desire.
>
> 4. Irony. This is a modern ingredient—the self-effacement and examination by which a man [sic] for an instant can go on to something else.
>
> 5. Wit and play . . . for the human element.
>
> 6. The ephemeral and chance . . . for the human element.
>
> 7. Hope. 10 percent to make the tragic concept more endurable.
>
> I measure these ingredients very carefully when I paint a picture. It is always the form that follows these elements and the picture results from the proportions of these elements.[13]

In conjunction with the earlier list from 1943, there can be no doubt about Rothko's uncompromising commitment to the chosen direction of his work, to what he sees as a deep obligation laid on him as an artist. This way of speaking would not be out of place in a description of the spiritual idea of "vocation"; but Rothko does not use such a religiously loaded term. He is, nonetheless, absolutely single-minded, some would say obsessive. The point for Rothko (as for Kierkegaard's Abraham) is that nothing less than full commitment will do. Nothing less can deliver the goal—whatever the cost—and for Rothko the cost had by now shown itself to be high. His health already in decline, not helped by his extreme commitment to long hours working

---

13. Rothko, *Writings on Art*, 125–26.

at his craft, Rothko had taken his art out on a precarious limb. He had taken a risk, pursued his aim without compromise, and generated a vast body of work which was honored and ridiculed in near equal measure. These vast planes of barely differentiated color were not what artists or their patrons, past or present, would typically have labeled works of "common sense." I am not alone, however, in my gratitude for his unswerving commitment, sustained consistently, it would seem, right through to the time of his death.

Minimalism is such an easy butt of humor: the apparently vacant canvas, the unspectacular rectangle of bricks,[14] the canvas distinguished by nothing but a tear,[15] and so on. As I said earlier in this chapter, one of my own pre-reflective reactions to Rothko was to feel that his canvases were a waste of space; but it is this courageous commitment to space that lastingly calls for our spiritual attention.

Another focus for Rothko's attention in Kierkegaard's retelling of the Abraham story in *Fear and Trembling* is Abraham's inability to give any credible account for his action, and his inability to respond to potential critics, other than with silence. Rothko, it would seem, readily identified with Abraham in his own inability to give a fully credible account of why his work had developed as it had; there is no off-the-peg "common-sense" justification for his chosen style, any more than Abraham could find a way to rationalize the moral scandal implied in the commitment to sacrifice his son; this is simply how Rothko, like Abraham, finds himself compelled to act. Like Kierkegaard's Abraham, Rothko also remained largely silent when confronted by his critics, further symbolized by his decision, taken around this time, no longer to title any of his paintings—based on the conviction that words are unable to do justice to their elusive content. Add to all this the "visual silence" of these large fields of minimally differentiated color, and we soon begin to identify "silence" as a recognizable hallmark of Rothko's life and work.

Humans, it seems, are easily alarmed by space, and also by the silence which can accompany it. It signals too blatantly, as Rothko repeatedly commends, intimations of mortality; it confronts us with death—itself frequently the occasion for conspiracies of silence. It is tempting to connect the sense of alarm around space and silence, fear perhaps, with an event

---

14. A reference to Carl Andre's 1966 "Equivalent VIII," which caused such a stir when it was purchased by the Tate in 1972.

15. A reference to Lucio Fontana's 1960 "Spacial Concept Waiting" purchased by the Tate in 1964. Whenever I have seen this image hanging in the Liverpool Tate, my mind turns to a line I had first read in the writings of John Macquarrie, in which he likens human freedom to a "hole" or "breach" in the fabric of being (Macquarrie, *In Search of Humanity*, 12).

that took place on October 7, 2012 at Tate Modern. Was it significant that in a rare and extreme breach of security, "Black on Maroon" (Mural No. 6) in the Rothko Room, was deliberately vandalized and sustained costly damage? The investigation that followed into the motivation for this attack revealed complex motives and remains inconclusive. I am struck, however, by the idea that such a superficially inoffensive painting should draw such acute attention, violence even. Is there something about the empty-but-not-empty space, the apparent "nothing," that cries out, that intimidates and causes offense? This is a question to which I will return.

I am reminded here of a central motif in Wassily Kandinsky's much quoted *Concerning the Spiritual in Art* in which he uses the image of a pyramid to begin to explain why it is that art's greatest pioneers and innovators often find their work faced with total ridicule when first exhibited.[16] Kandinsky equates the work of what he might have termed "also-ran artists" to the bulk volume of a pyramid, where their work stays safely locked within the limits of already familiar categories for interpretation. Just occasionally, and we guess Kandinsky thought himself to be amongst them, someone rises as it were to the apex of the pyramid and launches beyond its highest point into as yet uncharted territory. The mass of potential viewers, as well as lesser artists, still trapped deep in the body of the pyramid have no available conceptual apparatus with which to appreciate the new departure, and the result is invariably scathing rejection. Only with the passing of time, argues Kandinsky, is there a steady cultural "tickle-down," until eventually works which were at one time pilloried finally become the focus of huge popular retrospective exhibitions—sometimes, sadly, too late for the original artists to enjoy their well-deserved acclaim. The list of artists whose names could be used to illustrate this phenomenon is endless—Edward Munch, Claude Monet, Vincent van Gogh, and Pablo Picasso are amongst the better known. I am adding the name of Mark Rothko to this list—with the further observation that Rothko was well aware of what he was undertaking when he rose above the apex of the pyramid. Rothko, like Abraham before him, remains silent because it is simply impossible to justify this break with "common sense" until enough time has elapsed for a new language to take shape and for a viewing public to begin to internalize the new vocabulary.

Matter and Spirit

Returning now to Rothko's 1958 list, I am strongly drawn to his emphasis on the radical physicality of his medium. If there is indeed "spiritual" value

16. Kandinsky, *Concerning the Spiritual in Art*, 6–9.

in his murals, it has nothing at all to do with a simple dualism between matter and spirit, or receiving something from an immaterial beyond. *This* paint, *this* canvas, *this* lighting, *this* physical context of a gallery is where, for Rothko, the authentically spiritual happens—or fails to happen altogether. Something like this is a recurrent theme in several of our chapters concerned with the communion of saints. If we stand, typically in the company of other viewers, in the overwhelming presence of one of Rothko's large canvases, we can find ourselves drawn, as if through an open portal, into a strange and unexpectedly energized world. All the elements that prompt this experience are solidly rooted in the material realities of paint, gallery, and other human bodies. Something can happen, however, in just such spaces; in shared contemplation of an abstract image we can find ourselves awakened to an extraordinary sense of "communion"—communion with both human companions and with the larger world around us. It is in such moments that an abstract painting of the kind we associate with Mark Rothko can kindle a vision for the kind of space we are attempting to describe when we speak of "the communion of saints." The entirety of the shared experience we are having in the gallery becomes a visual metaphor for the elusive encounter with mystery that this phrase points towards.

It is this kind of experience that drew me in our earlier volume to emphasize the "strangeness" of the material universe we inhabit, the "superness" of the natural rather than anything necessitating a label like supernatural. Along similar lines, it has been greatly encouraging to engage with Marilynne Robinson's recent book, *The Givenness of Things*, in which she has provided fresh grist for the anti-dualist mill,[17] even if she does not herself consistently follow this through in her own theological work to what I understand as its inevitable conclusion.

Many of us know Robinson best for her ability to push words to new limits in her novels—the better known being *Gilead, Home,* and *Lila*—through which she draws her readers into imaginative worlds where carefully crafted, hugely empathetic characters enable us engage with subtle and elusive ideas of profound spiritual substance. But Robinson is skilled at more technical engagement too—frequently as an apologist at the interface between theology and the sciences. In *The Givenness of Things* she keenly draws our attention to what she calls ". . . the great strangeness of the human situation."[18] I like that. The overall approach in her book sits well with Rothko's emphasis on the physicality of his medium. Robinson's argument is that much which is now taken to be "reasonable" discourse in the world

---

17. Robinson, *Givenness of Things*, 214.
18. Robinson, *Givenness of Things*, 4–5.

of cosmological and quantum science reaches so far beyond the logic of everyday life (not unlike what Rothko called "common sense") that they make much religious language—now too often dismissed as "non-sense" on the grounds of not being rigorously scientific—actually look relatively clear and easily accessible to the human mind.

Robinson particularly cites "quantum entanglement," a key focus of current discourse on "complexity," as a prime example.[19] She recalls how early quantum physicists actually found themselves choosing the term "strangeness" to describe one of the now well-established parameters of such entanglement, a property of subatomic particles by which they can simultaneously flip their "strange" orientation, even when apparently located at opposite "ends" of the universe. Surely, she contends, if it is acceptable to argue boldly for this and other conceptually unthinkable notions, a "parallel universe," for example, one in which we ourselves might be associated with a remote *alter ego*, its biography unfolding in a radically different way from the one we know as our own, the idea of a human "soul" begins to look relatively simple and eminently reasonable—"common sense," you might say.

This is not, of course, of itself, an argument for anything, and Robinson admits that. We in this book strongly resist her attempt to reappropriate a concept of an immaterial "soul," which does nothing at all for the cause of resisting old dualisms; on the contrary, drawing on the arts, we ourselves are trying to conceive the reality of the communion of saints without resorting to a dualistic view of a detachable soul. What her apologetic usefully highlights—the reason I have called her as a witness in this chapter—is the arrogance of those who write off millennia of careful reflection on life's deeper mysteries as if they are now disproved by some blunt-edged scientism that, truth to tell, is not even qualified by its own criteria to engage with such issues at all. There is, she would argue, something very naïve in bids to discredit the strangeness and mystery historically associated with religious claims, whilst simultaneously expecting similarly unthinkable categories to carry the full weight of discourse in the worlds of science.

I have introduced Robinson into this conversation about Rothko, because she offers a fresh angle on our conceptualization of the relationship between the physical and the spiritual. She wants us to understand that the "physical" can be so very much more than many scientists have wanted us to believe. As she puts it:

> On scrutiny the physical is as elusive as anything to which a name can be given. The physical as we have come to know it

---

19. Robinson, *Givenness of Things*, 4–5.

frays away into dark matter, antimatter, and by implication on beyond them and beyond our present powers of inference.[20]

I am attracted to this because, in coming to the work of a visual artist, I am wanting to affirm that the solid physicality of paint on canvas, in its very physicality, and even in the most minimalist of formats, can become the locus of insight into deep levels of our human reality.

Rothko is, if nothing else, a committed distributor of paint—significant quantities, many layered, variously diluted and textured—producing huge areas crafted with great subtlety, and generating immensely more fine variations than any casual glance could possibly recognize; and it is this subtle variation in the very material of the paint itself that works the "magic" when we see it. So, in his later years, when Rothko distanced himself from the idea that art is primarily a "self-expression" of its author/creator, I understand him to be affirming the importance of the painted matter itself—along, of course, with the importance of the attentive viewer. The artist crafts paint to enable us, the viewers, to see the world in a new way—primarily the actual world, out there, and not merely the inner life of the artist.

This resonates well with my own preferred style of theological reflection, which invariably begins with the concrete physicality of the world and our sensory/sensual experience of it. Typically, I find myself beginning with a preliminary description of an actual encounter with the stuff of life: seeing a picture, reading a text, visiting a place, exploring a natural phenomenon, experimenting with a mathematical concept, meeting a person or community, and so on. It is, of course, impossible ever to achieve a finished description. My analysis is always inseparable from the entirety of prior experience and understanding I bring to each encounter. It can, however, become an important moment in a significant process, triggering a creative (and fully earthed) dialogue between the explorer and explored as we work with the tensions that emerge, and strive towards an ever richer analysis and understanding of our life experience. My hope, of course, is that I might in the end achieve more than Rothko's meagre 10 percent on the scale of hope . . . but more of that later too.

Being Drawn Into the World of a Rothko

In 2006 I decided to spend an extended period of time in Tate Modern's "Rothko Room" and to keep a minute-by-minute journal of my unfolding experience—both my own personal experience and also my observations

---

20. Robinson, *Givenness of Things*, 8.

of others coming and going during the span of 100 minutes. This was prompted by my growing interest in more contemplative styles of spirituality biased, that is, towards the apophatic rather than kataphatic end of the historical spectrum. At the core of apophatic approaches to prayerful contemplation is the idea that spirituality can be nourished by an engagement with silence and the space that can open up within it—the space between the words rather than words themselves. My 100-minute experiment had been encouraged by the enthusiastic testimonies of others who have found the open space of Rothko's murals to contribute positively to their spiritual experience.

I was interested to monitor how my own experience developed if I took Rothko at his word and committed myself to sustained proximity and attention to his canvases. The present-day Rothko Room contains nine canvases in all, hung in the original pattern approved by the painter, and I soon learnt where to locate myself in relation to each of the canvases so that they filled my field of vision, drawing me fully into their visual space. Much as we are encouraged to do in the presence of a traditional Eastern icon, I allowed my gaze to melt into the image. Much to my delight, I too found that the murals offered a fertile space—you might call it, as I suggested earlier, a kind of "visual silence"—within which potentially significant contemplative explorations began to take shape. I suspect that I might be numbered amongst Rothko's more receptive viewers, but I am quietly confident that others too could find such encounters spiritually valuable. These minimal visual icons free us from the normative constraints of all the conceptual formulations which pretend to provide us with shortcuts to transcendence and spiritual insight.

Something that quickly becomes apparent—and very much relevant to the communal dimension of our controlling theme, the communion of saints—is that exploring a Rothko does not turn out to be the highly individualistic experience one might at first imagine. This has several dimensions. Because of the intrinsically participatory importance of its viewers—and if my viewing takes place in a popular gallery as in the case of my 100-minute visit—interaction with other viewers is almost inevitable. I also bring friends and others who are present to my mind at the time, perhaps because of their personal trials or seasons of celebration. More than that, however, what I see deep-layered in these painted canvases is not an external "beyond," but something that is primarily informed by everything that I bring in my eye's mind.[21] In my case, as for other believers too, this

---

21. This provocative phrase was chosen by the artist Bridget Riley for the title of her book, *The Eye's Mind*.

includes a vast heritage of scriptural and other spiritual writings that have been born and tested for their lasting significance by whole communities of faith through many ages. For me, these are predominantly Christian and very often Baptist, but others are there too—a whole community of God's saints. Viewed in this way, I can now see some potential advantages in the original restaurant venue for Rothko's canvases, a venue already constituted by the communion of a meal, something very dear to those of us who often focus our understanding of the communion of saints in a eucharistic celebration; but perhaps a carefully curated gallery has no less power to do something similar, even if in rather different ways.

I found my time in the gallery passed extremely quickly, and in the end I was glad that I had set the 100-minute limit in advance, as otherwise it might have been difficult to decide when to draw the session to a close. Here are a few extracts from my notes:

> As I do my own gazing, No 4 begins to change, losing its brighter redness and becoming very dark. I begin to see some vibrating movement in the central space. The inner edges of the darker surround become very sharp in focus. I now begin to experience for myself that this whole environment is very pleasing . . .
>
> No 8 loses all its color differentiations, the verticals at the sides are becoming like monumental pillars marking the portal into a broad landscape . . .
>
> The red centre of No 9 becomes highlighted and emphatic, with vertical lines/bands moving side to side . . .
>
> Nos 1 and 9 are now presenting much brighter pillars of color at the centre—but it is No 4 which increasingly becomes the richest window of all, as if looking out onto another world . . .

A recurrent motif in my notes is that of the "portal," and a sense of seeing through a door or window into an energetic, warm, and inviting space. Not everyone will necessarily see the warmth as I do; perhaps this is something that I am able to see because, as I have noted, I already carry my own mental *cache* of images from the Christian tradition, including the intimation of an eschatological goal symbolized by an enormous banquet. The reliance of what a viewer brings to his pictures is no dereliction of duty on Rothko's part; he has committed himself to provide an original canvas, and now expects similar commitment from his viewers.

I am not the first to write about the power of these canvases to draw us into another world (rather more welcoming, I might add, than a modern cosmologist's invitation to a parallel universe), and I doubt that I will be the last. My understanding is that Rothko was very much aware of a potential in these images to generate reactions of many kinds in his viewers, and that the carefully crafted detail of these spaces, designed to encourage just such experience, was central to his discovery of a mature style.

Once again I do not want to give the impression that I think there is anything super- or un-natural about the painterly power of these images—any more, that is, than I would want to say that of other more traditional iconic images. What interests me is the potential for these very natural (thoroughly earthed, paint-earthed) images, under the committed gaze of expectant viewers, to become—as Orthodox worshipers are known to say of their icons, "windows on eternity"[22]—places where the attentive spirit can find surprising inspiration and increased confidence in a transcendent ground, above and beyond a merely surface material of reality. The "magic" is not in the presence of an auxiliary spiritual layer, as some dualistic views of the world might suggest, but in the complex physical and psychological dynamics of visual experience: painter, paint, and viewers, individually and together. Rothko's recipe for a painting suggests that he saw the raw materiality of paint on canvas and the sensory/sensual experience it evokes as, in itself, a possible source of hope—even if limited to 10 percent! Paint on canvas becomes an occasion for the human spirit to be warmed by intimations of transcendence, a place where resources for reflection on the strangeness of life can be nourished. In that sense images work metaphorically, much as do the words of poets, finding their way into our lives—through the eyes, however, rather than through the ears.

It is, I think, instructive to note some of the influences that we discover leading Rothko's work in this direction. Michael Compton records how it was in the actual process of working on the Seagram Murals that Rothko came to realize that he was being influenced by the staircase hall of Michelangelo's Laurentian Library, with its blind windows and deliberately oppressive atmosphere.[23] In June 1959, Rothko had broken from the project, traveling to Europe with his family. Some of the places noted in his memoir are very significant: Pompei with its somber murals, the Laurentian Library, already noted; but also, in Florence, the San Marco frescoes of Fra Angelico. In my own experience, there is something quite extraordinary about the vibrancy of the light that radiates from the San Marco frescoes, stimulating the visual imagination in ways not dissimilar to those of the Rothko murals.

---

22. See, for example, the work compiled by Gennadios Limouris for the World Council of Churches under that very title (Limouris, *Icons*).

23. Compton, *Mark Rothko*, 13.

Visiting for himself these particular European examples of portals, windows, and doorways, at the same time as painting the Seagram Murals, was not the first time Rothko had engaged with motifs of door and window. In his chapter "The World in a Frame" in the volume that accompanied a major Rothko retrospective at Tate Modern in 2008/2009, David Anfam explores how these motifs pervaded Rothko's painterly imagination from his early years.[24] This is especially interesting in respect of the Seagram Murals when it is also set alongside the progressive loss of figurative elements in Rothko's work, eventually completely absent in what I have termed his classic period. The human figure was never abundant in Rotho's paintings, but initially people were present, gradually reducing in number, finally fading to nothing through the late use of a lonely single figure. Rothko's own comment on this movement towards non-figurative painting reads as follows:

> I belong to a generation that was preoccupied with the human figure (. . .) It was with the utmost reluctance that I found that it did not meet my needs. Whoever used it mutilated it. No one could paint the figure as it was and feel that he [sic] could produce something that could express the world. I refuse to mutilate and had to find another way of expression. (. . .) My current pictures are involved with the *scale* of human feelings, the human drama, as much of it as I can express.[25]

In the transitional period there is a notable picture, "Untitled (Figure Standing at a Portal)" (gouache on paper, c. 1938–1939), in which a single figure, present as a face only, is shown looking at/into a picture/portal, which could well be compared to a preliminary sketch for a Seagram Mural.[26] One interpretation of this process of figurative withdrawal, one I warm to very strongly, is to see it as progressively leading towards the point where the figure, now entirely removed, is fully reconstituted in ourselves as viewers. This is, I think, an entirely credible interpretation, and one that helps to make sense of the experience of modern-day viewers of these otherwise empty portals. A human presence certainly remains thoroughly alive in Rothko's work, but precisely how to describe its working is far from easy. The starting point is our own presence as individual viewers, somehow drawn into the image through the portal that opens before us. Becoming aware of our own presence in the paintings, however, can

24. Anfam, *Rothko*, 45–57.
25. Rothko, *Writings on Art*, 126.
26. This image can be seen on the website of the National Gallery of Art, Washington, at http://www.nga.gov/content/ngaweb/Collection/art-object-page.69074.html, and is printed in Anfam, "World in a Frame", 54.

also modulate into an awareness of a wider community in which we are involved in the very act of viewing—which for Christians would be symbolized in the communion of saints. Many extant photographs of Rothko in his studio, repeated in many books and articles about his work, present him seated at a distance from a huge canvas, himself rehearsing the role of a future viewer of the finished picture.[27]

But what of my observation of others who visited the Rothko Room during my 100-minute sojourn? Again my notes are instructive. In particular, they highlight the importance of committed observation, which sadly contrasts with the more typical inability of people in the modern world to offer any real effort of attention of a kind that is necessary to lift the human imagination beyond the superficiality of a material surface. I wrote:

> At this point . . . a guide strides in with forty people in tow, and they scatter around the room, showing various of levels of disinterest. She brashly talks facts, tedious and uninspiring facts—where, when, who, the decision to give them to the Tate, historical categorization (modern, contemporary with Pollock), suicide—as if all this says something usefully definitive about the canvases. She never once shows any inclination to hint how or what it might be possible to see, what Rothko is inviting us to see with commitment to an appropriate kind of looking. How very sad! Not a hint of the holiness of it all—no cross-reference to the Rothko Chapel in Houston. All she can manage is to compare the canvases to prison windows. How depressing . . . and before you know it, whiz-bang, off they go to another gallery!

And some time later:

> Another party comes in—much more sensitive to the whole context, but again the guide never hints at anything spiritual . . . that might be going on . . . Again she introduces ideas of windows, prisons, feelings of enclosure; but not even a hint of transcendence—now beaming at me through No 4.

What a wasted opportunity. No more than a modicum of sensitive guidance might have opened a whole new world for these unsuspecting viewers. I have never once been tempted to view the vertical bands in a Rothko mural as prison bars; always I have seen them, quite intuitively, as portals and windows. I am left wondering about the measure to which these uninspiring gallery guides were misled by a temptation to project

---

27. For example a photograph by Hans Namuth, "Rothko in his East Hampton Studio 1964," in Borchardt-Hume, *Rothko*, 22–23.

the event of Rothko's suicide, with all its evident despair, back into his mid-life murals, thereby constructing these restraining bars rather than windows on transcendence.

One further dimension of the whole Rothko experience is undoubtedly sexual—also unsurprising in a resource that connects with the apophatic tradition and its long history of exploiting an overlap between spiritual and sexual experience. Rothko's recipe (in the second item of the 1958 list) had referred to the centrality of the sensual. It is plain to see in the basic forms in many of his murals—pillars, almost certainly phallic, and portals often suggesting places of entry into womb-like havens of shelter and security. None of the visiting guides mentioned anything sexual, any more than they mentioned anything spiritual, with respect to these works—as if inhibited by a double contemporary embarrassment and inhibition concerning the sexual and the spiritual. This was, I hasten to add, sharply contradicted by the behaviors of other visitors during my 100-minute stay—especially couples. At one point I noted:

> A young couple are hovering near the centre, wound together like Hindu statues—although still fully clothed—evidently engrossed both in the gazing, and in each other—a very innocent and really rather beautiful example of love-making one with the other as they gaze, repeatedly whispering observations and insights, often stroking each other gently and caringly. The sexual motif is up and running quicker than I had expected, and it is hard not to feel left out in the presence of their evident bliss. What a superbly appropriate activity for this context.

A useful way to make sense of this powerful meeting of spirituality and sexuality is to focus on the concept of "desire." Mystics repeatedly and emphatically tell us that God is only taken seriously when God becomes the supreme object of desire. But an object of desire is unlikely to sustain its attraction without some significant reward along the scale of human pleasure. In order to hold center-stage, being found at prayer and taking shelter in the house of God will have to prove an entrancing experience.

Sadly, in the modern world, there is so much to suggest that the experience of religion will be almost an opposite to the fulfillment of desire. Religion often looks tedious, and not a little boring, certainly in its institutional manifestations. Where modern western people typically experience the arousal of desire is not in an invitation to pray, but in an invitation to sexual union; not in the serenity of an ancient chapel, but in the exhilaration of a roller-coaster ride, either real or, these days more often, in virtual reality. But what if the two are at root so intimately related that, without in any way denigrating the enormity of sexual and physical stimulation and pleasure, it becomes possible to explain convincingly how union with God can also be a source of erotic and sensual pleasure too?

This is precisely what many of the mystics, at some level, appear to be reporting and, in so doing, merely reflect the glorious ambiguity of so much scriptural writing. Surely the rich sexual language of the Song of Songs, and many of the Psalms, is no accident of semantics—it is testimony to the intense and comparable satisfactions experienced through both prayer and sex. It is sad that so many commentators have felt the need to defuse it all with overly contrived allegorical and symbolic interpretations.

A really significant message for our time is that, whilst sex alone can lead to an immense anti-climax, dissatisfaction, and disappointment, giving priority to prayer and union with God not only has the potential to deliver its own intensity of sensual pleasure, but in turn can transform embodied sexual experience as well—overcoming the frustration caused by sex's ultimate failure to deliver lasting satisfaction alone.

As I complete this section, I am daring to suggest that the culturally alien experience of "space" provided by the paintings of Mark Rothko is a good place to begin to discover some energetic avenues into fresh spiritual insight. Rothko's murals can provide a remarkable focus for spiritual reflection, an invitation to taste the joy of life within a fresh and potentially revitalized spiritual horizon—an opportunity for pleasure which is simultaneously spiritual and fully embodied. As I have already suggested, the "presence" created by the spaces in a Rothko painting is a relational one; we find ourselves, strangely perhaps, drawn into a larger human community, journeying together towards a transcendent reality which is nevertheless always immanent in the world. It is this more expansive community, extending through time and space, which is symbolized for Christian theologians by the image of the communion of saints symbolizes.

"Nothing" Really Matters

Let us further explore the simplicity, the "plane-ness" of Rothko's typical canvas. My inclination is to relate it to another core element in apophatic spiritual traditions, with their special attention to "nothingness" and "the nothing"—the desire to affirm that "nothing" ("no-thing", that is), in some seemingly perverse way, really matters. There is a joke that now appears in several variations on the internet; it usually reads something like this:

> The French existentialist Jean-Paul Sartre was sitting at a café table working.

A waiter approached him. "Can I get you something to drink, Monsieur Sartre?" he asked. "Yes, I'd like a cup of coffee with sugar—but no cream", the philosopher replied. A few minutes later, however, the waiter returned and said, "I'm so sorry, Monsieur Sartre, we are completely out of cream—how about a coffee with no milk?"

Joking aside, however, Christian interest in "nothing" or "non-being" has a very long history. I was probably not alone, in being mystified for a long time by what felt to be an important saying in 1 Cor 1:28:

> God chose what is low and despised in the world, things that are not, to reduce to nothing things that are, so that no one might boast in the presence of God.

The RSV translation has here: "*even* things that are not." Whatever did Paul, the apostle, have in mind? Surely that even the "no-things" are important.

The earliest Christian theological reflections on the concept of non-being were largely the result of a dialogue with Neoplatonism, a major component in the Hellenistic mind-set of the early Christian centuries. Neoplatonism exploited a facility within the language of ancient Greece, which enabled it to distinguish two quite distinct ways in which the idea of non-being can be used (something we find much harder, if not impossible, in English). On the one hand the Greek language has the *ouk on* or absolute non-being, that which simply is not. Four-sided triangles, for example, are simply "not," oukontically—absolutely. But more commonly we find ourselves using the idea of non-being in a much more relative way—the Greek term is *me on*—which leads theologians, especially in the Eastern church, even to speak of a "meontic" tradition. When I say "it is not raining in Manchester"—unlike the four-sided triangles which simply cannot be—the "not rain" only takes meaning because "raining in Manchester" is a real possibility. In fact, it would not be possible to understand "not raining in Manchester" at all if it were not for a prior understanding of "raining in Manchester"—which is not beyond the possibilities of reasonable thought. So "not raining" has a relative kind of non-being—as in reality do the majority of things we refer to as not being. We might say—the Neoplatonists certainly did—that something with relative non-being is not "nothing"; although, lacking evident being of its own, it actually "taps into," "draws on," is "parasitic on" being and gains vital energy from it.

It soon becomes clear, then, that relative non-being actually defines a highly fertile conceptual domain—it points to some kind of space in reality where all manner of creativity takes shape;[28] it is a space where the conceptually possible but still not yet begins to find form. Could this, I wonder, be helpful in making sense of the creative space that is offered by a Rothko mural?

There is a fascinating passage in Sartre's *Being and Nothingness* where he invites his readers to accompany him on a visit to his local café in Paris—where I can easily imagine him engaged in refined intellectual conversation with his Parisian friends.[29] This is almost certainly the passage that inspired our opening attempt at a joke. On arrival in the café Sartre finds that his friend, Pièrre, whom he expects to meet there, is nowhere to be seen. He then proceeds to explore just how deeply significant the absence of his friend really might be—indeed how his absence, in its own strange way, actually makes his friend thoroughly present—a worked example of relative non-being. The absence of his friend influences his feelings, his activities, in fact his whole life very deeply.

Analyzing this experience, as Sartre does, can help us to understand why some minimal experiences, apparently of nothing, a seeming absence, might in fact become a very significant way by which we come to recognize a less obvious, but no less real, presence. Suddenly, the space at the heart of a Rothko canvas begins to reveal itself in a new light.

There is something about the absence of Sartre's particular friend which makes the experience acutely significant, more significant, for example, than numerous other possible absences which could in theory be credited to that café at that moment—the absence of all those people, unknown to him, who live in England and have never even thought of visiting Paris. So what are the structural conditions which make this particular absence so special? Sartre identifies several factors, some more obvious than others.

First, the dimension of expectation is seen to be highly significant—Sartre arrived at the café with an expectation of meeting his friend, something which he brought to the experience as prior knowledge and prior relationship. I have already been arguing how important it is to recognize the diverse baggage, the expectations indeed, with which we arrive in the presence of a Rothko mural. I have even suggested that what might be strangely revealed for a Christian believer in the presence of a Rothko, very much in the vein of "absent friends," is symbolized in the idea of a communion of

---

28. Martin Heidegger writes about a "shock" in the presence of non-being; this he expounds under the concept of *Dasein*, which acts as a kind of portal into the mystery and depth of being. The *locus classicus* is Heidegger, *Being and Time*, 61–64.

29. Sartre, *Being and Nothingness*. The story is first introduced on p. 33, and is then progressively interrogated and expounded through the following pages.

saints; this is a potential place for meeting not only with a hidden God but with hidden friends, hidden in God, too.

Second, Sartre identifies the importance of wonder—here primarily in the sense of questioning. Then, he draws attention to the experience of fear—so why is my friend not here; has something gone wrong between us? And finally, he points to the role of imagination; it is crucial that Sartre can imagine another possibility, namely that his friend is potentially present.

This might help to make sense of an experience, common to many Christian believers: that our sense of God's apparent absence—it might be more helpful here to speak of "hiddenness" rather than a total absence which would be oukontic rather than meontic—can be very significant for our experience of God's presence. More generally it helps us to conceptualize the very real potential latent in an apparently empty space. In his poem "Via Negativa," another well-known label for the apophatic tradition, poet and theologian R. S. Thomas famously wrote about "the interstices in our knowledge, the darkness between stars"[30] as a reliable place to conduct a search for the presence of God. In his poetic allusions to an experience of God, Thomas clearly favored the word "absence" over the less stark category, "hiddenness," but there is more than a little ambiguity here. In another poem, actually entitled "The Absence,"[31] Thomas writes of a vacant "emptiness" or void of his being into which God projects his presence, as energetically as gases that rush into an unsealed vacuum, so that the impression is of a God who is primarily hidden. This then, I suggest, is not an oukontic, absolute absence, but much more like what I have been calling meontic absence.

Whether, then, it is Sartre's absent friend, Pierre, or R. S. Thomas's absent God, we are encountering here something that is not merely nothing. The hidden is actively making itself known, and I am suggesting that something similar can also take place in the presence of a Rothko painting. Sartre's ontology would suggest that this should be a universal human experience: any viewer, religiously-minded or not, might expect to be drawn into a world where seemingly absent companions are in some sense "encountered," and a mystery is faced. But if I also enter a Rothko space in the spirit of a Christian believer, my mind already enriched by an inheritance from a mature faith community and its stories, this encounter will take on additional layers of meaning, offering a point of entry into the mystery that Christians have called the communion of saints. Rather like Sartre arriving at the café, I come with developed expectations, however limited. I certainly come with

---

30. Thomas, *Collected Poems*, 220.
31. Thomas, *Collected Poems*, 361.

questions. I come with fears—at root my fear of my own finite limitations (in both time and space) which repeatedly threaten to bowl me over with an overwhelming wave of meaninglessness. And I come with a certain capacity for imagination, an intuition of the possibility of holy presence. In fact, I might reasonably condense Sartre's four conditioning factors into the more famous Corinthian three—I come with faith and hope and love[32]—and these profoundly transform and shape my experience of apparent, but nonetheless deeply threatening, absence and emptiness.

Perhaps it is not too bold to say that they transform an apparent emptiness into a possibility for unprecedented fullness. A pithy saying which is commonly attributed to Sartre, "fullness is emptiness given direction," is often quoted in the context of essays on Rothko and his work.[33] I might find myself in the presence of empty space, but if I am simultaneously fed by a rich tradition which offers direction, perhaps this can become an occasion when fullness will make itself more fully known and in ever greater measure. That is certainly what mystics and the exponents of contemplation are repeatedly telling us.

The absence of Sartre's friend from the Paris café, then, the absence of R. S. Thomas's God from wind-blown ever-more-emptying chapels of the Welsh hillsides, and now the apparent emptiness of a Rothko canvas—all meet in an extraordinary and mutually informative way. How ironic that space, silence, and emptiness should become occasions for some of the most intensely significant presences in human experience. This grounds for us a real possibility that God might make God's own self known in the spaces—between words, within the images, and between people. This is never something we can control; it has to remain a work of grace; but neither is this a never-never space of cloud-cuckoos, not the utterly elsewhere of the *ouk on*, beyond all space and time. It happens this very day in the here and now, in the real world, where what seems like the contradictory signals of pain and fear have their own potential repeatedly to drive us to the edge of unbelief and despair.[34] We are back, then, at a meeting between arts and sciences.

32. 1 Cor 13:13.

33. For example, at the head of an essay by Jeffrey Weiss entitled "Rothko's Unknown Space" in Weiss, *Mark Rothko*, a superb collection incorporating a number of papers pertinent to the theme of this chapter.

34. I have tried in this section to avoid any confusion that might arise if we were to try and give account of another important theme in so-called "meontic" theology, the kind pioneered in Paul Tillich's *Systematic Theology* and in books like Nicolas Berdyaev's *Freedom and Spirit,* in which we are invited to make profound connections between non-being and the dynamics of evil. Whilst these are hugely important connections and need to be made, my judgment has been that they would detract from the main argument of this present chapter.

Both are dealing with the real material of the universe, and both can be the location for intimations of God, present if nowhere else in the intensity of an apparent absence.

Getting Back to Rothko

Mark Rothko's exploration of open spaces and their potential for spiritual significance did not end with the Seagram murals. In fact, they merely marked the beginning of an extraordinary process of productive development. "One must go further, one must go further," Kierkegaard had written.

For some viewers, the highlight of Rothko's total *oeuvre* will be the Rothko Chapel in Houston, Texas. This was another special commission, riding on the back of the Seagram murals, made possible by a benefaction from the Menil family. Photographs of the Chapel, which are all I have seen on my travels so far, clearly fail to do justice to the scale and the peculiar ambience of this installation.[35] Once again the canvases are huge, although this time their tones are significantly darker. Once again, Rothko prescribed every detail of the architectural space, the precise configuration of the canvases and the lighting which vitalizes their somber colors. The testimonies of many who have been privileged to spend time in this space confirm that something quite extraordinary has been created. I still find it quite remarkable that Rothko should ever have been invited to create such a specifically religious environment, and that he should have agreed to devote so much time and energy to its completion—given, that is, his reluctance to welcome associations of his work with the spiritual. The Chapel is not associated with any one religious tradition, but there is no doubting that the deliberate intention was to create a religious space, one in which an experience of transcendence might become a real possibility. Rothko, then, had chosen to put his mind and hand to the creation of a material environment in which the spectator might begin to see the world in a new way, a way that Rothko himself had already begun to anticipate through his own "spiritual" experience. In the extensive web-space allocated to Rothko on the USA National Gallery of Art website, we read:

> Certain qualities such as radiance or the duality of light and dark have a symbolic meaning in Western culture from which Rothko clearly drew. An impression of vast space is said to represent the historical concept of the "sublime", a quasi-religious

---

35. See, for example, Phillips and Crow, *Seeing Rothko*, 64–65.

experience of limitless immensity. The installation of these canvases also produces its own sacrosanct environment.³⁶

This ability to anticipate the sacred impact of his huge canvases surely lies at the heart of his genius as a painter.

I complete this chapter with reflections on a Rothko image that surely must stand as one of the most extraordinary challenges to artistic "common sense" ever painted. It bears the depressingly unpromising label "Untitled (Black on Grey)," and is part of a series of "Black on Grey" paintings that Rothko executed in the final year of his life, from 1969–1970. I viewed the particular example I describe here first-hand at the Royal Academy in London in 2016.³⁷ On first sight, it simply seems that rectangles of black and gray occupy half of the canvas each. Surely every person who has ever attended the most elementary lesson in art knows that to locate the only discernible feature in a painting across the exact center of the picture plane is to dice with the potential for total banality—increased by doing it in black and gray. But it works, against all the odds. It is, of course, like every Rothko, much more subtle than a brief encounter would have us believe. The expanses of black and gray have been worked and reworked many times over; there are multiple layers upon layers, and they sediment a vitality just waiting for release. The line across the middle is in reality a complex boundary between two distinct zones of "colorful" grays, and close attention reveals much fine detail to be seen. The picture is delivered on a full Rothko-scale, 80 inches by 69 inches, and to stand in its presence is to be drawn into a vast and mysterious space.

I have used this painting—or at least poor representations of it on digital screens—in a variety of lectures and classes, often including participants who are not easily inclined to perceive the sublime in such an apparently bland image. We sometimes find ourselves talking about the surprise that the black occupies the upper rather than the lower portion of the picture, a heavy weight bearing down on its flimsy gray support. Has it, perhaps, been hung upside down? Then, just as I begin to lose my audience completely, I introduce the simple possibility that it might be interesting to think of the horizontal as some kind of horizon. Usually some participants have already begun to think along similar lines, but occasionally there is an audible gasp at this point. I am quick to disown the idea that this is something that

---

36. Accessed at http://www.nga.gov/content/ngaweb/features/slideshows/mark-rothko.html#slide_39.

37. It is reproduced in Borchardt-Hume, *Rothko*, 193, and is from the collection of Christopher Rothko. It can be readily viewed online, for instance through the official Mark Rothko website.

Rothko would necessarily want us to do—I merely offer it as a possible way into a process of exploration. Soon we are talking about the vista of a night sky, perhaps seen looking back toward earth from the surface of the moon, and eyes begin to recognize previously unnoticed detail in the variations of texture and tone. Rothko himself was known to speak about these images in terms of death—as desolate, empty images.

I myself find these paintings far from desolate; rather, I find them strangely hopeful. The portal, if portal they suggest, opens for me onto a non-threatening, welcoming space. It echoes with the vastness of the same universe which catches up scientific eyes and minds in a spirit of wonder. Despite the explicit absence of human figures, I do not find it hard to imagine these spaces filled with presences, human and divine. This will not, of course, be the experience of every viewer; much depends on prior experience and commitments. Many viewers—whether or not they have religious beliefs—will find themelves in some way drawn into a sense of being "accompanied" as they enter the visual space of a Rothko mural. When I enter their spaces, however, I arrive already predisposed to find in this "accompaniment" strong resonances with my Christian understanding of the communion of saints. I am already open to hear echoes of the psalmist's famous words, "The heavens are telling the glory of God."[38] Thus the paintings become iconic windows, occasions when, always strangely, the rawness of material prompts fresh confidence in transcendence, an immanent well-earthed transcendence, and provides my imagination with an enriched vocabulary meaningfully to envisage a rich communal possibility of "life beyond life."

---

38. Ps 19:1.

4

A Death Observed

*St. Thérèse of Lisieux and the
Music of John Tavener*

Brian Haymes

In our previous volume exploring the doctrine of the communion of saints, an understanding of "covenant" from Baptist and other dissenting traditions proved to be a fruitful way into the doctrine, revealing important insights into pastoral theological practices and the multi-dimensional nature of our common life in God.[1] In particular, my fellow-authors and I argued for an understanding of both covenant and communion that centered on the living and the dead as participating in the triune life of God. Baptism into God the Trinity means being in an unbroken fellowship, a sharing of life, in this present life and in death, born of the eternal love of God. There is a depth to communion not often explored by any whose understanding of discipleship lacks this essential corporate nature of the Church. We, the living and the dead who are alive in Christ, remain one in God.

In this chapter, I seek to explore further this understanding of gospel and church in relation to our living before the horizon of death. Being human, we shall all come to face what the apostle Paul called the last enemy (1 Cor 15:26), that attempt to deny us life as God's gift in Christ, who is the conqueror of the powers of death. Each person's dying and death is their own and we come to it in many different ways. For some there is the immediacy of the bullet, the accident, the earthquake, something that gives us no time to prepare and may come at any age. Others face the steady decline of their physical powers as the soft machine of the body simply wears out. This may be accompanied by pain and the wish that such suffering be over.

---

1. Fiddes et al., *Baptists and the Communion of Saints*, 127–84.

Dying in the faith of Christ in no way insures us against any and all of these ways by which our earthly life comes to an end. My purpose in this chapter is to reflect on facing death in the communion of saints, among those who live and face death in God.

The way in which I propose to reflect on this theme continues my study of St. Thérèse of Lisieux, which I began in our earlier volume.[2] In her own words we have reflections on her movement towards death and her dying, closely observed by those who shared the life of the Carmel with her. It will be her death which I invite you to observe with me. But later I shall turn to another reflection on her dying, in the opera *Thérèse* by Sir John Tavener. What does he see and how does he set to music the dying of this saint? What does he observe? Then I shall reflect on how this opera was performed and interpreted by one group of musicians. Finally I shall reflect briefly on how these various observations of death might help us in our understanding of the communion of saints and even in our own dying.

Introducing St. Thérèse of Lisieux

At first blush Thérèse seems a very unlikely candidate for sainthood. She was born in 1873 to exceptionally devout parents both of whom had separately, prior to marriage, sought the religious life in monastery and convent. In the event, Thérèse was the ninth child (of whom five survived) of Louis and Zélie Martin.[3] Theirs was a comfortable middle-class life, Louis a jeweller and Zélie running a lace-making business. Economically comfortable, they were also deeply pious. This very religious household knew the influences of a declining scrupulous Jansenist climate of sin and guilt even as it also knew deep expressions of human love and care. Her older sisters were to enter the Carmelite monastery in Lisieux and eventually she sought to follow them.[4]

Her life was short. She died horribly of tuberculosis at the age of twenty-four. She did not initiate any new works of mission. She led no advances in theology. Hers was the quiet life of a sister in an enclosed Carmel. How and why did she come to be identified as a saint and doctor of the church?

Under obedience, she had set about writing the story of her life. This was at the request in particular of Mother Agnes, then prioress of the Carmel at the age of thirty-one. Mother Agnes was Thérèse's natural older sister Pauline. Eventually there were to be three manuscripts: the first was

---

2. Fiddes et al., *Baptists and the Communion of Saints*, 114–25.

3. In October 2015, Louis and Zèlie Martin were canonized by the Roman Catholic Church, the first married couple to be canonized together.

4. Another sister tried with difficulty to become a religious in several traditions.

autobiographical and dedicated to Pauline; the second was a letter on the theme of her spiritual life requested by another of her biological sisters in the Carmel, Marie; the third consisted of further autobiographical pieces dedicated to the woman who was prioress when she entered the Carmel and again when she died, Mother Marie de Gonzague. At her death various other letters, poems, prayers, and writings were also gathered together.

It was the practice among Carmelites to send to all the Carmels an obituary which told the story of sisters who had died. Mother Agnes prepared a document based on these three manuscripts which was then sent around in place of an obituary. Two comments are pertinent here. First, there is strong evidence to suggest that Agnes worked on the manuscripts to make them conform to acceptable understandings of sainthood. She was eager to promote her sister's reputation but in so doing she sometimes changed the emphasis and meaning of her sister's writing.[5] In the judgement of Guy Gaucher, "She fell victim to an excess of sentimental devotion which betrayed her. She was victim also of her own language, which was that of the late nineteenth century and flowed from the religiosity of her age: a handicap to be overcome."[6] Second, the "book" became a huge "best seller" with demand for copies overwhelming the Carmel at Lisieux. Then came the stories of healings, graces, miracles attributed to Thérèse, not least from those serving in the First World War in Flanders, many of whom carried a picture or token of Thérèse with them. This was the popularity of the "Little Flower," all that the readers of the day would have expected a saint to be. It was sentimental and uncritical, far at times from the truth. In fact, what had been written by Thérèse had been transformed by over seven thousand readings and corrections by Mother Agnes.

The recent careful critical scholarship of the last fifty years has told a different story, not least of her dying.[7] The three manuscripts which make up the *Story of a Soul* have been carefully identified and edited.[8] In so far as it is possible to be confident, I have tried to concentrate on Thérèse's own account of her dying, indicating "a toughness, a sharpness, a splendidly incurable independence of mind which transcended her meagre education, and which even in sickness and mortal agony did not desert her."[9]

5. See the brisk discussion of these matters by Jean-François Six, *Light of the Night*. Facsimile editions of the autobiographical manuscripts were only released and published in 1956.

6. Gaucher, *Story of a Life*, 2.

7. See Meester, *With Empty Hands*, and Nevin, *Thérèse of Lisieux*.

8. I have used the third edition of 1996, translated by John Clarke: see Thérèse, *Story of a Soul*.

9. Furlong, *Thérèse of Lisieux*, 130.

Thérèse's first encounter with death and dying came with the death of her mother when she was four and a half years old. She remembers being taken to see her mother by her father who called on her to kiss her mother which she did without a word. She did not speak with anyone about the deep feeling she was experiencing, looking and listening in silence. Later she was to admit that the first part of her life ended that day. On August 28, 1877 she announced that she had chosen Pauline, one of her older sisters, to be her "mother."[10]

There were some aspects of her growing up that need indicating. Her school years which began in 1881 she described as the saddest of her life. Her home life by contrast was full of happiness in spite of some morbid scrupulosity. In 1883 she suffered a strange illness involving much trembling and coldness, probably the nervous disorder of Sydenham's Chorea, sometimes popularly called "St Vitus Dance."[11] One of her sisters brought a statue of the Virgin into her room where she was often calling "Mama, Mama." On Whit Sunday three sisters prayed before the statue and in Thérèse's own words, "All of a sudden the blessed Virgin appeared to me *beautiful*, so *beautiful* that never had I seen anything so attractive; her face expressed an ineffable benevolence and tenderness, but what penetrated to the very depths of my soul was the '*ravishing smile of the Blessed Virgin*'. At the instant, all my pain disappeared . . . "[12] For the most part there was no recurrence of this illness. She acknowledged that, as she would put it, in those days her soul was far from mature. She was certainly some way from learning to receive love from God such that she understood that the energy of her actions came from the work of God in her.

Another event, so significant she called it her "complete conversion," occurred on Christmas night 1886. She indulged in the traditional family practice which was for the youngest children to put their shoes at the fireplace to receive gifts. Coming downstairs she overheard her father's remark that at least this would be the last time this happened. It was a sudden transformation: "In an instant Jesus, content with my good will, accomplished the work I had not been able to do in ten years." She saw this as the start of a new period in her life. She became less sensitive. "Jesus changed me in such a way that I no longer knew myself."[13] The awareness of God's loving strength in her was the grace of her complete conversion.

---

10. Thérèse, *Story of a Soul*, 65–66.
11. See Nevin, *Thérèse of Lisieux*, 254.
12. Thérèse, *Story of a Soul*, 65–66.
13. Thérèse, *Story of a Soul*, 98.

Periods of inner spiritual dryness were not unknown to Thérèse. She experienced the silence of God, a dark night: "like Jesus in the garden. I felt I was alone, finding no consolation either on earth or from heaven. God seemed to have forsaken me!"[14] Other experiences brought a special joy, one of which needs mention now for what would follow in Tavener's opera. In 1887 in Paris a woman, her maid, and a child were all viciously stabbed to death. A man was arrested for the crime, Henri Pranzini. He protested his innocence but was found guilty and condemned to death. This news story was carried by many papers and was known to Thérèse. She adopted Pranzini as her "first child," praying for him and arranging to have masses offered for him. "I felt in the depths of my heart certain that our desires would be granted, but to obtain courage to pray for sinners I told God I was sure He would pardon poor unfortunate Pranzini and that I'd believe this even if he went to his death without any signs of repentance or without having gone to confession. I was absolutely confident in the mercy of Jesus. But I was begging Him for a 'sign' of repentance only for my own simple consolation."[15] In the event, Pranzini went to the guillotine. At the last moment he called for a crucifix and kissed it twice before dying. Thérèse believed that her prayer had been heard and the sign she hoped for had been granted. This was the grace Jesus had given her, to pray for sinners. Her determination to pray for sinners through sacrifice intensified her desire to enter Carmel.

She had wished to enter Carmel from an early age and found herself facing opposition. Some simply said she was too young for such a commitment. Others were wary of so many sisters from one family in one small community. Thérèse's story is one of persistence, taking every opportunity to press her case and eventually she entered the Carmel at Lisieux aged fifteen. She was seventeen when she took her final vows.

The Little Way

In 1892 a serious bout of influenza struck the Carmel. Several sisters died. Thérèse came to play a crucial role as one of the few who remained physically strong. She was much involved in caring for the sisters and taking initiatives with funerals and other duties. This work seemed to take her out of herself as she noticed that her scruples, her worries over details, became less troublesome to her. Out of tiredness, she wandered in thought during prayer even to the point of falling asleep. Her immediate reaction was to worry. She faced her times of doubt and uncertainty about her faith, something which

---

14. Thérèse, *Story of a Soul*, 107.
15. Thérèse, *Story of a Soul*, 100.

was in fact a feature of her whole life. At a retreat given at this time the priest gave her great assurance: "He told me that *my faults caused God no pain, and that holding as he did God's place,* he was telling me *in His name* that God was very much pleased with me."[16] The result was no longer her frustration with the sense of loneliness, the critical judgments of herself and those from Reverend Mother, and the petty problems with her fellow sisters.

Yet she still dreamed of greatness: "I feel the *vocation* of the WARRIOR, THE PRIEST, THE APOSTLE, THE DOCTOR, THE MARTYR."[17] Thérèse imagined these possibilities, reflecting her strong egotism and ambition.[18] About this time she wrote a play on one of her heroes, *Jeanne d'Arc*.[19] But her masochism was being transformed and she evolved what came to be called her "Little Way." Life became more straightforward, liveable, free from impossible dreams and the world of her unreal imagination. She came to face life as it is and began to show kindness, compassion, unselfishness. She took care over the smallest of duties and did them for love. This was virtually a complete reversal of what she had been taught about great saints, of her own ambition.[20] Life became for Thérèse a much simpler matter of following what she knew to be the will of God in all things, in life's common tasks. She came to give herself to that way, abandoning herself to the claims of God in the lives of others. So she became free to be herself—and that she believed was pleasing to God. She even began to sense that her own poverty of gifts enabled her to be the representative of all who might feel small, poor, and inadequate in themselves. This was her littleness and offering it to God was her vocation, life as offering.[21] The meaning of "littleness" moves beyond simple humility, as childlikeness becomes for Thérèse a confident hope such that a child might have in her father. She worked this out as she became responsible for the novices in the Carmel, although she insisted on remaining in the novice state in the Carmel which she did until the end. She longed to turn all her actions into deeds of love, no small matter in the Carmel community life.

At about this time she completed the first manuscript as instructed by Mother Agnes and gave it to her, but Pauline's three years as Reverend Mother were coming to an end. There was an election, an uncomfortable

16. Thérèse, *Story of a Soul,* 174.

17. Thérèse, *Story of a Soul,* 192.

18. John Udris, *Holy Daring,* 8–16, draws attention to her boldness, *parrhesia,* a consistent feature in her life and writings.

19. There were national celebrations in 1894.

20. That she was aware of the romantic tradition of sainthood is evidenced in her poems.

21. Thérèse, *Story of a Soul,* 192–95.

experience for the Carmel since there was a division built around the family presence of the Martins.[22] After a series of seven ballots Mother Marie de Gonzague once again took the prioress's seat in chapel. Pauline locked the manuscript away.

The Dark Night and the Vocation of Love

In April 1896, Thérèse observed the Lenten fast "in all its vigour." Good Friday night, for the first time, she coughed up blood. Her first response was a conviction "that Jesus, on the anniversary of his own death, wanted to have me hear His first call. *It was like a sweet and distant murmur that announced the Bridegroom's arrival.*"[23] She was going to heaven. She reports what has happened to Mother Gonzague but asked for nothing special. She was enjoying a "living faith" in those days but this did not last. Not for the first time in her life, but now most intently, there came a thick darkness. The thought of heaven, once such a delight, became a matter of trial and doubt. She used the metaphor of being in a dense fog: "it penetrates my soul and envelops it in such a way that it is impossible to discover within it the sweet image of my Fatherland; everything has disappeared."[24]

Thérèse was suffering from tuberculosis, a painful but poorly understood illness in those days. She was examined by a doctor who was on one side of the grille and she the other, dressed in her full robes! It is not surprising that he offered a misdiagnosis. A second doctor pronounced her well and she continued in the full life under the Carmel Rule. It is around this time that she begins the second manuscript at the request of Marie her eldest sister, asking for an explanation of her "Little Way." A letter, it is addressed to Jesus. Reflecting on 1 Corinthians chapter 13, the importance of which to her would be difficult to overestimate, she saw that no gifts or abilities were anything without love; charity is the excellent way that leads most surely to God. From now on she would prioritize love over faith and hope.

> I finally had rest. Considering the mystical body of the Church, I had not recognized myself in any of the members described by St.Paul, or rather, I desired to see myself in them *all*. *Charity* gave me the key to my *vocation*. I understood that if the Church had a body composed of different members, the most necessary and most noble of all could not be lacking to it, and so I understood that the Church *had a Heart and that this Heart*

22. Thérèse did not have a vote.
23. Thérèse, *Story of a Soul*, 211.
24. Thérèse, *Story of a Soul*, 213.

> *was BURNING WITH LOVE. I understood it was Love alone* that made the Church's members act, that if *Love* ever became extinct, apostles would not preach the Gospel and martyrs would not shed their blood. I understood that LOVE COMPRISED ALL VOCATIONS, THAT LOVE WAS EVERYTHING, THAT IT EMBRACED ALL TIMES AND PLACES . . . IN A WORD, THAT IT WAS ETERNAL!
>
> Then, in the excess of my delirious joy, I cried out: O Jesus, my Love . . . my vocation, at last I have found it . . . MY VOCATION IS LOVE![25]

Henceforth Thérèse would live in trust of God's love and not in her own attempted goodness. Marie was forcibly struck by this writing of her little sister. It was certainly not what she would have expected given their family formation in the faith. Thérèse remained outwardly cheerful, participating to the full in the life of the Carmel but increasingly aware of her illness. She suffered serious doubts. An old dream found new life as she desired to share in the missions, wanting to go to a Carmel in Vietnam.

Her relationship with Pauline found new life. Eventually Pauline was to read what Thérèse had written under obedience. It was not the easiest of relationships, with a natural born sister who had at one time had shared with Thérèse a mother/child relationship, now in a small community of nuns where there was already some suspicion of family connections. Only as late as April 1897 did Pauline begin to record their conversations. Again, Pauline was struck by the attitudes her sister revealed; for example, she wanted no fuss or wreaths at her funeral! Thérèse remained loyal to the Carmel community, wanting to keep the Rule but the increasing weakness resulting from her illness made this more difficult—or was there an element of revision as Thérèse came to focus on what she really believed was important?

To put it mildly, the medical care she received left a lot to be desired. The doctor whom Mother Gonzague commended and used did not understand her condition and sought to cauterize her, a drastic painful treatment from which it took time to recover. Finally Thérèse told Pauline of her condition as it became harder to conceal the coughing and the blood. Pauline told Mother Gonzague of the early manuscript which led the prioress to instruct Thérèse to continue writing in the face of her impending death. Pauline was allowed to sit with her sister privately and alone together. So Thérèse began her third manuscript, writing at times candidly about her faith:

> My dear Mother, I may perhaps appear to you to be exaggerating my trial. In fact, if you are judging according to the sentiments I

---

25. Thérèse, *Story of a Soul*, 194.

express in my little poems composed this year, I must appear to you as a soul filled with consolations and one for whom the veil of faith is almost torn aside; and yet it is no longer a veil for me, it is a wall which reaches right up to the heavens and covers the starry firmament. When I sing of the happiness of heaven and of the eternal possession of God, I feel no joy in this, for I sing what I WANT TO BELIEVE. It is true that at times a very small ray of the sun comes to illumine my darkness, and then the trial ceases for *an instant,* but afterward the memory of this ray, instead of causing me joy, makes my darkness even more dense."[26]

The focus of her reflection and writing became her vocation to love, not least her sisters in Carmel. She noted Jesus' readiness to love, and even to lay down his life for his friends, "the poor ignorant fishermen." It led her to face the fact that she did not love her sisters but God loved them. She came to understand that "charity consists in bearing with the faults of others (. . .) That charity must not remain hidden in the bottom of the heart. Jesus has said: *'No one lights a lamp and puts it under a bushel basket, but upon the lampstand, so as to give light to ALL in the house.'* It seems to me that this lamp represents charity which must enlighten and rejoice not only those who are dearest to us but *'ALL who are in the house'* without distinction."[27] Thérèse admitted she found such love impossible, but she saw that Jesus could love them in her. "Oh luminous Beacon of love, I know how to reach You. I have found the secret (. . .) I am only a child, powerless and weak, and yet it is my weakness that gives me the boldness of offering myself (. . .) Yes, in order that Love be fully satisfied, it is necessary It lower itself, and that It lower Itself to nothingness and transform this nothingness into *fire.* O Jesus, I know it, love is repaid by love alone."[28] This was the joy of the new commandment to love. She lived less by obedience to the Rule and more by this command from God. She trusted more in the activity of God in her life, that of love but her inner life became more arid. She found saying the rosary difficult but there was help in the common prayers in choir. The fervor of others made up for her own lack of devotion. Sometimes prayer became impossible—she slowly recites an "Our Father."[29]

Mother Gonzague gave her a spiritual brother, soon to be a mission priest. Thérèse was delighted by this, the second such responsibility for a priest that had been entrusted to her. She knew it was part of the Carmelite

---

26. Thérèse, *Story of a Soul,* 214.
27. Thérèse, *Story of a Soul,* 220.
28. Thérèse, *Story of a Soul,* 195.
29. Thérèse, *Story of a Soul,* 254.

calling to pray for priests. How was she to do this? She was given an answer from the Song of Songs, "DRAW ME, WE SHALL RUN after you in the odour of your ointments."[30] She realized that this work never happened alone to any soul when captivated by the love of Jesus; it is always "we" who are drawn by Christ: "I have no other treasures than the souls it has pleased You to unite to mine." She wanted to be able to pray the high priestly prayer of Jesus in John 17.[31]

With this, the language of the manuscript changes. No longer is it addressed to Mother Gonzague but to Jesus, with boldness. She reflects further on what it is to be "drawn" by Jesus into his love. She asks to be drawn further into the flames of his love, that he live and act in her. If she burns with his love then she will be active indeed in her mission calling and the more the souls who are given to her or who approach her will "run swiftly in the odour of the ointments of their Beloved." She recalls the love shown by Mary Magdalene and how she was praised by Jesus in contrast to his correcting of his ardent hostess. She believes all the saints have known this, the significance of prayer: "The Almighty has given them a *fulcrum: HIMSELF ALONE; as lever: PRAYER* which burns with a fire of love. And it is in this way that they have *lifted the world*; it is in this way that the saints still militant lift it, and that, until the end of time, the saints to come will lift it."[32]

The manuscript comes to an incomplete end, written in pencil since holding a pen became impossibly difficult. Whether Thérèse meant it or not the final words seem to be a summary, at least of these difficult days of pain:

> Most of all I imitate the conduct of Magdalene; her astonishing or rather her loving audacity which charms the Heart of Jesus also attracts my own. Yes, I feel it; even though I had on my conscience all the sins that can be committed, I would go, my heart broken with sorrow, and throw myself into Jesus' arms, for I know how much He loves the prodigal child who returns to Him. It is not because God, in His anticipating Mercy, has preserved my soul from mortal sin that I go to Him with confidence and love..."[33]

---

30. Song 1:3–4.
31. Thérèse, *Story of a Soul*, 254–55.
32. Thérèse, *Story of a Soul*, 258.
33. Thérèse, *Story of a Soul*, 258–59.

Facing Death

Thérèse steadily declined in health and strength. She was taken to the infirmary. Dr. de Cornière, the friend of Mother Gonzague, still misdiagnosed her illness, thinking it an incident of lung congestion and not tuberculosis. To be fair, little was known about the disease and out of fear it carried a certain social stigma. As far as Thérèse was concerned it was not the illness as such that mattered but that she was being consumed by the divine love. It was as if she echoed Job: "though He slay me, yet will I trust Him."[34] She had come to believe that the way of redemption lay through suffering but this was not the way of bodily penances. She focuses on the Songs of the Suffering Servant in Isaiah. She read the text in the Vulgate translation which translates Isa 53:3 not as the iniquitous hiding their faces from the sufferer (so the NRSV) but as Christ being the Sufferer whose face remains secret and hidden.[35] The cross of Jesus was not some self-imposed punishment. It was the act of love. Thérèse sought to bind herself more and more to Christ, embracing the crucifix not only at the feet but wholly at the face.

Pauline kept her company, keeping watch like a mother. She wrote their conversations down[36] although she was often surprised by Thérèse's attitudes and viewpoints, not least her joy. For example:

> Mother Agnes: "Are you afraid now that death is close?"
>
> Thérèse: *"Ah! Less and less!"*
>
> Mother Agnes: "Do you fear the Thief? This time He is at the door!"
>
> Thérèse: *"No. He is not at the door; He has entered. But what are you saying, little Mother? How can I fear one whom I love?"*[37]

This was not the kind of response expected from one schooled in the rule of the Carmel. The disease grew worse with Thérèse coughing up glasses of blood. This badly affected Pauline but Thérèse was aware that this fear was more for Pauline herself than for the patient who maintained, for the most part, a calm gaiety. She was aware that she must protect the community from her doubts. She enjoyed her gift for mimicry. Pauline was not the only one confused by her sister. Marie Guérin, a cousin, also a sister in

---

34. Job 13:15.

35. Thérèse, *Story of a Soul*, 152. Vulgate: *quasi absconditus vultus eius et despectus.* Cf. Nevin, *Last Years of Saint Thérèse*, 41.

36. There is doubt as to the authenticity of some of these conversations.

37. Thérèse, *Story of a Soul*, 262–63.

the Carmel, wrote to her father finding it impossible to understand Thérèse's seeming joy at dying. For Thérèse, it was time to raise questions with Pauline about the possible publication of the manuscripts and the kind of secrecy which should surround them until after her death.

Dr. de Cornière went away on holiday. Another doctor, brother-in-law of Marie Guérin himself visiting on holiday, asked permission to examine Thérèse and finally the disease was properly identified. He recognized the pain she was in and prescribed some relief. At this late stage, however, the tuberculosis had invaded her intestines. She never received the treatment which was needed and available. Still, Thérèse continued to wrestle with her doubts and talked of what faith meant to her. She longed for daily Eucharist, an activity of which Mother Gonzague disapproved but by August 19 she was unable to receive at all. Still Thérèse affirmed that since all was of grace she was content.

Members of the Carmel, especially her family sisters, would visit her with much of their traditional pietistic comfort. Thérèse commented to Pauline on the falseness of so much of this legendary material, especially concerning Mary the mother of Jesus. She said that if she were permitted to preach she would speak of Mary but in terms of her reality in life, not the popular escapist legends.[38] She seemed to have a presentiment about her activity after death. Then on July 17 she made her now-famous prediction: *"I feel that my mission is about to begin, my mission of making others love God as I love Him, my mission of teaching my little way to souls. If God answers my requests, my heaven will be spent on earth up until the end of the world. Yes, I want to spend my heaven in doing good on earth."*[39]

The pain increased, so much so that Thérèse became annoyed and critical, crying out in agony. She never prayed for any miracle for herself. Mother Gonzague would not permit morphine to ease the pain. Thérèse received Holy Viaticum. She remained *"in the night, that underground passage, before the wall."*[40]

At the end, the community was present around her bed. She smiled at them, saying nothing. For over two hours the death rattle tore at her chest, she shivered, and it became increasingly difficult for her to breath. She clutched the crucifix. The strain told on the sisters so the prioress sent them away. But it was not long before death came. The community reassembled, knelt at her bedside in time to hear her say, gazing at the crucifix,

---

38. Thérèse, *Her Last Conversations*, 161–62.
39. Thérèse, *Story of a Soul*, 263.
40. Thérèse, *Story of a Soul*, 266.

"Oh! I love Him! My God, I love you!"[41] She closed her eyes and died. To the mission priest for whom she prayed she had written on June 9, "*I am not dying; I am entering into life.*"[42] Within years her fame was enormous and she became an outstanding example of a saint raised to the altars of the church by popular acclaim.

Only God knows the truth of our lives. We cannot know what was going on in the depths of Thérèse, living and dying in Christ. Undoubtedly her religious upbringing was one that she valued but came to find it less than she needed. She lived with the experience of a wall between herself and God, or being in a dark tunnel, such that she had to live with many doubts, to feel at times what it was to be an atheist in a world without God. The small world of the cherished special child of her upbringing was left behind as she learned the truth of being one with all humankind, but a humankind shared and loved by God in Christ. The love she was called to share was very different from the sometimes sentimental love of the family home. It was cross-shaped. It necessarily involved suffering. It was for others. She wished to take her place at the table of sinners, willing to join them in hell out of love. For her, heaven came only with the end of all things in Christ. As Elizabeth Dreyer summarizes her journey, "From the child who kept count of her sacrifices and dreamt of a divine reward, she became an adult with insights into atheism and despair."[43]

Of herself she said, "When I want to rest my heart fatigued by the darkness that surrounds it by the memory of the harmonious country after which I aspire, my torment redoubles; it seems to me that the darkness, borrowing the voice of sinners, says mockingly to me: 'You are dreaming about the light, about a fatherland embalmed in the sweetest perfumes; you are dreaming about the *eternal* possession of the Creator of all these marvels; you believe that one day you will walk out of this fog that surrounds you! Advance, advance; rejoice in death which will give you not what you hope for but for a night still more profound, the night of nothingness.'"[44] She tells of her desire for Jesus to be loved even in hell. She would consent to see herself plunged into hell alongside sinners so that even there He would be loved eternally.[45] Her conviction was that Jesus had made her see this reality of unbelief and had brought her to participate in its darkness, so that she might live in this state of darkness for the sake of unbelievers. Paradoxically, this

---

41. Thérèse, *Story of a Soul*, 271.
42. Thérèse, *Letters*, 1128.
43. Dreyer, *Accidental Theologians*, 114.
44. Thérèse, *Story of a Soul*, 213.
45. Thérèse, *Story of a Soul*, 120.

is a new joy, the joy of not consciously perceiving her own belief. She knew agony without any mixture of consolation.[46] She had thoughts of suicide.[47] In these ways we may say that she was Thérèse *of the Holy Face*, desiring to be a visible reactualization of the passion of the Suffering Servant.[48] Like Jesus. Her suffering was an expression of her love, and so she welcomed suffering and made it an offering. Her self-witness shows us that she did not fear death although she endured excruciating pain in dying. There were moments of sudden dread, but she believed she was in the hands of God. In her own mind, she longed to suffer and to die of love.

Sir John Tavener and the Context of the Opera, "Thérèse"

John Tavener was one of the most significant of British composers in the twentieth century.[49] He was born in London in 1944 into an economically strong family that owned a successful upmarket building business. He was close to his parents, the relationship with his mother Muriel being particularly intense. There was music in the family, his grandfather owning a studio which contained a pipe organ. John quickly showed a precocious musical talent, the family saying that John "sees with his ears."[50] His aristocratic godmother took him to a performance at Glyndbourne of *The Magic Flute* when he was twelve, and he was overwhelmed by the experience. He attended a school with a notable music tradition, and fellow students included John Rutter, Brian Chapple, and others who would make their own significant contributions to British music making. During his school days he was composing, influenced at the time by Stravinsky, an influence that was to wane in later years. He won a scholarship to the Royal Academy of Music in 1962, studying piano and composition. An early success came with the dramatic cantata *The Whale*. This brought a contact with the Beatles and consequent productions on the Apple label. He began to receive commissions. The late 1960s and 1970s was a time of fruitful productivity. He was on the way to celebrity status.

The Christian faith was something he knew from birth. His father and later he himself played the organ in Presbyterian churches but slowly

---

46. Thérèse, *Last Conversations*, 204.
47. Thérèse, *Last Conversations*, 196.
48. Gaucher, *Passion of Thérèse of Lisieux*, 216.
49. For a mostly autobiographical account see Tavener, *Music of Silence*. Cf. Haydon, *John Tavener* and Dudgeon, *Lifting the Veil*.
50. Dudgeon, *Lifting the Veil*, xi.

he was introduced to Roman Catholicism. However, he could not imagine experiencing any religion without music. He also had a metaphysical bent, looking for a theory of everything, a metaphysical unity in all that is. For Tavener, any true conception of God had to be universal, or catholic.[51] A key figure in those early days was Father Malachy Lynch, a Catholic priest with a devotion to St.Thérèse who also had living contact with Sufism. This Irishman lived for tradition. Upon Father Malachy's death, at the funeral, a *Little Requiem* came unbidden and nearly completed into Tavener's mind.[52] It was the first of several occasions when he claimed this kind of inspiration happened.

Tavener came to believe that creativity was always in the hands of God.[53] Another friend, Jean Anderson, introduced him to the poetry of St. John of the Cross and he was taken to the Maundy Thursday service at Westminster Cathedral which he described as most desolate and primordially moving as the image of Christ is taken from the altar, laid in the tomb, and no longer with us. During these early years Tavener often thought of death. Whether he was aware of it or not he harbored Marfan syndrome, a threatening hereditary disease. He suffered a mild stroke in 1974 and underwent heart surgery. The issue of death was rarely far from his mind and music. The works of this period leading up to and including *Thérèse* face the questions of any continuing existence after death, anything that might suggest that there is a beauty and ecstasy in death which is more than the ugliness and pain that can come with dying. "After Father Malachy's death, I felt I wanted to write an opera based on St Thérèse of Lisieux; this intense twenty-four year old saint who appears to do nothing at all during her earthly existence."[54] He received a commission for the work from the Royal Opera House with the active encouragement of Benjamin Britten. Piers Dudgeon suggests that "John never meant this work to be a celebration of Thérèse's life, but rather a cry for what was missing in his." Tavener told him, "I needed a liturgical element to make sense of it all."[55] So, for the first time, he had to work with a librettist.

Gerald McLarnon, that librettist, was a creative but not an easy colleague. He was an Irish playwright, nurtured as a Roman Catholic but who had converted to Orthodoxy. With the zeal of the convert he could be highly critical of Catholicism. Tavener recalls that when he first broached the

51. Tavener, *Music of Silence*, 119–28.
52. Tavener, *Music of Silence*, 28.
53. Tavener, *Music of Silence*, 130–38.
54. Tavener, *Music of Silence*, 28.
55. Dudgeon, *Lifting the Veil*, 77.

subject of Thérèse, McLarnon replied, "Oh God—which one? Not that awful little flower!," hoping it might be Teresa of Avila.[56] Tavener explained his reasons, stressing Thérèse's struggles with faith, the apparent ineffectiveness of her earthly life and the notion of her eternity doing good on earth. They worked from 1973–1976 on the libretto, sometimes painfully so. Together Tavener and McLarnon made visits to Lisieux but there was little creativity as a result. On one visit they were able to talk with one of the nuns, Sister Marie-Lucille, who had been close to Thérèse's sister Celine who had nursed Thérèse when she was dying. Through a grille they told Marie-Lucille of their plans for the opera. She heard them out in silence and then taking a piece of paper wrote the one word *athéiste*.[57] They at first thought the word was meant for them but later they discovered that it referred to Thérèse's assumed loss of faith. I myself have shown above that, for Thérèse, faith as a gift of God remains. What falters is her own awareness of having belief. Thérèse never had stronger faith than when she had no conscious perception of her belief, but it seems that the sisters could not make this distinction.

McLarnon remained uncertain about the project and wanted to introduce the anarchic atheist French poet Arthur Rimbaud, who had explored mysticism, into the work. Tavener at first resisted this possibility and they seemed to have reached an impasse. They appealed for the help of another friend, Clive Wearing, and he it was who suggested using the *Song of Songs* which became the basis of the love duet between Christ and Thérèse. It was this insight that gave Tavener the crucial language for the work which became a dialogue between Thérèse and the Beloved, while the presence of Rimbaud remained. Tavener admits that during these years he was writing himself away from Catholicism;[58] McLarnon introduced him to Anthony Bloom, Metropolitan Anthony of Sourozh, who oversaw his conversion to Orthodoxy in 1977. *Thérèse*, along with the *Requiem for Father Malachy* and the *Canticle of the Mother of God*, turned out to be a watershed in Tavener's life.

Thérèse was first performed at the Royal Opera House on October 1, 1979, continuing for three more nights. A preview article in *The Musical Times* ended by suggesting that because of their demanding of the audience a response to what is a raw musical and dramatic exposition of a spiritual life, Tavener and McLarnon were playing for high stakes: *Thérèse* would either be awesome or would fail.[59] In the event, the judgment of the reviewer was that the performance was excellent but the life of the saint was not at

---

56. Tavener, *Music of Silence*, 29.
57. Haydon, *John Tavener*, 110.
58. Tavener, *Music of Silence*, 31.
59. Griffiths, "Thérèse," 814–16.

home in an opera house. "Too many devices seemed to be applied," wrote the reviewer, asking, "If we are invited to take part in some mystical ceremony or ritual—an experience that has always interested Tavener—do we need an opera house?"[60] The implication was that a religious context would be more appropriate. The work, however, is highly dramatic as Tavener seeks to use the entire space and possibilities provided by its original venue, the Royal Opera House. So how do Tavener and McLarnon tell this story?[61]

The Story of Thérèse as Opera

Tavener headed the full score with the words of the Russian Archimandrite Sophrony, "Let us not forget, that the way to this superabundant love lies through the depths of hell. We must not be afraid of this descent, since without it, plenitude of knowledge is unobtainable."

Thérèse is an opera in one act but with three distinct parts. Tavener describes the work as architectural, involving three symbolic journeys. There is no doubt from the very beginning that the subject is deeply serious, and that matters of life and death, heaven and hell are at hand. The drama is set over the Easter festival of 1896. The long opening section focuses on the "descent" of Thérèse as she sinks into the divine darkness. It begins with the passion of Thérèse, the stage all in darkness but male voices singing slowly *pianissimo* Alleluias with steady percussion accompaniment. Lights come up. Thérèse, who is always on stage, lies on her bed, center stage, wearing the night habit of a Carmelite. She clutches a cloth scapular. Either side are seven white and seven black figures. The black figures appear headless while the white figures are faceless nuns standing with their backs to the scene. Christ (a tenor) enters singing *Veni* from the dome of the opera house, quoting from the Song of Songs.[62] He is joined by Thérèse who sings *Death*. Eventually she raises the scapular. It is stained with blood. Christ still sings and is heard by Thérèse who responds: *Behold, the bridegroom cometh!*[63] She tries to rise. The black figures move with menace and mockery singing repetitively: *Night of nothing!* Thérèse sings, *Blind then and dumb, I'll take the cross and climb the hill of Golgotha.*

The scene changes. The area behind the bed is lit, a hill of bones and skulls. Christ stands on the hill, dressed in purple. He strikes a crucifixion

60. Dean, "Music in London," 932–33.

61. The libretto is published by J. and W. Chester/Edition Wilhelm Hansen, London Ltd, 1979, and quotations are made by kind permission.

62. "Come [to my garden, my sister, my bride]": Song 5:1. See also Song 1:4.

63. Matt 25:6.

pose as he sings *Eli, Eli, Eli*.[64] Thérèse looks up terrified and in a childlike manner sings *Baby goes to bye-byes.* The white figures approach her bed. They sing *Christ is risen!* Thérèse continues, *Baby goes to bye-byes.* Almost hysterically the white figures continue to sing *Christ is risen!* Christ appears again on the hill of bones, arms extended singing the cry of desolation. He disappears and Thérèse uncovers her face. Now in panic she sings *Mama! Mama!* She twitches and jerks. She sings *Christ have pity of your little g g g g girl!* The white figures continue to respond with *Christ is risen!* Thérèse opens her eyes but she does not see Christ. The black figures sing *Christ is dead!* The white figures sing *Christ is risen!* Thérèse calls for pity, she stops twitching and looks at the white figures. She says she is in a tunnel of black stone. The black figures cry *Atheist.* The white figures sing *Christ is dead!* Thérèse cries *Agne* (an exclamation of pain), *Mama! Have pity!* Black and white figures together cry *Atheist.* Thérèse unaccompanied sings *I do not know how to die.* Christ appears again, standing as if nailed to the cross, over the bed of Thérèse. He sings *Eli, Eli, lama sabachthani!*[65] He comes down from the hill to the foot of Thérèse's bed. He sings *Ecce tu pulchra es!*[66] Thérèse, with hand extended, sings *Behold thou are fair, beloved!*[67] At which point he removes his crown, mask, and robe and appears as her father Louis.

So begins the first journey with her father. Almost as if he is teaching her to walk, they move backwards and forwards. Both of them sing *Draw me after. Let us hasten.*[68] Twice Thérèse stops, asking if he is her father. Will he lead her through the black stony night to morning? *Or oblivion!* replies her father. The stage becomes light and on to it as a harlequin figure dances Rimbaud, teasing her. The music then draws on children's songs. He begins to recall her childhood, in particular a moment when Thérèse claimed she saw the letter T in the planets. "Look Father," she had said, "my name is written in heaven." To which Rimbaud replies, *Astronomical arrogance of one little flower.* Thérèse sings to herself, *A child! I saw as a child!* A dancer begins to dance, as if chasing a little bird and catching it, only to release and imitate its flight. The dancer makes herself very small. Rimbaud sings *Cockadoodledo* and the dancer rises as a firebird with eyes set on the sky. Rimbaud cries *Arrogance! Arrogance! Arrogance!* To which Thérèse replies, *A child! A child! I was a child!* And a group of children sing, in French, a song of a child loving to recall childhood days, the flowering of innocence,

64. "My God, my God, my God": Matt 27:46.
65. "My God, my God. Why have you forsaken me?": Matt 27:26.
66. "Behold, you are beautiful!": Song 1:14, Song 4:1, 4:7, 6:4.
67. Song 1:15.
68. Song 1:4.

the Lord always surrounding her with love. The dancer poses as a lectern and Thérèse reads of her childhood, of being only a little bird yet with an eagle's eye and and daring to gaze on the Divine Sun. Again, with vicious irony Rimbaud calls out: *LEVIATHAN arrogance of one little chicken.* She responds: *A child! I saw as a child!* Again Rimbaud accuses her of arrogance, of being able to show to the wisest the way of perfection. Thérèse again reads from the imaginary book, making the claim of which he accuses her, and Rimbaud shuts the book with savage delight: *GARGANTUAN arrogance of one little girl!*[69]

Then the incident of Thérèse's falling ill with St. Vitus dance is recalled: *Dance of St Vitus, Dance of your scalded pride, dance, dance, dance!* Thérèse, with little screams calls: *Have pity on your little girl! Agne! Mama!* This journey through childhood ends recalling the miracle of the Mother of God. Thérèse sings, *A Miracle cured me, a miracle! God's mother smiled on me; O smile again now in this night.* Rimbaud dances around her and with great flamboyance, grandeur, and irony sings, *A miracle cured the child. And you spewed that miracle out into the bucket ears of Carmelite nuns—at the tickle of flattery you vomited out Eternal life.* Thérèse admits that is the truth: *I shall sit with sinners now and with dark souls for whom God is dead.*

The second journey begins with her father and Rimbaud. Thérèse sings, *A sky of stone is on my head* and Rimbaud adds *The tunnel shrinks as you go downwards.* They talk together with her father and a male chorus sings in Spanish about a man leaving his house unseen. It recalls the incident of Thérèse seeing her father in distress. Rimbaud asks: *Where have you seen him?* Thérèse responds: *His face is hidden. No one sees him.*[70]

Then voices call from the darkness: *Pranzini.* Pranzini stands center stage, arms extended like a cross. This is the criminal Thérèse has adopted as her spiritual child. From the crowd come two women and a child. Rimbaud asks Thérèse: *you know that face?* Thérèse replies: *I know that soul! God snatched him from the rim of hell.* Then in some drama, with funeral marches, the three murders of Pranzini are retold in gruesome detail at the end of which Rimbaud faces her with a choice: *Choose, Thérèse! Great saints must choose!* Thérèse moves as if she has the girl's head in her hands. She moves towards the cross. Rimbaud sings, *The reptile head of granite blood, that wears a mask of human skin.* Thérèse in an agony of choice cries *Jesus!*

---

69. It might be asked whether McLarnon, through the voice of Rimbaud, is himself being unfair to Thérèse. Another interpretation of the little bird and the eagle might be in terms of her humility, her littleness which nonetheless shows boldness. See Udris, *Holy Daring*, 6. Humility is one of Thérèse's main themes; one of her plays about Joan of Arc is entitled, "The Triumph of Humility."

70. Echoing perhaps Isa 53:3—see the discussion above.

Jesus! with great passion. She is now facing Pranzini. She sees no reptile face but something holy and wonderful. She falls to the ground and bows at Pranzini's feet. One of the women walks away, and so does Pranzini, while her father walks to where Pranzini stood.

Thérèse, her father, and Rimbaud begin the third journey, to the words *Let us hasten–draw me after, see we hasten.* Thérèse, holding her father's hand sings *The tunnel's gone (. . .) the stone sky.* Rimbaud sings, *Your journey's end.* She walks on. Both Rimbaud and her father move away from her. Thérèse announces: *I've seen the holy face! Where?* asks Rimbaud. *In a child, in a criminal,* she replies. *In a dream!* sings Rimbaud. Her father again takes her by the hand. Thérèse stops, singing *I have seen Christ's face on earth.* Christ and Rimbaud are close to the hill on the stage with their backs to it. Rimbaud sings the striking lines, *Saints are the strong ones, artists are no longer needed!*

There is silence as the hill opens and Rimbaud disappears, and Christ too leaves. A deep note is sounded. Christ reappears as Christ in glory, with a golden face mask and a glittering robe. Thérèse does not turn to him but sings: *My word! My work! My heaven shall be on earth, serving God on earth till time dies on earth.* Christ exits and there is darkness everywhere as the music which is to mark the "ascent" of Thérèse is first heard. There are walls of barbed wire, marks of Flander's battles and concentration camps. The color red predominates. Thérèse sings again with her back to the vision: *My heaven shall be on earth serving God on earth till time dies on earth.* She turns and sways at the sight. She raises her hands and cries triumphantly with all her might: *My God, my God, Thou hast not forsaken them.* Two lines of naked skeleton-thin men shuffle in, herded by seven faceless others carrying machine guns. They sing, *We do not know how to die.* They are lined against an invisible wall between them and the hill. They are killed. The soldiers sing, *They do not know how to die* and the mountain opens and they disappear in smoke. The soldiers also go into darkness. Thérèse sings: *My God, my God Thou hast not forsaken them.* Groups of little children come and play games, until all freeze in white light. Then darkness and Thérèse stands alone. She goes up to the hill, raising her hands in mute appeal. She lowers her hands and turn around facing front. She prostrates herself, stretching out her arms in the form of a cross. The light above her contracts, becomes radiant, seeming to draw her up. She stands radiant in the light and so the opera ends with the song of ecstasy, a duet as Thérèse and Christ sing together. It ends with Thérèse singing *Love* and Christ singing *Veni.* All the lights go out and, as at the beginning, the steady beat of Alleluias is heard.

A Performative Interpretation of the Opera

When Tavener's opera *Thérèse* was first performed at the Royal Opera House it was not hailed as a success, although BBC 3 carried a live performance. As far as I am aware no public commercial recording of the work has ever been produced. However, Rhonda Kess, an American teacher of music theater at Trinity College of Music, where Tavener was still nominally a professor, presented *Thérèse* in a shortened version of her own editing. It was the college's Christmas production, staged in the small Rudolf Steiner Theatre on the nights of December 5 and 6, 1991. This was the first performance since the first production in 1979. Tavener was present at both performances and declared himself pleased with the production. There are video tapes of the performances of both evenings, although the quality of reproduction is not very good. The tapes can be viewed by arrangement at the College Library, as I and my fellow-authors did in 2015.[71]

It is obvious from the recordings that conditions were cramped for both performers and musicians. These limitations meant that much of the drama of the Covent Garden production as it was envisioned in the published libretto was impossible. However, it was a bold student presentation, given the considerable demands Tavener makes on the performers.

There were several changes made from the original libretto for this production. The cuts meant the opera was reduced from ninety to sixty minutes in length. Visually, there was no place for the "hill" which is an important feature of the original, standing for the hill of bones, the hill of Golgotha. In the production there were two "Thérèses," one who was permanently in bed at the front of the stage. Other changes and omissions prove to be very significant in comparison to the original libretto. All references to the hill of Golgotha and Thérèse's cries of terror in the journey of descent are excised. The various contributions of children singing and playing are likewise omitted. The main emphases in the college's production are on Rimbaud, who is now visually set in the context of a circus, and on the story of Pranzini whose three murders are all fully played out. However, what is hardly present at all in these scenes is the making of the sign of the cross, which is an often-repeated action in the original libretto. Further, verbal references to Christ and the cross play little part in this shortened version.

This is the most serious and significant of the changes made because now Thérèse's story appears more of an individual human struggle in a search for meaning. While the part of Rimbaud is strongly presented, and makes an imaginative contribution to the story, the work has become a

---

71. We are very grateful to Clare Kidwell, a librarian at Trinity Laban College, for help with visits to view these tapes on October 7, 2015.

narrative of existential *angst*. Unlike Thérèse's own writing, which is reflected in the original libretto, the image of Christ to whom she dedicates her life in the service of others is seriously diminished. The meaning of the story as Thérèse told it is in the Christology but it is this that has been edited out, consequently changing the meaning of her death. Being in Christ is the basis for the communion of saints, of which we catch a glimpse in the presence of Thérèse with soldiers on the front line of battle, sharing in the suffering of the world in life and after her death because she is participating in God through Christ. In her own words, as preserved in the libretto: "My work! My heaven shall be on earth." In the shorter version we are told a secular story with little religious and theological content. Christ, so central to Thérèse's life story—Thérèse of the Child Jesus and of the Holy Face—is so distant and hidden as to be absent, not in the theological sense of a felt absence in Thérèse's agony of faith, but simply by not being significant to the drama of life.

Mother Thekla, a nun in the enclosed Orthodox Monastery of the Assumption in North Yorkshire who became a spiritual guide for Tavener, had expressed reservations about the opera. She never thought that even the original libretto engaged with her idea of being and becoming a saint, and she would surely have been more critical of the shortened version. Certainly the spiritual themes implicit in Thérèse's writings and in Tavener's opera are here reduced to near oblivion. By contrast, in Tavener's own words:

> The final section is a gigantic 'time' mirror of the opening section. Thérèse I left alone, apparently abandoned on the fields of annihilation where battles have been fought, in concentration camps where human beings have gone beyond despair, and finally she witnesses the total extinction of this world. Side by side with devastation, she contemplates rebirth, understanding that there is no tragedy in God, and none of the despair that destroys. Reaching her lowest ebb, humanly speaking, Thérèse prostrates herself and kisses the earth. An enhanced recognition of human suffering somehow brings her to her feet, and the opera ends with a cry of triumph, a song of love to God, sung for the suffering in the world. The music closes as it began, with Alleluias sung in Church-Slavonic, sounding from the dome.[72]

Tavener was working out much of his own convictions at this time. He was disappointed by the Roman Catholic Church, its legalism and scholasticism. To his mind, issues of papal infallibility and a pharisaical Vatican smacked of that human pride that cursed the human race. He wrote

---

72. "Musical Note," in McLarnon, *Thérèse*, 3.

Thérèse at a difficult time of his life when he was disillusioned by much of the West's culture and civilization. He shared something of Thérèse's doubts and longed to stand in her place, nevertheless, of faith in God. The piece in many ways is a completion of this part of Tavener's life.

Thérèse and the Communion of Saints

Thérèse found her "Little Way" liberating. She had moved from a rule-bound over-scrupulous way of life that shaped her family life and that of the Carmel, to a freedom to love called for by the presence of others. She saw this not as her love but as the love of Jesus that she perceived in the cross and that she believed was now indwelling her. A life aimed at personal achievements gave way to a participation in the love of Jesus for the world, a feature of the lives of all saints. The love of Jesus was the love of God. She wanted to love as God loved, and this was a direct simple passion; indeed, she was aware that her thoughts were something out of the ordinary for the Carmel tradition. There are no serious reflections on the Trinity in her writing, but this faith was the given structure of her life, worship, and love. Living "in love" was a dwelling "in God," and in that location she could offer prayer for a suffering world. This is precisely the nature of the communion of saints, summed up in the text she chose from Song of Songs as a clue to intercessory prayer: "Draw me; *we* shall run after you." Perceptively, McLarnon and Tavener selected these words to mark the "three journeys" of Thérèse.

There was nothing sentimental here. Such sentimentality she knew from her home and was aware of as Carmelite sisters came and spoke easy words of "comfort" to her at the end. She had come far from such religiosity. She knew there was no love without cost and pain to the lover but this was sharing the love of Jesus. She came to realize that martyrdom was not one single act but rather a life lived in persistent love.

Tavener's Thérèse has her faced rubbed in childish sentimentalism by Rimbaud. She does not try to defend it, claiming she was only a child. For her the way to heaven lies through the hell of suffering, her own and that of the world. Admittedly, her childishness, pride, and ambition are always there just below the surface, and there is a darkness surrounding her dying. Yet, for love she nailed herself to the earth for the saving of humankind ("My heaven will be spent on earth"). The religion of escapism moved aside for the way of costly discipleship.

Both Thérèse and Tavener trusted in a God whose mercy was stronger than sin, suffering, and death. They shared a deep conviction about the reality of the communion of saints. Tavener surrounded himself with icons of the saints and was known to visit shrines in order to venerate relics.[73] Thérèse understood that she faced her own death held in that communion, which meant the eternal love of Jesus Christ. She believed that she would meet again with "Papa, Mama, the four little Angels. I believe I am enjoying for ever a real and eternal family reunion."[74] As she participated in love so she shared the love at the heart of all things, especially in the church. It was not her love of its sometimes difficult members that became her focus but the possibility of sharing the love of Jesus for them. Jesus' love for all the world was the love of others in her, even for those she herself could not love.

It is this community of love, alive in Jesus, that she believed "lifts the world." Thus the prayers of the saints are essential to the world's life and hope. Thérèse was astonished that Christ, true God and true human, not only gives and offers love but seeks to be loved, begs like a mendicant for response. By Jesus' cry, "I thirst," she found ignited within her a strange and living fire.[75] She sees in this what we might call an interpenetration of lives as she engages with others in and through Christ. As in the Trinity space is made for each to be themselves in God so she can live with the difficult sisters, and with herself, held in love as early sentimentality gives way to a deeper sense of God in others. Her own "favorite" saint was Teresa of Avila after whom she was named. With Teresa and St. John of the Cross she could live in the dark places in a trust of God who in Christ knew the desolation of unloved love.[76]

I do not know if Dietrich Bonhoeffer ever read anything of Thérèse's writing but I am struck by the resonance with her thought in his famous letter on the day after the unsuccessful attempt on Hitler's life:

> I discovered late, and I'm still discovering right up to this moment, that it is only by living completely in this world that one learns to have faith. One must completely abandon any attempt to make something of oneself, whether it be a saint, or a converted sinner, or a churchman (a so-called priestly type!), a righteous man or an unrighteous one. By this-worldliness I mean living unreservedly in life's duties, problems, successes and failures, experiences and perplexities. In so doing we throw ourselves completely into the arms of God, taking seriously not our

---

73. Tavener, *Music of Silence*, 53.

74. Thérèse, *Story of a Soul*, 88.

75. Thérèse, *Story of a Soul*, 99.

76. Nevin, *Last Years of Saint Thérèse*, 1–36 offers a discussion of the considerable influence of Teresa of Avila and St. John of the Cross on Thérèse.

own sufferings, but those of God in the world—watching with Christ in Gethsemane. That, I think, is faith; that is *metanoia*.[77]

Tavener too was affected by the difficulties of trying to live by a form of the faith he did not find wholly sufficient. He enjoyed playing what he called the "soupy" hymns of the Free Churches but liturgically he needed something more. He was much affected by a brief first marriage he entered into in 1974. He, with Thérèse, sought a life and future with others, dedicated to the praise and glory of God. He had not yet found that as he wrote the opera but he sensed the importance for Thérèse, and perhaps for himself, of the agony that goes with faith. His later works such as *Akhmatova Requiem* (1979) and *Eis Thanaton* (1985) still faced the reality of death but they do so in fuller recognition of the saints and their role in the church. For both Thérèse and Tavener faith is no easy journey but it is made at the loving invitation of One who calls *veni, veni*, a call to enter the love that the saints know and share, the love that does not let the world go.

I began this chapter by reflecting that the idea of "covenant," drawn from the dissenting tradition of Christianity in England, has the capacity for stretching the bounds of the fellowship of the church to include not only the living but the dead. It also has the potential for crossing the boundaries between the local assembly and wider manifestations of the body of Christ. Appeals to maintain unity between congregations have been often based on the understanding that the "communion of saints" (members) in one local community is interdependent with others, since they are all held in one covenant and so one communion.[78] Both Thérèse and Tavener, with different sets of languages, understand the love of God to range much wider than particular ecclesiological limits. In Tavener's mind the range became increasingly universal, exceeding any particular confession of the Christian church, as all creation is gathered up in the "cosmic dance of the resurrection" into the salvation of God.[79] For Thérèse, much more was at stake than the survival of the Carmel, or even the church as a whole. From the first she saw herself as engaged in mission, praying at first for missionary priests, and then focusing eventually on those whose lives were marked by unbelief. Thus it was that Thérèse asked that her "heaven" be spent on earth doing good for the sake of others with whom she came to identify, so lowering herself "to nothingness."[80] It is the judgment of Thomas Nevin that "the table of sinners provides the ground for Thérèse's ever-renewable mission. She becomes the

---

77. Bonhoeffer, *Letters and Papers from Prison*, 369–70.
78. Haymes, "Communion of Saints," 51–56.
79. Tavener, *Music of Silence*, 181.
80. Thérèse, *Story of a Soul*, 263, 195.

saint of the dispossessed, all who sit in darkness, including those who care to gloat in it. At the same time she, she speaks to those within the folds of faith who fell troubled and bereft of hope, who find themselves lacking the warmth and sustenance of faith. Thérèse is the saint . . . of those who fear to acknowledge that their faith has been weakened or lost altogether."[81] Thus Thérèse's desire to suffer, so misunderstood by her sisters in the Carmel, echoed for her the costly passion of Christ for the forsaken.

---

81. Nevin, *Thérèse of Lisieux*, 320.

5

The Journey and the Dwelling

*After Death in the Musical Images
of Elgar and Brahms*

PAUL S. FIDDES

THE DOCTRINE OF THE communion of saints affirms that, in some way, we have fellowship with the saints in light, with all "saints" (understood as all believers, being made progressively "holy" by God) and with named saints, whose lives have stood out as a focus of God's gracious activity in the world and who stand on the church's calendar. The church has traditionally linked this communion with the possibility of reciprocal and mutual prayer between all those who are in God through Christ, whether living or dead. But this raises the question, "How do the saints live on?" What kind of condition of existence makes credible the notion of a fellowship of prayer?

We cannot know the answer to that question scientifically, in the sense of empirical investigation and validation. We can only come to some reasonable proposals by using imagination, constructing pictures which are in accord with the images and concepts given us in the Scripture which has shaped the faith and imagination of the church through the ages, within which process we can believe the Spirit of God to be at work. Imagination can be a response to the self-unveiling of the triune God as much as discursive reasoning. Music, the visual arts, and poetry offer a medium for this response, and I want to consider two images that music has embodied: the journey and the dwelling.

Elgar: the Journey of the Soul

The image of a journey through and after death has rarely been better expressed than by Edward Elgar, in his Oratorio *The Dream of Gerontius*. Composed for the Birmingham Music Festival in 1900, this is a setting of the poem of the same name by Cardinal John Henry Newman (1801–1890) who, while a priest of the Church of England was a leader of the Anglo-Catholic Oxford movement; the poem was written, however, long after Newman's conversion to Roman Catholicism in 1845. Elgar's music is strongly influenced by Wagner, and the similarity between the Preludes to *Parsifal* and the *Dream* (especially the opening section) has often been remarked upon. In both works the solos and the choruses are thoroughly integrated, unlike conventional oratorio where they are separated as set pieces, so that the *Dream* makes its impact as drama. The leading theme of this drama is a journey. Part I is to climax with Gerontius passing from this life, accompanied by a chorus consisting of his priest and "assistants", all bidding him: "Go forth upon thy journey Christian soul! Go from this world!"

At the beginning of the poem Gerontius, an "old man," is near to death, hearing a "visitant . . . knocking his dire summons at my door," and he rouses himself to travel "through such waning span/ Of life and thought as still has to be trod" before the next phase of the journey after death. The music begins with a long, slow, and somber line in D minor played pianissimo by the clarinets, bassoons, and violas, similar to the opening theme of *Parsifal*, which Elgar's friend August Jaeger calls a "Judgement" theme.[1] In his analysis Jaeger identifies and names no less than fourteen themes which emerge in the Prelude and which are almost all to be played out in the whole work. The opening themes express Gerontius' changing moods on the verge of death, and Jaeger names those following "Judgement" as "Fear," "Prayer," "Sleep," "Committal," "Miserere," and "Despair."[2] When, for example, the theme appears that will accompany Gerontius' anguished prayer ("be with me, Lord in my extremity") the music builds to an urgent climax with organ underpinning and thudding timpani.

Now, this shift from theme to theme, each appearing many times in whole or in fragments, accentuates the sense of a forward movement and so evokes the sense of a journeying onward. Elgar is creating a flexible vocal style in which the music of the soloist adapts constantly to the words in the way that we find in recitative, but here it is melody rather than spoken recitative which sets the opening lines in which Gerontius runs through a

---

1. Jaeger, *Dream of Gerontius*, 4. Jaeger was nicknamed "Nimrod" by Elgar in *The Enigma Variations*.

2. Jaeger, *Dream of Gerontius*, 4–6.

range of feelings of desperation, terror, appeal, and finally exhausted calm. Among the themes propelling this forward momentum is the one Jaeger names "Committal."[3] This has an extraordinary rhythmic fluidity, and it evolves throughout Part I, growing and developing in its noble statement until it bursts out at the end of the movement with its affirmation of Gerontius' journey: "Go forth upon thy journey Christian soul!"

First the priest (bass) declares that he is to go in the name of the Trinity, Father, Son, and Holy Spirit. At the words "Go in the name of Angels and Archangels," the chorus joins in, building to a massive triple forte on the words "go forth." He is also to go in the name of "all saints of God, both men and women." "Go on thy course" they exhort, in the name of patriarchs, prophets, apostles, evangelists, martyrs, confessors, holy monks and hermits, and holy virgins. He is to journey on in the name, in the company and with the support of the triune God and all the saints.

> *Proficere, anima Christiana, de hoc mundo!*
>
> Go forth upon thy journey, Christian soul!
>
> Go from this world! Go, in the Name of God
>
> The Omnipotent Father, who created thee!
>
> Go, in the name of Jesus Christ, our Lord,
>
> Son of the living God, who bled for thee!
>
> Go, in the Name of the Holy Spirit, who
>
> Hath been poured out on thee!
>
> Go, in the name
>
> Of Angels and Archangels; in the name
>
> Of Thrones and Dominations, in the name
>
> Of Princedoms and Powers; and in the name
>
> Of Cherubim and Seraphim, go forth!
>
> Go, in the name of Patriarchs and Prophets;
>
> And of Apostles and Evangelists,
>
> Of Martyrs and Confessors; in the name
>
> Of holy Monks and Hermits; in the name

---

3. Jaeger, *Dream of Gerontius*, 6, 15.

> Of holy Virgins; and all Saints of God,
>
> Both men and women, go! Go on thy course;
>
> And may thy place today be found in peace,
>
> And may thy dwelling be the Holy Mount
>
> Of Sion; through the same, through Christ our Lord.

With the final words the accompaniment softens to a single melody for the first violins, and then orchestra and voices swell up gently on the words "through Christ our Lord," bringing a movement that began in D minor to an end in D major. *"Go forth upon thy journey, Christian soul"* Gerontius has been bidden. And journey on he does.

Part II begins with a hushed introduction, one of the finest things Elgar ever wrote, and Gerontius feels as though he has awoken, refreshed from sleep. "I feel in me an inexpressive lightness" he sings, and this lightness is articulated (if not fully expressed) in a melody in F major (marked *dolce e legato*) and in a triple time (3/4) which is musically lighter than the quarter-time rhythms of Part I. While a forward momentum was evoked by the constant shifting of themes in the first part, here it is delivered more by the skipping rhythm. For while the soul of Gerontius remarks "how still it is!/ I hear no more the busy beat of time" and celebrates a "deep rest," he is in fact in motion. The lightness betokens swift travel, and Gerontius finds himself borne onwards by a gentle pressure, held fast in someone's hand: "A uniform/ And gentle pressure tells me I am not / Self-moving, but borne forward on my way." In an extended conversation between Gerontius and his guardian angel, when many questions are answered, Gerontius exclaims: "What lets me now from going to my Lord?" The angel replies "Thou art not let [hindered] but with extremest speed art hurrying to the just and holy judge."

He passes through the heavens, wondering why he has no fear of meeting his Lord. On he goes, traveling through the outer regions of the court of divine judgment, passing malignant and false spirits singing a mocking fugue, who fail to distract him with their temptations. As Jaeger points out, Elgar contrasts the passage of the soul onwards to the throne of God with the stationary position of the demons who can make no progress, by having their jeers grow more and more faint to our hearing.[4] On Gerontius journeys towards the presence of God himself whom he desires with a fervent love to see face to face. The soul hears distant singing, the first sounds of a choir singing "Praise to the Holiest in the height." The angel announces that they "have passed the gate, and are within/ The House of Judgement." The

---

4. Jaeger, *Dream of Gerontius*, 24.

pace quickens, and Gerontius adds another image of movement; the surging music reminds him, he says, of "the rushing of the wind—/ The summer wind—among the lofty pines." Marking their progress on the journey to the "veiled presence of our God," the angel introduces the singing of the great hymn "Praise to the Holiest in the Height" as he sings in ecstasy, "And now the threshold, as we traverse it,/ Utters aloud its glad responsive chant." All the voices join together triple-forte, singing "Praise to the Holiest" accompanied by full orchestra. While the hymn begins with a massive announcement of the first musical subject in what Elgar called "the great Blaze," it does not remain static, but underlines the overall sense of movement by swinging into a second subject in a different tempo on the words "O loving wisdom of our God!" Two subjects intertwine in an intricate way with four- and eight-part harmonies, until with a last repetition of the refrain the voices and orchestra recombine in C-major for a final, resonant chord.

As Gerontius comes finally before God, angelic voices on heaven and the voices of friends on earth combine in prayer to plead for mercy. Elgar now builds up the "judgement" theme throughout the orchestra, rising to an enormous crescendo. He writes in the score: "For one moment, must every instrument exert its fullest force." The sight of God is overwhelming; as the angel had warned, the soul is safe and quickened by God, but also at the same time "consumed." As the soul of Gerontius sees God in glory and holiness he cries out: "Take me away!"

As Elgar sets this exclamation, it is not a cry of fear but one of deepest love: it is as if he desires to be with God but knows he is not yet ready. He has come thus far on his journey, and we are reminded of this by the inclusion of many of the musical themes explored so far in his response that follows the opening words, "Take me away!" But his journey is not complete. Poet and musician, Newman and Elgar, both Catholics, believe that he must pass through the waters of purification, the cleansing waters of purgatory. The angel promises that he will, "through the flood thy rapid passage take, sinking deep, deeper into the dim distance" and will after the night of trial be brought home to the God whom he has come to love in Christ.

Newman and Elgar are weaving together the motifs of a journey and a fellowship of intercessory prayer between the living and the dead, the prayers bearing Gerontius forwards. In the Prelude, what Jaeger calls the "prayer theme" is thundered out by the full force of the orchestra, including organ. "It seems," commented Jaeger, "like the whole church's agonized supplication, 'Jesu, have mercy! Mary, pray for me!'"[5] Nor is the intercession sought only from Mary, or from the "Angel of the Agony." Later, as Gerontius enters the

---

5. Jaeger, *Dream of Gerontius*, 6.

throne-room of God, we hear the echo of the prayer of the assistants singing at the bedside of Gerontius in Part I; the same theme, the music of the *Kyrie Eleison*, appears again with the words "Be merciful, be gracious, spare him Lord." Yet we feel that the aspect of intercession is subordinate to the motif of the journey. We recall that on its earlier appearance, the *kyrie* theme was followed immediately by the great *Profiscere* chords, "Go forth, Christian soul," and here, in the majestic throne-room, it is the journey into God's presence that is foremost. As Jaeger notes again, while the "prayer theme" is given "remarkable prominence" in the Prelude, it does not occur in the main body of the oratorio.[6] Comparing the emphases of Newman's poem and Elgar's version of it, Charles McGuire suggests that "for Newman, the narrative form of Gerontius' soul moving through this realm towards its judgement is . . . not as important as the lessons taught throughout the journey," whereas in contrast "Elgar constructed his libretto to avoid the lessons, concentrating instead on Gerontius' journey . . . "[7]

This overall picture of the soul's journey, I suggest, has both advantages and problems for our own spiritual life. It can assure us, positively, that life beyond death is a voyage of adventure and discovery. It indicates that to be a person is always to be in a process of growth and development, never standing still, that there is always something new to come. The saints who have died are in a state of holy activity, moving on. Though they are in the nearer presence of God there are things to do for God, for themselves, and especially for others. The communion of saints is a journey with saints as companions on the way.

The biblical picture from which this journey comes is the journey of Christ himself as portrayed in the letter to the Hebrews. The author depicts Christ as our High Priest who is also the "pioneer of our faith" (Heb 11.2); he has gone ahead of us through the sufferings of the cross to "take his seat at the right hand of the throne of God." We then are to "run with perseverance the race that is set before us"—that is, we are to follow Christ, both the "pioneer" and "perfecter" of our faith into the heavenly sanctuary. Or rather, we are to allow Christ to take us *with him* into the innermost presence of God:

> Since then, we have a great high priest who has *passed through the heavens*, Jesus, the Son of God, let us hold fast to our confession . . . *Let us therefore* approach the throne of grace with boldness, so that we may receive mercy and find grace to help in time of need (Heb 4:14–16).

---

6. Jaeger, *Dream of Gerontius*, 6.
7. McGuire, "One Story, Two Visions," 90–91.

As Charles Wesley memorably paraphrased this thought: "Bold I approach the eternal throne/ And claim the crown, through Christ, my own."[8] The prevailing picture of the book of Hebrews is of the believer as entering the divine presence *with* Christ, who has blazed the trail through his own human trust in the compassionate God. He has passed through the heavens, and we can travel with him.

The journey of the soul, as expressed in the Dream of Gerontius, is a gift from the Catholic tradition. But *reformed* Catholics, with a debt to the Protestant Reformation as well as to a Catholic heritage, will also find problems with this portrayal. In the first place, Newman and Elgar imagine that the journey will come to an end. It only lasts as long as purgatory. Yet if it is true that persons made in God's image are always as active and adventurous as God is, then the journey will *never* come to an end. The deeper we come into God, the more there is to be discovered. God never ceases to create new things, and we can share in that creativity. God, God's self, is on a journey, and we can travel on with God.

Second, the picture of purification can easily become one of punishment. A healthy picture of growth and development in the spiritual life can become one of merely suffering penalties. This then runs the danger of turning praying for the dead into a kind of transaction or contract when so many prayers and masses are calculated to release the soul from so many years in purgatory. We know how this doctrine became an abuse in the Middle Ages, when payment to the church could supposedly release the soul from punishment. In the weaving together of the journey and intercession motifs there is a hint of this transactional process when the angel assures Gerontius that "Masses on the earth, and prayers in heaven / Shall aid thee at the Throne of the Most High."

Third, this picture can draw a sharp distinction between the saints and all other Christians, between *the* saints who are named and celebrated in the public tradition of the church, and *all* saints. *The* saints, it has been often thought, are those who can enter directly into fellowship with God without having to pass through purification. All others must continue their journey. Yet fellowship with God and journeying with God belong together, and all are involved with both.

Finally, in this picture the last judgment and the resurrection of the dead have been lost from sight: judgment has become the judgment of the individual soul at death. The dualistic account of the human being on which Newman relies, envisaging the release of a soul from the body

---

8. Charles Wesley, hymn (1738), "And can it be that I should gain/ An interest in the Saviour's blood?"

at death, means that the human person is diagnosed as being *incomplete* without a body which is finally granted in the resurrection from the dead.[9] In Aquinas' form of this argument, the soul is restless until its desire to be united with the body is fulfilled. Augustine had maintained that this desire, until satisfied, will actually hold the soul back from its full enjoyment of the vision of God,[10] though Aquinas hesitates to go this far.[11] There is then, traditionally, a problem of two judgments, about which we can see that Aquinas shows some embarrassment. As Christian thinkers had increasingly developed a personal eschatology in which the soul is judged at the point of death, this seemed to make the public eschatology of the Last Judgment redundant. As Simon Tugwell puts it neatly, "By the end of the twelfth century, then, it was clear that there was one judgement too many."[12] Newman and Elgar are still, it seems, entangled in this impasse. Newman devotes many lines in his poem to an attempt to explain the relation between individual and universal judgment, but as Diana McVeagh points out, Elgar simply omits this complex thought.[13]

The Christian story is that the whole physical universe will be transformed and re-created by God when evil is overcome. There will be a last judgment ushering in this new creation because judgment is not so much the awarding of rewards and punishments, but the bringing of the truth to light. The exposure of the truth about all human lives will be the basis on which a new world can begin. Bringing truth to light will prompt repentance and a remaking of relationship with God. Judgment leads to healing. But this vision of a corporate resurrection leaves us with the problem of the state of the saints before the Last Day, to which I will shortly return.

Brahms: the Dwelling of the Human Person

We turn to a second picture of the destiny of persons beyond death, the image of dwelling with God and dwelling in God. This is beautifully expressed by another composer, Brahms, in his German *Requiem* (written 1845–1850). This work seems quite different from the Elgar; there is little explicit church doctrine here, with Brahms drawing simply upon Scripture

---

9. This is stressed in Geach, *God and the Soul*, 25–28.

10. Augustine, *De Genesi ad litteram* (Commentary on Genesis), 12.35.

11. Aquinas, *Summa Theologiae*, 1a2ae.4.5; cf. 3a.59. A modern philosophical version of a temporary disembodiment of the soul can be found in Davis, "Resurrection of the Dead," 122–27.

12. Tugwell, *Human Immortality*, 131.

13. McVeagh, "Making of Gerontius," 212.

to make universal affirmations about human life. He has replaced the Latin Requiem mass with verses from the German Bible. Brahms told Carl Martin Reinthaler, director of music at the Bremen Cathedral, that he would have gladly called the work *Ein menschliches Requiem* (A Human Requiem). In his correspondence with Reinthaler, when Reinthaler expressed concern over the lack of dogma, Brahms refused to add references to "the redeeming death of the Lord," as Reinthaler described it, such as John 3:16.[14] In the Bremen performance of the piece, Reinthaler took the liberty of inserting the aria "I know that my Redeemer liveth" from Handel's *Messiah* to satisfy the clergy.

While the prayer in the Roman Catholic liturgy to give "requiem" (rest) does not occur, it is replaced by the word *selig* (blessed) in the first and final movements—that is in the locations one would expect to find "requiem" in the mass. The first instance applies to the living rather than the dead, introducing the text "Blessed are they that mourn, for they shall be comforted," but the second applies to the dead, introducing the text "blessed are those who die in the Lord." In fact the transition from anxiety ("those who mourn") to reassurance ("they shall be comforted") occurs in all the movements except 4 and 7, the central one and the final one, setting up a dialectic which can also be seen as being between human suffering and joy.[15] This Requiem is not, as is sometimes claimed, directed towards comfort in this life only. In fact, this transition from sorrow to joy in movements 1–3, 5–6 can be understood as a journey from the sorrows of this life to *eternal joy*. The journey made by the bereaved from grief to peaceful acceptance is thus reflected in the larger journey from life to afterlife. Musicologists have frequently pointed to the opposing forces in this work, contrasts which are harmonic, tonal, and rhythmic. These can be readily understood in terms of stages on the spiritual journey. For instance, the three movements that begin in a minor key end in the parallel major key. The actual moments of shift from the minor system to the major system occur appropriately when the texts shift from mortal turmoil to the eternal salvation that can only be found in death: i.e., "Aber des Herrn Wort bleibet in Ewigkeit" in movement two; "Ich hoffe auf dich" in movement 3; and "Herr, du bist würdig zu nehmen Preis und Ehre und Kraft " in movement 6. There is a similar technique at work here to the musical depiction of journey in Elgar's *The Dream*. The movements that do not show this pattern are the central movement (4) and the final movement (7), and I want to suggest that these

---

14. See Musgrave, *Brahms*, 1–2.
15. See Tuck, "Brahm's *Ein Deutsches Requiem*," esp. 5–6.

portray something different, or perhaps complementary, namely the image of "dwelling" in God.

At the center of the Requiem is a movement (4) consisting of three verses from Psalm 84:

a. How lovely is your dwelling-place,

O Lord of Hosts!

b. My soul longs, yes, even faints

for the courts of the Lord:

my heart and my flesh cry out

for the living God.

c. Blessed are they that dwell in your house:

they will always be praising you.

These three verses selected from Psalm 84 stand in parallel to the three clauses in the *Sanctus* in the Requiem mass.[16] While the three sentences of the Sanctus with its *Hosanna* are very brief, and although Brahms' sentences are longer, each section still contains one sentence of Scripture.

Sanctus

a. Holy, Holy, Holy, Lord God of Hosts.

b. Heaven and earth are full of thy glory.

c. Hosanna in the highest.

Theologically, this replacement by Brahms moves emphasis from a contemplation of the holiness of God to the beauty of the dwelling-place that God promises, though God is of course still present as the provider of the dwelling. Indeed, we might conceive of the triune God as making space within God's own self for human beings to dwell, though it is unlikely that Brahms himself had made that theological connection. He seems more concerned with evoking a "place to be" for human beings, and paints this in tonal colors.

The section employs not a contrast between keys, registers of the voice or rhythms, but a homophonal approach employing imitation and parallel octaves. Much of the orchestration doubles the voice parts or provides simple rhythmic accompaniment (although there are short polyphonic

---

16. See McDermott, "Requiem Reinvented," 82.

sections which decorate the basic homophony). At the beginning the orchestra announces a yearning phrase for the setting of verse a., which is inverted to become a broad lyric melody. A second theme sets the same text a., in which the tenors imitate the violins, and the basses imitate the tenors at the same pitch. Because the timber of the voices is different there is a beauty in the diversity of tone, but there is no opposition. A middle section or development sets the text b., and we soon return through modulations to the tonic and have a recapitulation of the first two themes which were used to set a. The second theme has now become a straightforward tune which is played and sung at the same register by orchestra and chorus in turn, setting the first part of text c. ("Blessed are they that dwell in your house"). The second part of this text is now set to a fugue, which moves into a quiet coda which includes the words and music of text a., and which concludes with a singing of matched octaves between the voices. Again, contrast and opposition are reduced to the minimum.

Thus, the music supports the words in depicting a broad space in which a person can be. The image is a dwelling-place rather than the journey which is portrayed in the surrounding movements. The advantage of this image is that there is something undefined about the idea of "dwelling" in God. It allows for a sense of mystery; it does not map out the future in detail; the image of "dwelling" leaves a great deal open. One music critic has supposed that Brahms must have viewed the dwelling-place of movement 4 not as a reality but as "an idyllic dream fantasy," but in response the theologian Paul Minear discerns that Brahms' choice of texts points away from any simply "mortality/immortality option to more imaginative and profound appraisals of the human alternatives." The texts do not perceive life as an individual's resuscitation from the grave, but the "gift of a loving God."[17]

Dwelling in the love of God thus leaves open the mystery about the exact form of survival of a person after death. Newman's *Dream of Gerontius* reduces the element of mystery by a definite philosophical scheme; it works with the idea of a disembodied soul, floating out of the body as a butterfly leaves a cocoon. It exhibits the dualism that originates in the Greek philosophy of Plato. Newman's epigram to his poem expresses the Platonic sentiment of "coming out of the shadows into reality," and the poem assumes his philosophy of the world as "economies of the visible" in which creation exists primarily as a symbol of the invisible world.[18] In the *Dream*, the soul is borne forward, feeling the qualities of subtlety and agility which theologians traditionally attribute to incorporeal existence. We should note that, to some

---

17. Minear, *Death Set to Music*, 81–82.
18. Carballo, "Towards a Non-Dialectic Poetry of Dogma," 58–62.

extent, Elgar has moderated this dualism. In a letter to Jaeger, he commented that "I've not filled his [Gerontius'] part with Church tunes and rubbish but a good, healthy full-blooded romantic, remembered worldliness."[19] In his contrast between Newman's and Elgar's versions of the poem, McGuire comments that "Elgar radically altered the philosophical thrust of the poem, shifting the focus of the Oratorio away from Newman's vision of the afterlife towards Gerontius as a suffering human figure . . . foregrounding the poignancy of Gerontius' physical experience."[20] Nevertheless, the Newman-Elgar *Dream* remains the journey of a now disembodied soul.

Many Christian thinkers have adopted this theory. In fact, some people think it is the only Christian understanding of life beyond death. But we are truer to the witnessing of the Hebrew Bible to the psychosomatic unity of the human person, and truer to the New Testament concept of the resurrection of the body, if we think that soul and body are always bound up together and can never be separated.[21] The soul is the dimension of the human personality that is open towards God, but it always needs the body to survive. Death must mean an end to the whole person, soul and body, and we are right to feel deeply, to grieve, at the seriousness of this event. It is not to be trivialized as a mere door for the soul to pass through. This leads to a hope that God will overcome death in the resurrection of the body—not just a revival of the body as we know it but a transformation of the whole person into something new, what St Paul calls a "spiritual body" (1 Cor 15:44).

Because the human body is part of the whole natural world, this resurrection must involve the renewal of the whole universe and cannot happen immediately after death. It still lies in God's future. Paul, for example, looks forward to a time when the whole of creation will be "set free from its bondage to decay and will obtain the freedom of the glory of the children of God" (Rom 8:21). It is, he says, groaning under the burden of suffering at the moment, and awaits with eager longing for the revealing of the children of God who are themselves transformed; in that day it will be changed in itself, raised to a totally new level of existence.

If this is the picture then, as I have already indicated, there is a puzzle about the survival of the saints until the day of resurrection. We cannot think of them as individual souls existing without bodies, and so the only way we can speak of them is to say that they "dwell in God." We live in God now, and we shall go on living in God after death. The saints are alive in the

---

19. Elgar, Letter to Jaeger, August 1900, cited in Young, *Elgar, Newman and the Dream of Gerontius*, 118.

20. McGuire, "One Story, Two Visions," 85.

21. See Fiddes, *Promised End*, 80–84.

fellowship of the Holy Trinity, held between the relations of the Father, the Son, and the Spirit. As we suggested in our first book, God maintains their identity, keeping alive all the hopes, aims, values, gifts, loves, and characteristics that they expressed in life. God represents them, keeping their personalities in being until God resurrects them in a new creation as individuals in a new community. God stands in for them. We might be inclined to say that God "remembers" them, but the word scarcely seems enough; the memory of God is life-giving in a way that our memories are not. God represents the saints in such a way that we can pray *with* them; also we can say that they pray *for* us and we can pray for them.

Brahms, it seems, follows a quite Reformed position in imagining the dead as waiting for the resurrection in their dwelling-place. But at the same time he invokes the image of the journey, so that putting the two together as the hearer, we find each interpreting the other. We hear the "dwelling" of the central and the last movements in the context of the "journey" in the other movements. This is vividly expressed in the juxtaposition of sections 6 and 7.

At the beginning of section 6 the choir sings quietly a verse from the book of Hebrews: "For here we have no city that remains, but we seek one to come" (Heb 13:14). They begin with an image of dwelling, in the present and the future, but the thought is one of journeying as strangers and pilgrims in this world. This is underlined by the music, which shifts vaguely in its harmonies and melody, hovering around the key of C minor. This is followed by the intervention of the baritone declaiming Paul's words about the last trump and the resurrection of the dead from 1 Cor 15:51–55: "Behold I show you a mystery. We shall not all sleep, but we shall all be changed," and this message is repeated by the choir. The voices make a grand modulation, from C minor to E minor with stupendous effect, no less shattering than any attempt to imitate the last trumpet with brass instruments. The text is a dramatic image, of change from one state of life to another.

Brahms is using the baritone soloist to introduce successive episodes within the movement, creating a dramatic dialogue between soloist and choir, and provoking a constantly unfolding drama. At this point the baritone interrupts again with syncopated rhythms, declaiming "Then shall be brought to pass the saying that is written" and the fury of the chorus resumes with "Death is swallowed up in victory," the volume of sound accented with *sforzando* markings throughout. As one musicologist puts it, "In Beethoven-like fashion, Brahms extends the drama again and again, leading toward moments of resolution that immediately turn and move back to the fury."[22]

---

22. McDermott, "Requiem Reinvented," 73.

Another commentator writes, "The chorus drives death into a corner by a series of rising modulations—Death, where is thy sting? Grave, where is thy victory?—[and] at last the revelation bursts forth."[23] This disclosure is another New Testament text, from the book of Revelation (Rev 4:11): "Thou art worthy, O Lord, to receive honour and glory and power. . ." The verse is set in a grand double fugue in 2/2 time, recalling the climactic grand fugues to which the corrresponding text in the Latin Requiem, *Cum Sanctis*, is often set. But there is nothing static about this fugue. The lines pile up in their repetition, one on top of another, so that the impression is of a vast staircase or set of steps that are being climbed.[24] The first notes of entry by each voice successively make a climbing series, first in thirds, then in fourths, and lastly in single interval rising steps, until the destination is reached with a lyrical expression of the final clause "for thou has created all things. . ."

With high drama this movement thus portrays the transition from earthly sorrows to eternal joy, in text and music. It thus gives the impression of a journey. But the final movement *Selig sind die Toten* (Blessed are the dead) has no such drama, and like the central movement (IV) neither text nor music mark a transition from suffering to bliss. Brahms chooses a text from the book of Revelation (Rev 14:13) that contains a promise of "rest," echoing the "dwelling-place" of the earlier movement: "Blessed are the dead who from henceforth die in the Lord: yes, says the Spirit, they will rest from their labors; and their works follow them." One critic comments that "it is a movement of peace," similar to the *In Paradisum* that we often find in traditional requiems.[25] This music conveys a mood of quiet assurance and steady confidence, consonant with the image of rest. The movement begins with choral unisons, first by sopranos against a surging accompaniment that extends throughout the range of orchestral sound, and then their theme is answered by the basses over a repeated eight-note accompaniment. The whole chorus expands the text in the dominant key, coming to a quiet close which is followed by a dialogue between low voices and the brass, to the words: "Yes, says the Spirit, they will rest from their labors." In accord with the image of rest, this is not a dramatic dialogue such as the previous movement offered. It is solemn, gently rhythmic, delivered by the voices almost in a monotone. The phrase is then taken up in a gentle *cantabile* (singing style) in the bright key of A major.

The first section—"Blessed are the dead"—is recapitulated in the tonic of F, but then something astonishing happens. There is a modulation into

---

23. Tovey, *Essays in Musical Analysis*, 222.
24. This might be recognized to be a "Handelian" style.
25. McDermott, "Requiem Reinvented," 63.

E flat, only one tone below the tonic. The musicologist Donald Tovey comments that "this is a relation used by great composers only when it may appropriately convey a sense of something seen through a veil,"[26] and it appropriately evokes a sense of seeing "through a glass darkly" into the state of rest which the dead in the Lord are enjoying, shrouded as it is in mystery. In this key there is then a return to a musical theme of the very first movement; there it set the words "blessed are they that mourn," and here it now sets the words "blessed are the dead." This return to an opening theme is reminiscent of the return of the opening *requiem aeternam* in the requiem genre, underlining the parallel between "blessed" and "requiem," in a movement about "rest" (i.e., requiem).

The advantage of the image of "dwelling" (here dwelling in a heavenly city) is that it leaves open the mystery of *how* we can go on living after death. What matters is that the dead are "in the Lord"; the place of dwelling or rest is in God. The disadvantage of this picture of dwelling is that it tends to be static, unmoving. It is associated with the image of "rest" and this can often—wrongly—be understood as non-activity, and even as sleep. When the author to the Hebrews writes that "a rest remains for the people of God" (Heb 4:9) he is taking up the Old Testament promise of rest given to Israel: God promised them "rest" in the land of Canaan, and this certainly did not mean non-activity as they were to build a nation there. Rest means relief from anxiety, release from oppression and satisfaction for the soul. So Jesus promises "Come to me, and I will give you rest" (Matt 11:28–30). Rest, however, along with "dwelling" can become an immobility, a getting stuck in a state of slumber. So the image needs to be balanced and corrected by the image of a journey. For Brahms, journey and rest interpret each other through the juxtaposition of movements in the requiem. He gives greater prominence to the image of rest than Elgar does, finding it conducive to his reservations about any dogma of life beyond death. Nevertheless, Newman/Elgar while putting the image of the journey to the fore also include allusions to rest: Gerontius immediately after death feels a "deep rest so soothing and so sweet" (though it is simultaneously a pressure of movement); Gerontius anticipates a "motionless" state in purgatory, and the angel refers to his immersion in the waters of the lake as "sleep" (even though he is also taking a "rapid passage through the flood"), and the souls in purgatory sing the psalm "Lord you have been our refuge in every generation."

---

26. Tovey, Vocal Music, 224.

A Fellowship in Prayer with the Saints

How then are the saints alive? We use imaginative pictures which correspond to the truth, but which cannot be taken as exactly mimetic of reality: the saints "dwell" in God and they are on a "journey" to God's future. They are journeying first towards resurrection and then they will journey on to new quests and new adventures in God's new universe, only because they are held in a dwelling-place within God.

This mutually corrective imagery perhaps corresponds to attempts by theologians (first by Maximus the Confessor, then by Aquinas, then in modern times by Wolfhart Pannenberg, Jürgen Moltmann, and Hans Urs von von Balthasar)[27] to describe some kind of paradoxical "motion at rest" in God. There must be movement, since the Trinity denotes a "generating" movement from the Father, a "returning" movement by the Son, and an "opening up" movement by the Spirit. On the other hand theologians have rightly wanted to attribute some kind of "stability" or "constancy" to God. When described as "stasis," "simultaneity," or "stillness" (memorably expressed in T. S. Eliot's phrase, "the still point of the turning world"[28]), these latter concepts inevitably attribute a kind of immobility and immutability to God which is not coherent with God's involvement in time and history through creation and redemption. The musical presentation of eternal life beyond death we have been exploring opens the possibility that we might conceive a kind of stability in the movement of God which is analogous to the relation between "tension" and "resolution" that we find in musical rhythm.[29]

Returning to the question of a fellowship of prayer with the saints, we find this has the aspects of both movement and "rest." It only makes sense in the double context of images of journey *and* dwelling-place. In the first place, intercessory prayer depends on having a "place" within God. In prayers of intercession we find that we are dwelling in a zone of inter-connection. This kind of prayer is supremely social. We are being swept into a current in which nothing is separated from anything else, no one from anyone else. We find we are being urged by the Spirit to pray for those far away in the world, some of whom we have never met; we find that we can enter with empathy into the experience of the hungry and needy of the world, and that this opens up an awareness of the hungry and needy parts of ourselves. We who pray for others find that we too are being prayed for as we enter the community of

---

27. Maximus, *Quaestiones ad Thalassium* PG90, 760A; Aquinas, *Summa Contra Gentiles* 4, 11; Pannenberg, *Systematic Theology*, 2:93; Moltmann, *Spirit of Life*, 303-4; cf. Balthasar, *Theo-Drama*, 5:91-95.

28. "Burnt Norton," in Eliot, *Poems*, 181.

29. See Begbie, *Theology, Music and Time*, 39-44.

prayer. Intercessory prayer is an experience of connectedness and mutuality, because it is praying "in God" who lives in relationships. In intercession we meet others in the interweaving of the Father, Son, and Spirit or—we might say—in the movements of the divine dance.

While Brahms does not refer to the idea of mutual prayer in developing his image of "dwelling," he is certainly concerned with the mutuality of love between living and dead, and we have argued previously[30] that intercessory prayer is simply an expression of love and concern for the other before and in God. God acts in the world through love, not coercion or intervention; in love God seeks to persuade created beings to cooperate with the purposes that God knows will enable them and their environment to flourish. As God makes room in God's own interweaving relations of love, God humbly permits our love to enhance and even amplify God's own, increasing its effect in the life of those who receive it. Intercessory prayer is thus an adding of our love to God's own love which is already operative in the world at every level of existence. This is not a question of increasing the quantity of divine love, as if this were somehow deficient, but a consent to the humble decision of God in creation to allow the love of created beings to augment uncreated love.

There is, of course, no sign of such a *theology* in Brahms, but there is the reality of dwelling in a place where love can be shared with others, regardless of the boundary of death. In commenting on movement 6 of Brahm's *Requiem*, Minear notes that "what these pilgrims seek transcends any limitation to individual destinies; what is to come, what their souls long for, is a city."[31] He goes on to suggest that the repetition of music from the first movement in the seventh indicates "a desire to bind those who die with those who mourn their deaths," and perhaps it denotes that "this bond, which death appears always to break, is forged by the common bond to God."[32] The texts that Brahms has chosen, he urges, do not deal with an individual's demise and fate, but "with the Creator's purpose for his creation and the creation's participation in those purposes."[33] The musicologist Michael Musgrave points out that, while only one of the three short texts in movement 5 refers directly to the love of a mother for a child, Brahms has imbued the whole movement (perhaps written as a memorial to his mother who had recently died) with the sense of loving relationships.[34]

30. See Fiddes et al., *Baptists and the Communion of Saints*, 81–84.
31. Minear, *Death Set to Music*, 77.
32. Minear, *Death Set to Music*, 80.
33. Minear, *Death Set to Music*, 81.
34. Musgrave, *Brahms*, 22.

In the second place, prayer requires participation in a journey, which nothing less than Christ's own journey. I suggested earlier that the picture given us in the book of Hebrews is of the believer as entering the divine presence *with* Christ, who has blazed the trail through his own human trust in the compassionate God. The journey of Christ is thus also a *prayer* to the Father in which we are invited to join, a prayer which enables our praying who, as Hebrews (7:25) puts it, "approach God *through* him." In Heb 7:25—8:1 we are presented with the picture of Christ "sitting at the right hand of God" and praying, as the Great High Priest, to God the Father in the heavenly sanctuary. We might say that our prayers ride upon the praying of Christ into the Most Holy Place. Christ as High Priest leads the prayers in the heavenly worship; he does not pray alone. The heavenly intercession of Christ is portrayed as enabling our own praying and approaching God; our prayers are wrapped in the prayer that is already going on within God. Elsewhere Paul speaks of Christ as the supreme "Yes" from God and to God: "it is through Christ that we say the Amen [i.e. the "Yes"] to the glory of God," immediately adding that he has "given us his Spirit in our hearts" (2 Cor 1:19-22). We say "Yes" and "Our Father" through the "Yes" and the "My Father" of Christ. This is what it means to pray, in the New Testament formula, "To the Father, through the Son and in the Holy Spirit."

Now, the prayers of God's people can only be understood as effective in the context of the intercessions of Christ. In prayer we join with the prayers of all God's people, because they all—to be prayer at all—participate in the intercessions of Christ. It is in Christ, in the relations of the Trinity, that our prayers meet. We realize that all saints share in the adoration of God, that we are part of a heavenly worship, of myriads alive and dead (as far as this life is concerned) who cry, in the words set by Brahms in his *Requiem*, "Thou art worthy, O Lord, to receive glory, and honour and power" (Rev 4:11); Newman, in the *Dream*, has added his own version of the heavenly worship with his great hymn "Praise to the Holiest in the height." Though Newman and Elgar do not portray the praying of Christ himself, the prayers of the human assistants, the angels, and Mary that carry Gerontius forward into the heart of this worship are grounded in the mercy of Christ. We may say that the prayers of the saints that glorify God ride on the movement in the Trinity which is like a son responding in love and obedience to glorify a father, and our own prayers are supported on this surge of adoration. Here again the pictures of dwelling and journey come together: it is because the saints dwell in God that they can share the journey of Christ in prayer.

And how shall we describe this "dwelling"? The characteristic way that the saints who have died once glorified and praised God in their lives, their concerns for others, their particular ways of self-giving, their love which they expressed for those near to them and those far away, including those they never personally knew—all these aspects are kept alive in God as their prayers. The human love that they added to the uncreated love of God, and which had a powerful effect on the world, is still enriching the transforming love of God and making a difference. In this sense, the saints who have died are still praying for the world; they are interceding because Christ is interceding. All those who have been gathered into God are praying for us. They are praying that the kingdom of God will come, crying, "How long, O Lord?" (Rev 6:10), and they are on a journey to its coming.

6

One World

Brian Haymes

EARLIER IN THIS VOLUME I reflected on the life of St. Thérèse of Lisieux, and especially on her experience of facing death. I had been introduced to this saint by Graeme and Sue Parfitt, both Anglican priests and at the time joint secretaries of the Anglican Fellowship of St. Thérèse. On two occasions, the first in 2006, my wife and I went to Lisieux with members of the Fellowship to learn of the saint and to share retreat in the Carmel. We have since made other more personal visits but it was these initially unplanned occasions that caused me, a Baptist minister, to think further about the doctrine of the communion of saints and its significance.

Soon after our first book on the communion of saints was written, containing a piece by me on St. Thérèse, Graeme died. Among other pastorates, he had been a much-loved vicar of St. Stephen's Parish Church, Southmead, Bristol, and it was to this place that we went for the funeral service. The printed Order of Service for Worship indicated that it was a *Requiem Eucharist and Funeral Office celebrating the life and ministry of Graeme Stanley Parfitt*. I have attended many funerals in the course of my ministry, some in Anglican churches, but this was the first funeral at which I would share in Holy Communion. I was not ready for the deep impression the service of worship was to make on me. Reflection on the experience of this Requiem will, I believe, help us to bring together the chapters already offered in the present volume and lead us to further consideration of one important theme for the communion of saints—that we live in one world created by God, and not in two different realms.

A Requiem Eucharist: Bringing Things Together

The printed order of service for worship was simple and direct. The front cover included a photograph of Graeme and the text "Arise my love, my fair one and come away for now the winter is past, the rain is over and gone. The flowers appear on the earth; the time of the singing of the birds has come and the voice of the turtle dove is heard in our land."[1] The large congregation sang well-known hymns. During the first hymn the clergy processed into the sanctuary: the vicar, curate, preacher, and the bishop of Bristol. There was no choir. The service was initially one of the word, with prayers of approach, confession, invocation. We heard Scripture read and then came the sermon. This was a proclamation of the Christian faith. For sure, there were references to Graeme but it was not a series of reminiscences such that remembering Graeme was the center of it all. By contrast to some other kinds of funeral gatherings where several people might offer their memories and reflections on the deceased this was a service of worship offered to God by a congregation made up of the living and the dead. The sharing of memories came afterwards, with refreshments and conversation.

The service moved from word to sacrament according to the Anglican prayer book. All the time, at the front of the church, before the communion rail and the Holy Table, was Graeme's coffin. On top of it were placed symbols of his life among which were included his Bible and prayer book, his priest's *vade mecum*, a photograph of St. Thérèse, and a large builder's tape measure, recalling his considerable DIY abilities.

So we moved into the eucharistic liturgy in a simple uncomplicated form, the congregation saying the responses. Then we were called to the Holy Table and forward we went, to stand before the Table alongside the body of Graeme, and there we were offered and received the bread and wine, gifts of God for the people of God. It was this that I found to be so unexpectedly moving. Here was communion, covenant love, those in Christ—the dead and alive in Christ—finding life in the gracious gift of God, sharing the living hope at the heart of the gospel of God. We returned to our places. For myself, I could not speak. It was a realization of the communion of saints way beyond anything I had previously known at a funeral, or communion service, or any other act of Christian worship. Here we were with the living, with the body in the coffin, with Mary, the saints, martyrs, angels, and archangels, all united in God, Father, Son, and Holy Spirit.

The service was brought to its conclusion with prayers, a final hymn and words of blessing spoken by the bishop. The body remained there before

---

1. Songs 2:10b–12.

the Holy Table while the congregation retired for refreshments, the sharing of conversation, and the greeting of friends before the family left quietly to lay Graeme's body to rest in burial.

I have since learned that such a service was unusual in the Anglican tradition in that it is mostly only priests, but not exclusively so, at whose funerals Eucharist is celebrated. It was noticeable that there were many clergypersons present, expressing a solidarity among ministers I have not often observed among my own Baptist people. The bishop is usually in attendance at a priest's funeral but the local incumbent presided at the sacrament.

I have seldom been moved so much in an act of worship in recent years as was the case at Graeme's funeral. It was not the kind of requiem mass which is offered for a soul in purgatory. It was a gathering of the church offering worship to God, to hear the word, to receive the sacrament and to pray, in full funeral recognition of the deceased and the grief of mourners. The focus however was firmly on the triune God and our participation in the life of God by grace. As such the whole service was an experience of that larger world of the communion of saints. It was the most "satisfying" funeral I had attended for a long while. For months afterwards I found myself reflecting on why this was so.

In particular, it was the theological liturgical focus on God that was most striking. This stood in contrast to other funeral or thanksgiving services I had attended in recent years in various contexts where the focus has been on the deceased, giving the event a more anthropological than theological emphasis. Large photographs and highly personal music choices dominate. In my recent experience, more and more funeral services have become opportunities for various contributions to be made, often by family members and friends at such a time of mourning and bereavement. Such occasions are not without deep significance for the mourners, reflecting their deep loss in a context where faith in Christ has little living content. The bereaved is well remembered and given a "good send-off."

This may well be part of the growing general sense of a loss of God, possibly even in the churches. Today, in more informal styles of worship, preachers may often reveal more about themselves in the sermon than properly proclaim the good news of God. Intercessions may be reduced to the health conditions of members of the congregation or a list of current political and moral concerns. As such, these occasions have seemed to me to come very near to reflecting the practical atheism of the times in which we live in the western world. A funeral thus becomes a backward looking stance of thanksgiving. There is little forward hopeful look. Is this because there is no living conviction of resurrection in the face of death? Or, possibly and strangely, is there a vague half-remembered fear of a coming judgment?

Or is it that uncritical popular dualisms have a stronger grip on our minds than we realize?

While the church properly rejoices and celebrates all forms of human goodness, life, and love, such that occasions of memorial, thanksgiving, and celebration of life are entirely appropriate, before the face of death other depths need to be sounded. The message of the church is that of the apostles, prophets, and martyrs, witnessing to what God has done in history, particularly in the raising of Jesus the Messiah from the dead. Before the face of evil, threatening despair and death, God brings forth life in resurrection. By the Spirit, the church, built on Jesus Christ the chief cornerstone, comes to lay the dead to rest in sure and certain hope of the resurrection of the dead to eternal life. This is something we cannot do for and by ourselves. It is the work of God. Because God is as God is in Jesus, we have a gospel to proclaim, especially in the face of decay and death. It is the word of life, of the One who brings us out of darkness into his marvellous light (1 Pet 2:9). The living and the dead together in Christ are held with a love that will not let us go. The Church at Southmead had taken opportunity to remember Graeme and celebrate his life, as they had been called to live out their baptism, in the presence of the triune God. Many were the reminiscences and moments of laughter, many the expressions of gratitude, but these came later in the context already set by the worship of God in the communion of saints. We remembered God and God remembered us before we set about our personal and corporate expressions of gratitude and grief. The first word spoken to us was of God and the last word was the blessing of God. We proclaimed Christ as Word of life standing against death and all that robs us of God's gift of life.

For this Baptist, however, it was the sharing of Eucharist that was so significant. It was itself a celebration of our life in God. Together, with the body of Graeme so obviously with us, we received and shared the gifts of God for the people of God, we were one in Christ in the Spirit, the many living as one body, eating the one loaf and sharing the one cup. The sacrament proclaimed the gospel. I asked myself why we have not done this among the people called Baptist.

In this act of worship I was particularly struck by the way some matters which can easily fall apart were being held together, in particular, word and sacrament, life and death, earth and heaven. Simplistic dualisms, such as that of the soul leaving the body to ascend to heaven at death, were replaced by deeper convictions of the purposes of God in creation and salvation. Being a Baptist, I had been nurtured in a mainly word-dominated understanding of the faith in contrast to a sacramental approach, failing properly to hold table and pulpit, earth and heaven together. Can Baptists, I reflected, grateful for our heritage and all that we have received, move beyond such dualisms to a fuller experience of the life of faith in the triune God? Can we look beyond the historic distinctions we have been used to drawing to find a more complete integration of themes that are often forced apart? We cannot but come bodily, with all the joys and sorrows that the flesh means. With all the saints we pray for the coming of the kingdom of God and in our embodied lives we express its present life.

Making such a theological journey will bring us to challenge long-cherished approaches, none perhaps more so than the issue of what it means to be "saved." I think it can be fairly claimed that in much popular Christian thinking today, and not only among Baptists,[2] there is a deeply unbiblical dualism. It concerns the distinction between soul and the body and their separation from each other.

The Problem of Dualism

The New Testament scholar N. T. Wright characterizes the popular view of the Christian gospel as meeting a fundamental need for us to "get to heaven" when we die, a view compounded by a Platonized view of the soul as separate from the body. On this (mis)understanding, our basic human problem has to do with our bodily sinful selves and the aim is for the soul to escape all this temporal matter and find forgiveness and peace with God in an existence outside time, space, and materiality. Release from the body becomes the means of escaping "the world and the flesh" for the life of the spirit. This uncritical Platonism becomes "the context for what (. . .) is a basically paganized vision of how one might attain such a future: a transaction in which God's wrath was poured out against his son rather than against sinful humans."[3] This, Wright argues is quite erroneous as far as the Bible is concerned where we find not a disembodied "heaven" disengaged from earth but a calling to share God's renewed creation, the new heaven and earth of Rev 21:1. We do not go to heaven when we die, assuming all the right conditions have been fulfilled in our particular case, but rather heaven comes to earth in the new creation called resurrection. Creation remains the arena of the divine purpose.

Dualism may well lie at the root of the disastrous separation of word and sacrament. Just how this came to be in history need not concern us here but it was possible because of the dualistic distinctions made between

---

2. Some formal statements in this tradition are careful to avoid dualistic thought, for example, *The Baptist Faith and Message* of the Southern Baptist Convention (2000).

3. Wright and Langton, *Day the Revolution Began*, 34.

body and soul. In the practices of much of the western church, receiving the sacrament, validly administered through approved channels, became the way of salvation. Sacerdotalism and sacrament went together. Conversely, among the Free Churches, including Baptists, in England there was a predictable reaction—especially to nineteenth-century Tractarianism—which showed itself in a diminishing of baptismal and eucharistic practice and theology. The present state of affairs means that, although there is a resurgence of never quite forgotten sacramental theology among us, the practice is such that word and sacrament are not often held together. At Graeme's funeral liturgy there was an understanding of God in Trinity such that the God who made and makes us, who became incarnate in the Son Jesus, and who was active in the Spirit from the beginning—this triune God in whom Graeme had been baptized, lived, and died—was present with God's people in bread and wine, giving a foretaste of the coming new creation when death is no more. Such an emphasis on interconnectedness is effectively expressed in an agreed statement in a recent ecumenical report between the Roman Catholic Church and the Baptist World Alliance:

> Communion with the triune God and with the whole church of Christ is continually actualized in the Eucharist/Lord's Supper. In the celebration, those participating are sharing communion not only with each other in the local congregation, but with the whole church of Christ in time and space. "because there is one bread, all of us share in one body" (1 Cor 10:17). Because we hear the word of God in the Eucharist/Lord's Supper, this is a sharing in both word and sacrament (or ordinance) at the same time.[4]

Prompted by the Requiem Eucharist of Graeme, I reflected that one practical way of resisting dualism is in the very choice of place for a funeral. By comparison with fifty years ago,[5] many funeral services of Baptists are now held at the crematorium, involving the family and close friends. A more public memorial or thanksgiving service may be held later, perhaps on the same day as the committal. There is something understandable here in terms of family grief. Only a few of the family mourners may actually be part of the community which gathers to worship in the local church which may have become a strange place for the rest of the family. On the other hand, the situation should be different for those who share the worship of God in a building where the deceased person has regularly come to worship;

---

4. *The Word of God in the Life of the Church*, 41–42.

5. I restrict the period of comparison to the years of my ordained ministry. I am aware of the variety of funeral customs through the years and in different geographical contexts.

they will find the place full of memories and symbols which affirm the faith of the dead and the living, held together in one communion of saints. In the Christian liturgical assembly, the life of the congregation gathered by the covenant God is regularly nourished by both word and sacrament. It is to this company and in this place that people come to celebrate the birth of children, the gift of marriage, baptism, and to affirm week by week the triune God who welcomes us into God's life and love. This building is for the congregation of members a "home," unlike the crematorium which may impose constraints of time and provide few physical symbols of the faith by which people live, and it will notably lack the Holy Table. The church's building is the place for the worship, praise, and service of God, while the crematorium is little more than the place of disposal, a house of death. That is, after all, its only purpose. It is not where the church is called to meet on the first day of the week, and that place of gathering is surely where the funeral service should happen.

However, by no means do all friends and members of the immediate natural family necessarily share the faith in God Christian worship implies, and in which their loved one has participated as a member of a church "family" beyond the biological one. Should therefore Eucharist be celebrated in the funeral liturgy, invitations to sharing communion at such a time of grief may only increase feeling of awkwardness, even painful distance, when already deep emotions are being stirred. This becomes a pastoral issue of some consequence, and sensitivity is needed. However, not to include Eucharist in the funeral means that the theological significance of our own embodiedness is effectively denied. It is this flesh and blood, the life we call creation that God called into being and shared in Jesus Christ.

It is essential that we take a non-dualist view of the world, for at least three reasons. First, the vision of God as offered in the Bible and the historic creeds of the church stress God's being committed to matter—and to such matter mattering for God. In the beginning God creates the heaven and the earth (Gen 1:1). Working with this crucial biblical picture means this fundamental work of God cannot be a concern of passing indifference, resulting in inconsequential and inevitable waste. Moreover, such creativity is not one solitary explosive work from which God then withdraws into non-material existence, safe in God's own house and home, but rather is only the beginning of God's constant engagement with matter, the work of God's hands, sustaining and taking up all that is into the divine purposes. The ways in which the Bible bears witness to the work of God makes very little sense if creation and history do not ultimately matter. This is underlined in the doctrine of incarnation: the Word that was in the beginning becomes flesh and dwells among us (John 1:1–14). It is the basic Christian claim that the critical unique revelation of God happens in creation and history. Jesus the prophet from Nazareth in Galilee is obviously a human figure, one who weeps when a friend dies, who has opportunities for mental and physical growth, who bleeds when he is cut and eventually comes to death and the grave. What particularly is challenged in these emphases is any suggestion of twin causative forces of good and evil, suggesting good and evil as joint creative principles at work. Boldly such dualism is rejected in Isa 45:7: "I form light and create darkness, I make weal and create woe." The point being made is that there no other final "principle" in the making and forming of the world, although the Hebrew idiom here leaves out all the intermediate secondary causes that lie behind human woe, such as the freedom of human beings to do harm and the randomness of nature. Certainly the Bible sometimes uses dualistic language for its own purposes (for example in Paul's contrast of *flesh* and *spirit*) but this is not to develop any kind of dualistic systems.

The foundational witness of the Bible is to one creating saving God, to human engagement at all times with who and what God has made and is seeking to bring to fulfillment. It comes therefore as no surprise that when the fulfillment of all things is pictured in biblical imagery, as in Revelation 21, any new work of God involves what has been. Nothing is abandoned as waste and worthless. The new comes to the old and what is thought to be dead and gone is caught up again into the redeeming purposes of God which involve all creation and history.[6] Dry bones live. This extraordinary claim may push our imaginations to the limit but there is little doubt that the Bible makes it. The eschatological vision, like that of the beginning of all things, engages heaven and earth together in God. Again, it follows that the faith Christians hold, grounded in this biblical witness, is sacramental. In flesh and blood, in the water at the pool, in bread and wine at table, in friendships and marriage, we know this truth that God engages us in and through this created world of matter. We have these sacraments because we are embodied persons, sought by God, existing in a material world full of what Clark Pinnock called "sacramental possibilities."[7] Thus the biblical vision of God is non-dualist.

A second reason for rejecting dualism relates to the culture we share in the world in which we presently live. A key descriptive word for our time is "holistic," expressing the interconnectedness of all things. So, for example, modern medical science recognizes the inseparable interplay of mind and

---

6. So Moltmann, *Way of Jesus Christ*, 303.

7. Pinnock, *Flame of Love*, 120. For further Baptist studies on the sacraments see Cross and Thompson, *Baptist Sacramentalism*; and Fowler, *More than a Symbol*.

body. Treating a person acknowledges that "person" means both "body" and "mind." Those who are suffering after the recent terrorist bomb attacks in European cities receive treatments for their broken limbs and torn flesh, but also counselling care in recognition that we are embodied selves. This cultural perspective, reflecting the biblical emphases, is reflected in the assumptions of modern science. We live in one interconnected world. This is not to suggest that everything is open to empirical enquiry but it does affirm that there is no potentially separate "ghost in the machine," as one influential philosopher put it.[8]

What then of all talk of God acting in the world, a fundamental assertion of Christian faith? This is sometimes understood in a dualistic way as God's "intervening" from "outside" the material world. We are resisting all forms of dualism in this book and emphasizing embodiment, God's and ours. Traditionally the Christian faith has rightly asserted that God is not part of the world in such a way that God can be found and examined as some thing or being. The distinction we wish to stress is between God, the unique "uncreated Creator," and humankind as the "created creators." Things go wrong when humankind loses the art of being a creature. The God of whom we speak is ever active in creation and it is by this self-revelation that we dare to speak of God at all. With this perspective we resist any talk about God as a Being separate from the world; God is distinct but not separated. So, in speaking of God, Paul Fiddes stresses metaphors of inseparable participation and relationship between God and the world, between the Creator and the created, while not confusing them.[9] This, we believe, is following the biblical trajectory. Thus, for example, if we were to think of creation as a written text, then we might think of it as being held in the "author," the triune God.[10] Biblically, we cannot think of the world without God nor of God without the world. Such is the embodied nature of the fundamental relationship.

It is this embodiment which brings us to challenge all speech about God as intervening in creation, of making occasional excursions into a world from which God is otherwise assumed to be absent. In contrast we assert that it is the initiating agency of God, working together with human response, that sustains the creation through which the divine purposes of love and salvation are worked out. God has freedom to do new things but the way is not of coercion or compulsion but of love. In this regard we

---

8. The phrase is that of Gilbert Ryle's, used in critique of Descartes in Ryle, *Concept of Mind*.

9. Fiddes, *Seeing the World and Knowing God*, 25, 65, 149, 188, 293.

10. Fiddes, *Seeing the World and Knowing God*, 294.

take the cross of Jesus, the suffering love revealed there, as being crucial in God's self-revelation. God acts out of an abundance of love, costly love, calling the creation to new life. With God there are ever new possibilities. This constantly searching agency brings order and beauty out of chaos, offers forgiveness in the face of despair and even resurrection life from the dead. Healing, restoring, reconciling, peace-making—these are the marks of what Jesus called God's reign (Isaiah 61 and Luke 4). Easter morning may come as a disconcerting surprise to the disciples but the larger reading of the Scriptures suggests this is no new intervention so much as a further way by which God in freedom works at the saving and renewing of creation. Dualistic thinking results in a spasmodic God of occasional engagement with the world, while non-dualistic readings of the text render a more faithful and credible account.

Resisting Dualism Through the Creative Arts

A third reason for our resistance to dualism brings me to reflect on the contribution of my fellow-authors in previous chapters in this book. I mean the witness of the creative arts to the importance of the material. At the risk of overstating the obvious, it is clear that none of the works cited, whether in visual art, music, or literature, could happen without embodiment, both in their creation and appreciation. All our bodily senses come into play in engaging with them, and—through them—with God. What we see, touch, taste, hear, and smell affects not just our minds, our inner being, but our whole embodied selves. Dualistic approaches always require a separation of God from the world, where a non-dualistic approach leads to surprising discoveries about God's relationship to the world.

Richard Kidd's essay on Paul Nash's art[11] amply illustrates the profound inter-connectedness of all that is. What might be separated theoretically into matter and spirit is found to be interrelated in our lived experience. Certain places prompt the sense of recurring identifiable patterns. Memories are evoked which repopulate deserted places. There is a "strangeness" in our seeing which takes us beyond empirical *analysis* but not beyond the body. We are drawn into mystery, to places that appear to be empty but which contain a presence. All this amounts to the impossibility of reserving the "mystical" to an *additional* sense because it is already inherent in the sense of seeing, in ways of paying attention to the other.[12] The fact is that what some call the "inner life" is impossible for us without the physical.

---

11. See chapter 2 above.
12. Writers on prayer often commend the practice of "attention," and notably Weil,

In another essay,[13] Richard Kidd writes about spending extended time in the "Rothko Room" at the Tate Modern Gallery, where he found for himself that exploring a Rothko painting is much more than a specifically individual experience. His personal seeing was not apart from others whom he found he brought with him in memory. Inescapably he was in community in his engagement with the painting. No less, he reflects, does he come to an act of viewing apart from convictions about life and love informed by the tradition of faith he shares. Perhaps most surprising was his realization of the relationship between the spiritual and the sexual, although he was hardly the first to come to this perception. He offers a vivid description of the young couple for whom the intense gazing at one picture was inseparable from their touching and holding of one another. The desires of our "hearts" seek and find tactile expression. He suggests this has important insights for those who like the Hebrew psalmist "desire" God. Does it make sense to think of this emotion without the world of matter?

Both Richard Kidd and Paul Fiddes in their essays underline the importance of place. In his reflections on Hardy, Joyce, and Eliot,[14] Fiddes draws out the significance of places where the role of memory makes the past present, even pointing to the future. Visiting particular places prompts the memory and the imagination which recalls a history of living in patterns of historic moments and gives a sense of the interconnectedness of time and community. We may be apparently alone in our reading, viewing, and listening, but we are present with others who have been here before and those who are yet to come.

Thus, while some imagine that the effect of the creative arts goes on only in the inner life of the individual, in fact they witness both to the importance of the material and to the fundamental reality of community, with the two aspects intertwined. Dualism can never give such rich accounts of our human experience of being alive in a world like this, which is a world existing in God. Our primary theme in this book, as in our former jointly-written volume, has been the communion of saints, and our argument is that this doctrine, its credibility, and its importance, depends on its coherence with a non-dualistic view of the natural world and our human lives.

Gravity and Grace, 105–11.
13. See chapter 3 above.
14. See chapter 1 above.

The Saints in a Non-dualistic World

The definition of "saint" is contested within the Christian church. In our earlier volume we explored the way that Baptists and other Dissenting Christians, from their beginnings, were quick to use the word;[15] however, far from using the term to identify a specialized, limited group of Christians, they focused on what they saw as the basic New Testament use of the word, meaning all church members, those sharing the life of God in and through Christ. Earlier, apostles had written their letters to "the saints" at Corinth, Ephesus or wherever. The church is described as composed of "saints" (Acts 9.32). Baptists and others did not mean by this designation a community of exceptionally moral and godly people. They knew all too well that the saints who constitute the church were and remain sinners on the way to salvation. Their definition of saint was primarily theological before it was moral. So the saints were those who had been sought and found by God, blessed with the gracious gift of faith, living in Christ, sharing the life of the triune God. It was their belonging in God that meant they were a holy people in spite of their persistence in sin. When, helpfully, the church noticed that there were "saints among the saints"—named individuals—in whose lives the grace of God found special focus in their particular circumstances, again the basis for their being called "saints" was not in their own merit but in their sharing in God. Being in God, being in love, carried huge moral implications of course, and so the New Testament suggests communities of love and faith, with members living in God and thereby differently from their contemporaries (1 Pet 4:1–4). However, it was not this practical holiness of life that came first. It was their being in God that was the ground of their thankfulness and response. The result was a strong central focus even if the edges remained blurred. It is this corporate existence "in God" that is portrayed by the "communion of saints".

Now the point is that the meaning of "being in God" is seriously reduced when it becomes the survival of a disembodied soul. If the love and life of God can be known and entered into in our present bodily life, and if there is nothing in life or death that can separate us from the love of God for us (Rom 8:38–9), then the communion of saints is more than the church on earth waiting to become the church in heaven. Instead we are confronted with one church, one, holy and catholic because in life and death it is *embodied* in God.

Far from this requiring some dualistic separate realm of spirit in contrast to flesh, the biblical evangelical understanding properly involves

---

15. Fiddes et al., *Baptists and the Communion of Saints*, 14–24.

a unitive view of God and creation. As I have already pointed out, in the biblical narratives God is never portrayed as being alone, as it were. God is not known in God's separated self—where that is spoken of we are in the realm of speculative philosophy. The story the Bible tells is of the deep interconnectedness of all things in God, the One in whom all else lives and moves and has its being. God, as we have consistently argued, loves matter. This world of God's making belongs to God as do all the world's people (Ps 24:1). It is in and through this world of matter which comes to us as a gift that God continues the divine creativity, not as some occasional visitor but as the living ground of all that is and ever will be.

So the Bible tells the story of God's creation and salvation of the world which finds focus, not in some new spiritual energy let loose upon a few, but in history, notably in a people and a man, Jesus. The orthodox Christian claim is that this Jesus is the promised Messiah of Israel, the Christ of God and that God was in Christ reconciling not souls but the *world* to God (2 Cor 5:19). The church makes other associated claims, such as, that Jesus is the active Word that was in the beginning "by whom all things were made" who now comes to dwell among us in flesh and blood (John 1:1–18). As the human being he was, Jesus was killed, crucified, and buried. But God, ever active in the world, not least in the acts of Jesus, raised him from the dead. As they later thought about it the first Christians came to see that this was not some surprise intervention but a further and crucial expression of God's steady involvement with creation. The world of the flesh was never despised except by humans who had lost the art of being creatures, no more was it abandoned nor ignored by God. Eventually, as they puzzled about this remarkable Jesus and what God seemed to be doing in and through him, not least in their continuing and developing experience of God's gracious power in their lives which they called Spirit, they suggested formulations that tried to hold all this together, the doctrine of God in Trinity. Whatever else the doctrine means, it is a clear disavowal of dualism. Christ Jesus is the one through whom God is pleased to reconcile "all things," in heaven and on earth (Col 1:15–20). All things, all created things, are held together and find their *telos* in Christ. Nothing falls outside this creating, saving, re-creating, loving work of God in Christ. There can be no complete dualist account of this crucial story.

In his introduction to this book, Paul Fiddes recalls the theme of covenant, which was the particular form taken by the comunion of saints among dissenting Christians in England such as Baptists and Congregationalists. Meeting in covenant-communion requires the medium of the material world. Those holding to a covenant ecclesiology have urged the importance of the "visible church," and the local community of "visible saints" which does not exhaust the reality of the church universal but in which the body of Christ takes significant form.[16] Our stress in this book has been on embodiment, in the conviction that the Word which became flesh is always seeking such concrete expression. The church is composed of flesh and blood people responding to the gracious call of God in Christ. They are called to be visible saints who have a holy calling in the world, and whose "spirituality" takes embodied form. Two illustrations from history may underline this point.

The first concerns John Bunyan and his Baptist-Congregationalist congregation in Bedford in seventeenth-century England. On the face of it this may seem an odd choice since Bunyan's most famous writing, *The Pilgrim's Progress*, is usually understood as the story of an individual Christian making his personal journey of faith. The fact is that a more careful reading reveals how life in God is inescapably corporate.[17] *The Pilgrim's Progress*, one of the earliest creative works of English fiction,[18] pictures the Christian life in inescapably social terms, as the disciple journeys through life facing many temptations and finding grace in time of need. The disciple, Christian by name and calling, is joined with others in the covenanted community— named, for example, Evangelist, Help, Interpreter, Piety, Prudence, Charity, Faithful, and Hopeful. For all that Christian has found his personal burden of sin taken from him he knows he is not free to do simply what he wants and desires. With others, and only with others, he lives under the rule of Christ, facing opponents who are recognizable from the social and political situation of the time.[19] He is to honor God in his daily work as much as in his singing of hymns. He only ever hears of this way of life through the witness of others[20] and living this way is only possible with others. To "spiritualize" Bunyan and his famous book is to diminish him and his calling in God. He is credible because of his non-dualistic understanding of his calling.

For a second illustration we may recall some Baptist missionaries, William Knibb in Jamaica in the nineteenth century and Len Addicot and Eric Blakeborough in Angola in the twentieth. Knibb found himself a servant of the Baptist Missionary Society at a time when its declared policy was to avoid upsetting the policies of any lawfully appointed government. For the most part Knibb was loyal to this position until he found himself involved in political struggles not of his own making but as a consequence of his

---

16. See *Orthodox Creed*, articles 29–30, 318–19; cf. Nuttall, *Visible Saints*, 65–81.
17. See Freeman, *Undomesticated Dissent*, 61–2.
18. See Roger Sharrock, "When at the first I took my Pen in hand," 71–80.
19. Freeman, *Undomesticated Dissent*, 45–55.
20. This was true of Bunyan himself, meeting members of the Bedford covenanted community: see Bunyan, *Grace Abounding*, 14–15, 25–26.

Christian calling. To preach and plead for the "spiritual" salvation of slaves was not enough. "Soul freedom" was considerably less than the full liberty of the children of God. This could not, Knibb concluded, be all that it meant for Jesus to come to set the prisoners free.[21] So Knibb's ministry took a crucial political turn of agitating for emancipation, one which was a consequence of a non-dualist understanding of creation and salvation.

A similar response is found in the work of Addicot and Blakeborough as they engaged with the Portuguese rule in Angola in the 1950s.[22] They knew from visits and interviews with missionaries from Angola that atrocities were taking place. Godly mission called for a political response. Hence they raised petitions, wrote letters, addressed meetings, informed the press, and challenged the policies of the British Parliament. They too found themselves in controversies not of their own seeking but like Knibb they knew that discipleship meant political embodiment as God's salvation involved all creation.

These same principles of embodiment and relating which are at the heart of communion then lead to reflection on the Christian conviction of the resurrection of the body, the good news of the new creation. This is the New Testament perspective where material reality is never left to waste but is taken up into a new kind of living. It is beyond our knowing as to how and in what form God brings forth the new from the old dust of the earth but the conviction abides that the love of God which neither life nor death can destroy takes bodily form in new creation. A non-dualistic account of the communion of saints, as a fellowship of living and dead which is embodied, requires a belief in the ultimate resurrection of the body. Conversely, a doctrine of the communion of saints is required by a non-dualistic account of the relations of God and the world for which we have been arguing. The interconnectedness of all things in God, of which the creative arts give us strong hints, means that nothing can be lost because nothing can separate us from the love of God, who is the one source of all that is.

We will not speculate in this book about the *form* of the new creation but we affirm it. And one central feature will be the communion of saints, already a communion of those presently living on earth and those who have died in Christ, all held together in God. It has been a consistent feature of our exploration and arguments that we can only know God though others, through what is created and given. We believe this too must continue in some form or another beyond death, as well as the complementary truth

---

21. Stanley, *History of the Baptist Missionary Society*, 74–82; Hinton, *Memoir of William Knibb*, 50–51.

22. Stanley, *History of the Baptist Missionary Society*, 450–58.

that we can only know others through God. We can only have imperfect images for our communion with saints who have died, before we all attain to the resurrection of the body, but we must resist any kind of soul-body dualism in which a disembodied personality survives the impact of death. The key conviction is that we survive "in God," not in some aspect of ourselves. Two ideas that might then help us to unpack this affirmation are first, as set out by Paul Fiddes in his first chapter—and as adopted by us in our first volume—that before the resurrection God "represents" the saints, or "stands in" for them, maintaining their personalities, gifts, and love; such is the sheer livingness of God that this amounts to a real fellowhip of prayer with the saints. Second, the New Testament scholar Joe Kapolyo has illuminated the Petrine concept of an "inheritance" in Christ (1 Pet 1:1–3) by drawing on the traditional Zambian belief that we can "inherit" our ancestors.[23] In our first volume we suggested that we might find a convergence between the two traditions, so that saints here and now might share with God in the "representation" of saints who have gone before, inheriting and embodying something of their character, gifts, and virtues, and carrying on their mission to the world.[24] This would not be because of any dualistic understanding of someone else's spirit inhabiting a body, but because they and we are united in Christ in God, part of a network of embodied relating. The continuing existence of saints in God will be embodied in some way because the God who is ever active in creation uses the medium of created bodies to fulfill the divine purpose.

Embodied Existence in God

I offer one last illustration of how a non-dualistic approach to the world and belief in the communion of saints are mutually reinforcing, returning to themes in my chapter on St. Thérèse of Lisieux. Prior to his becoming a monk, and entering Gethsemani monastery, Thomas Merton taught at St. Bonaventure's College in the English Department.[25] In one corner of the campus was a small shrine to St. Thérèse of Lisieux. Merton did not find it attractive, judging it to reflect poor artistic taste. No more was he helped by the popular designation of the saint as "The Little Flower." However, the college librarian had a deep devotion to St. Thérèse and he encouraged Merton to read more. As is the case with many who have made this journey his early engagement with *Story of a Soul* only suggested that this was more of

23. Kapolyo, "An Inheritance Kept in Heaven."
24. Fiddes et al., *Baptists and the Communion of Saints*, 154.
25 I am drawing heavily here on Mott, *Seven Mountains of Thomas Merton*.

provincial middle-class French catholic piety, poorly written. This was to change with his reading of Henri Ghéon's biography written in 1934.[26] At the same time, Merton was teaching on James Joyce who, in his novels, understood the word *epiphany* in a secular sense to express the sense of the numinous, the moment when the ordinary reveals itself as extraordinary. (Paul Fiddes recounts one such moment in a Joyce story in his opening chapter.) It seemed to Merton that this significant intellectual insight in Joyce actually described the natural world in which St. Thérèse lived. This was remarkable, given the limited context of her life. She was no campaigner, showing no engagement with the church against the anticlerical forces in France. However, she lived in the conviction that she was sharing an epiphany in every moment of her life. She saw what others could not see. Merton found that her simplicity of practice in relationships and unaffected self-awareness challenged his considerable self-absorption.

Thérèse spoke to Merton of the cross. She suffered from tuberculosis and nervous disorders but she resisted absolutely the cult of the invalid. Indeed she seemed to have given up her own salvation, her joy of heaven, for the sake of others. She neither sought nor received religious consolation for herself. She lived for Jesus whom she loved in others. She saw things differently and embodied holiness. For Joyce in literature and Thérèse in convent life, sacredness, and grace was found in everyday epiphanies—that is, in embodied existence. Certainly, for Thérèse, in spite of the excruciating pain she endured, her deepest sense was of living in a world which was itself in God. Just before she died, at a time when she could not sleep because of the pain, her sister Cèline asked what she was doing. Thérèse told her she was praying and added that she was saying nothing to Jesus, only loving him. Life, including its bodily pain, was an offering freely given in the joy of loving and being loved.[27] Thérèse's sense of existence was of being in one world in God. Her hope (as we have seen) was to spend her "heaven" on earth doing good, that is, continuing sharing the life in God.

This emphasis on non-dualistic interpretation of the Christian faith suggests, we believe, consequences for the life and work of the church, called and living in God as Trinity. Returning for a moment to my own tradition as a Baptist, I believe that our ecclesiology needs to take more seriously the interconnectedness of all things in God to which a "one-world" perspective and the communion of saints both bear witness. Early Baptists were quick to affirm the communion of saints, and while they might well have seen this

---

26. Ghéon, *Secret of the Little Flower*. A new translation is entitled *The Truth about Thérèse*.

27. Ulanov, "Religious Devotion or Masochism?", 140–56.

phrase in limited congregational terms, they certainly realized the reality of inter-dependence.[28] But, over history, strong congregations have not always helped the weak, and many Baptist churches have failed to adopt strategies of responsibility towards national and international Baptist bodies, let alone wider ecumenical relations. We have failed to hold a necessary tension between the local assembly with its freedom under the rule of Christ, and the "more than local," ultimately the universal body of Christ. Sometimes Baptists have introduced structures to make such cooperation possible but these have often had pragmatic foundations, and are motivated by a quest for efficiency rather than by a theology of the one church as a communion of saints, interconnected in Christ within the triune God.

Existence in this triune God is embodied, a fact that carries huge moral, political, ecological, and ethical implications. Those who are baptized into Christ are members one of another, and (as my opening story of a Requiem Eucharist illustrates) to share the gifts of God at the table given for all the people of God is an embodied existence. My hope is that all churches, and not just the Baptist ones I know best, may begin their debates about renewing forms of church life with a vision of living in God without dualisms—beginning, that is, with the communion of saints.

---

28. Haymes et al., *On Being the Church*, 35–45, 52–54.

7

Hiddenness

Richard Kidd

Hiddenness is massively significant at every stage in human development. As parents and carers know to their delight, there is a brief period in early life when children are completely oblivious to everything that is hidden from their view. The hilarity associated with so-called "peek-a-boo" games totally depends on familiar objects appearing, as it seems to the infant observer, out of nowhere. At this early stage of life, "out of sight" is, it seems, entirely "out of mind"; indeed, "out of sight", you might say, is indistinguishable from "not existing."[1]

With increasing access to imaginative powers, however, soon a child is able to form and hold in the mind's eye even things that are entirely out of sight, a crucial development but one that brings with it a potentially painful ambiguity. On the one hand, it leads to further possibilities for delight in play, multiple variations on the theme of "hide and seek"; on the other, a facility for imagination also releases some sinister possibilities. Soon a child can imagine all manner of frightening scenarios that might or might not exist in reality: in the corners of a darkened room, for example, or behind the trunks of crowding trees.

Initially most of these apparent threats are easily exposed and their destructive powers can be put to rest: shining a light into dark corners or sending out a scout to check behind trees. Before long, however, the same

---

1. The development of Object Permanence in early sensorimotor stages was first researched in detail by Jean Piaget and his findings are explained in Piaget, *Construction of Reality in the Child*. Although some later research has suggested that Object Permanence begins to develop earlier than Piaget originally suggested, perhaps as early as 3–4 months, Piaget's basic understanding that Object Permanence emerges in parallel with a facility for representational thought, not fully developed until 18–24 months, has remained largely unchallenged.

capacity for imagination enables even darker possibilities to surface; for example, what might be lurking around and beyond the boundaries between life and death? Now imagination is raising questions that can never be settled by merely empirical evidence, the result of planned reconnaissance; at this level of complexity, it seems, definitive evidence of existence or non-existence is not in our gift. Only by engaging the self-same facility for imagination is there another way to explore things so radically hidden from our sight.

Imagination and Exploring the Hidden

In chapter 5, Paul Fiddes begins his reflections on the music of Elgar and Brahms with an introductory paragraph that highlights the priority of imagination for explorations that take us beyond the power of empirical analysis. He emphasizes, for example, that questions concerning the communion of saints, the core issue in this book, will never be settled scientifically; of necessity, such questions will demand the use of imagination to construct pictures capable of penetrating the *impasse* of hiddenness. This, he points out, is what the faith and imagination of the church has been doing throughout the ages, shaping a scriptural canon that we now inherit and against which we can measure our own endeavors. Imagination is fundamental to every chapter in this book, whether the focus is verbal, visual, or aural. Our conviction is that deliberate engagement with carefully crafted imaginative forms is essential to further our exploration and understanding of the subtle and elusive questions that cluster around life's most pressing but seemingly intractable concerns.

Hiddenness and the need for imaginative engagement shows itself, of course, in much everyday human experience. It is not just God's being that is in some way hidden from us, but also deep-level truths about every human being that we encounter. This is a hard lesson to learn and many people never seem to learn it; choosing rather to live in denial that it is so. It is all too common for people to assume that they fully know the inner truth about their neighbors: presuming to know their preferences, making decisions on their behalf, and assuming a transparency that never really exists. In reality, it does not matter how long we have been in a particular relationship or how intimate our connections with significant others, our human companions always have the ability to surprise us and, at their core, retain a measure of hiddenness that we can never penetrate—and most of the time we thank God that it is so.

In the process of our various explorations, whether our concerns are focused on God or on other people, it emerges time and again that humans do not cope easily with hiddenness. Beginning in our early years, hiddenness always provokes ambivalent experiences and responses. The "thrill of the chase" that first surfaces in a playful adventure of "hide and seek" does not necessarily disappear in later life. That surely is what energizes the cosmologist's search for a "theory of everything,"[2] a search that is pursued with enthusiasm, with or without any firm conviction that such a theory will ever be found or indeed that it actually exists. A similar drive energizes our quest to understand and know more deeply the people with whom we share our lives. In the case of theologians, there is a powerful urge to map the boundaries between truth and error, belief and unbelief. The possibility that no final or definitive answers will ever be found does not seem to discourage the search. It is so much a part of what it means for us to be human; the search itself satisfies a deep longing to create a reliable map of this vast arena of unknowns. The unfolding history of imaginative arts, from earliest music and cave paintings through to the present day, has been crucial in the progress we have made, enabling surprising levels of insight into areas previously hidden.

Hiddenness, a Darker Side

The shadow-side of our imaginative gifting—something that applies to scientists and theologians alike—is that we easily find ourselves overwhelmed by the feelings of insecurity that can confront us in such a vast and bewildering universe. The thrill of discovery experienced by scientists as they strive to understand the origins of the moon that circles our globe, for example, is inevitably shadowed by growing concern about the probability of further asteroid collisions with planet earth. The same powers of imagination that enable us to chart the history of planetary bodies simultaneously opens a Pandora's box of possible terrors.

When it comes to the exercise of theological imagination, the stakes are incredibly high. Again we find evidence for the thrill of a chase, but we also find unspeakable fears. Karl Rahner was surely right when he identified

---

2. This term came to popular attention in the original version of Stephen Hawking's landmark book *A Brief History of Time*. In a penultimate chapter entitled "The Unification of Physics" (155–69), Hawking admitted, " . . . it would be very difficult to construct a complete unified theory of everything in the universe all in one go" (155), but his words did not end the quest, either for himself or many of his colleagues, and it was an obvious choice for the title of the 2014 film of that name, loosely based on Hawking's life and work.

the "hiddenness of death" as key to death's uniquely fear-generating power.[3] Everywhere, it seems, "the hidden" occasions possibilities for exhilarating adventures and also debilitating fears; it drives much that is best in human endeavor, simultaneously threatening to crush all our future hopes. Hiddenness emerges as both friend and foe, energy of life and harbinger of despair.

From a theological perspective, the question of hiddenness is inseparable from a question about human limitation, possible limits to the ability of finite minds to conceptualize potentially infinite realities—and these are not questions that are alien to the world of science: be it the practical limits imposed by Heisenberg's Uncertainty Principle,[4] or the theoretical limits suggested by Gödel's Incompleteness Theorems.[5] In the disciplines of theology, this is sometimes addressed as the limited capacity of beings to conceptualize "being-itself," of which we ourselves are but an instance—a bit like picking ourselves up by our own bootstraps. It is also addressed in discourse about the relationship between creatures and a Creator, which acutely focuses the asymmetries between the human and the divine. In all these instances, it is the exercise of imagination that enables us to continue our exploration around seemingly intractable boundary issues; rather, that is, than simply finding ourselves immobilized by our evident limitations. Scientists, we find, are undeterred, continuing to work at models of "before the big bang"; and theologians continue to work with imaginative metaphors to explore the communion of saints.

Questions around hiddenness also acutely focus our attention on concepts of God. Because this book takes transcendence extremely seriously, believing it a meaningful category, almost every chapter has needed in one way or another to revisit the concept of "mystery." Each time we have done this, we have needed to work with finely-honed distinctions to avoid an easy confusion between mystery and mere mystification. Our conviction that mystery is an essential component of any coherent discourse about God means that we have needed to distance it from the idea that mystery is merely a temporary inconvenience which can one day be bypassed or removed. We have also needed to distance it from the idea that mystery is merely a factor in human perception, purely a consequence of finitude and limitation; rather, we have affirmed the all-pervasive importance of mystery rooted in the being of God. In various chapters this has surfaced as we have affirmed the metaphorical nature of religious language, and also as we have

---

3. Rahner, "Hiddenness of God," 227–43.

4. I first referred to the implications of Heisenberg's work in our earlier book, Fiddes et al., *Baptists and the Communion of Saints*, 39.

5. See above, chapter 2, 29.

discussed deeply painful human experiences of radical doubt and God's apparent withdrawal or absence.

Hiddenness or Absence?

Experiences of God's "seeming absence" connect all the chapters in this book. Clearly my choice here of the word "seeming" is crucially important, and leads us further into the exploration of hiddenness. Absence is a very stark word indeed, but it is not difficult to understand why some writers feel the need to use it. In so many ways, it matches very well the extreme severity of the human experiences that have prompted it. In chapter 3, I began to make a distinction between an "experience or feeling of absence" and an "ontological truth concerning hiddenness," and it is to that particular distinction that I return in this section.

Use of the term absence assumes a massive prior judgment about the meaning of what it means for God "to exist," a judgment, I would argue, that remains beyond intrinsic human limitations. There are tentative parallels, I suggest, to a child's inability to make a distinction between the existence or non-existence of things that surface in the early exercise of imagination. Most theologians would agree that a final answer to a question about God's existence or non-existence is not in our gift. Faith or trust in God is a step that we reasonably take on the basis of our ability credibly to imagine God's existence, and any claim to determine God's absence will inevitably be subject to the same limitations. In choosing the term hiddenness, we are attempting to account for the full force of our experience without making a leap beyond our capability to be certain about ontological realities.

Theologically, the case for the term hiddenness is very strong. The possibility of divine absence cannot possibly make sense unless our concept of God enables us to think of God in radical separation from God's world. If, as we have repeatedly urged in this book, we set our face against this uncritical dualism, instead preferring metaphors and images that center around a concept like participation, then the truth is that God and the world are inseparable, and it is simply impossible to conceive of God as totally absent. The word "hiddenness" enables us to speak about our human experience without demanding this dualistic division between God and God's world, as also the word "mystery" which functions in a similar way.

In Conversation with Musicians, Poets, Writers, and Painters

In the chapters of the first part of this book, I and my fellow-authors reflect on different ways that "hiddenness" and "mystery" can be explored through the exercise of artistic imagination, including a variety of forms that result from the work of artists who profess little or no Christian commitment. In our experience this is not a limiting factor in their value as a stimulus to theological reflection. Whatever their provenance, there are always limitations on the capacity of particular metaphors to elucidate the truths towards which they point; whilst they provide significant insights, they always have the potential also to mislead—especially when a literal meaning is pushed too far. There is, however, a cumulative effect, that builds confidence that we are on the trail of something important and worthy of further attention. When Paul Fiddes brings together insights into the mystery of life beyond death distilled from the music of both Elgar and Brahms, we discover more than simply the sum of two separate parts. The combined possibilities that "the saints 'dwell' in God and they are on a 'journey' to God's future"[6] hugely expands the imaginative potential as we seek to explore a credible understanding of the communion of saints. The larger vision creates space for the confidence of faith, despite the hiddenness of God and the hiddenness of our neighbors, living and dead. Neither insight, individually or in composite, is exhaustive and there is no sense in which "mystery" is finally dissolved or "hiddenness" ultimately dispelled, but together there appear fresh suggestions of ways we might conceive a hopeful future for God, God's people, and God's world, despite all the pressure that sometimes pushes us towards despair.

Similarly in the first chapter, where Paul Fiddes reflects on works by Thomas Hardy, James Joyce, and T. S. Eliot, he does not claim that these reflections lead directly to a fresh doctrinal re-formulation, but it is quite clear that they enable significant movement in a direction of deepening insight. Hardy's poems inspired by the memory of Emma and Joyce's evocation of Gretta through the memories of Gabriel are clearly not in themselves works of intentional religious endeavor, but together they are able to fuel a receptive religious imagination with an abundance of rich metaphorical resources. Eliot, of course, especially in the *Four Quartets*, is inspired more deliberately by religious motivation, but it is the interactive conjunction between Eliot, Hardy, and Joyce that bears the richest fruit. Through his reflection on Eliot's fourth Quartet, "Little Gidding," Paul Fiddes is able to build on the stories of Hardy and Joyce concerning individual experiences of communion with

---

6. See chapter 5 above, 118.

the dead, leading towards a larger vision for human communities, united through prayer, in a particular historical context. Once again, no claim to the abolition of the veil of hiddenness is made, but confidence is built through the accumulation of imaginative forms, offering additional credibility to our trust in a universal communion of saints.

My own chapters explore the potential of visual imagery to uncover similar hidden depths in human experience. In my work on Paul Nash a major theme is the evident sense of human presence, even in pictures without explicit human figuration. In reflecting on Nash's images, I was concerned to show how he enables us to see the deep connectedness between humans and the landscapes they occupy, both in times of ease and in times of great distress. Tapping Nash's imaginative skills enabled me to strengthen ways that as a Christian theologian I was able to envision hopeful, interconnected futures for God, God's world, and God's people. At first sight, for example, in Nash's seemingly bleak picture, "We are Making a New World," all we are able to see are charred remains and ubiquitous mire. After careful reflection we begin to see connections between different times, different places, and different forms of life; indeed, there are already the seeds of hope in a new possibility of life. It is not necessary, a theologian might say, to see God or to see the entirety of human community before we can begin to imagine energy and hope gathered in a vision of the communion of saints.

In considering the paintings of Mark Rothko, I aimed to draw on their peculiar power to evoke a sense of transcendence, his huge canvases creating gateways or portals through which, in company of other viewers, I found myself, with them, invited to engage with a wider and deeper hopeful vision of futures. It was itself an amazing imaginative leap when Rothko began transfer the figurative presence in a picture from the canvas to the viewers who stand before it. In one sense humanity is absent, but in another not only is it substantially present, but it is present in a community of viewers who find their hiddenness one from another strangely uncovered in the presence of his work.

In all these four chapters, then, reflecting on the work of artists—musicians, poets, writers, and artists—we have discovered imaginative forms, rich in verbal, visual, and audible metaphors that are capable of strengthening our confidence in an immanent and transcendent communion of saints, as yet largely hidden from our sight. Again, I repeat, it is not that the hiddenness has been removed, but as Paul Fiddes put it, with reference to Eliot: "The point is that his imaginative exploration of the relation between stages of time, in the context of prayer, enables the theologian to find new depths in the doctrine of the communion of saints."[7]

The Apophatic Way

There is, of course, already a substantial Christian literature that deals with issues of absence and hiddenness, and two particular concepts stand out in their need for consideration in this chapter: the *via negativa* and the "dark night of the soul," usually gathered under the umbrella label we know as the "apophatic way." Both of these concepts have a long history and have been hugely fruitful as resources for ways of exploring lives of contemplation and prayer. Sometimes, however, writers have been too hasty in assuming that these concepts reinforce a particular view of absence: both the absence of God from the person at prayer, and the absence of individuals at prayer and their neighbors. The idea of prayerful retreat too quickly evokes thoughts of an isolating individual experience when, in fact, grappling with the difficulties of prayer is often best done in a prayerful community, even if that community is committed to silence.

The *via negativa* was never designed as a way into a denial of God's presence, certainly not a denial of God's existence, but was the description of a model of contemplation, a "way of being," in which the focus on divine presence minimizes the significance of measurable experiences of material and spiritual providence. As such, it has always stood in sharp contrast to the "kataphatic way," which encourages disciples to put much greater store by tangible religious experience(s) and sensory images. Many spiritual writers, of course, advocate an integrated model of prayer that takes both of these "ways" with measured seriousness.[8] In reality, both are concerned with God's very real presence, and neither inhibits the potential discovery of deep relationships between people in community.

The apophatic way is, to be sure, most comfortable with habits of austerity, the deliberate practice of silence, but God's hiddenness is not taken to be a sign of God's actual absence, and silence is not a measure of human relationships. It is an almost universal testimony of people who attend individual guided retreats, very popular these days in monastic centers, that after many days living in silence side by side with people that have not previously met, deep bonds of mutual connection and understanding arise, even without speaking. My own experience is that at breakfast on the final day,

---

7. See chapter 1 above, 22.
8. See Turner, "Apophaticism, Idolatry and the Claims of Reason," 18–21.

the discipline of silence lifted, the community of retreatants find themselves in possession of surprisingly deep, ready-formed relationships.

In the exercise of apophatic disciplines, it is expected that seasons of felt absence can provide opportunities for significant personal and communal learning and development along the journey of faith. Everything I have said about the *via negativa* applies equally to the experience of the "dark night of the soul," which is always in danger of trivialization when taken out of its proper context. The dark night, far from suggesting the ontological absence of God, only arises in contexts where there is serious engagement with the mystery of divine presence, and the disciplines of life through which it can be explored. Many of those who have provided us with written guides to aid us in our own dark nights are people who have spent much of their lives in spiritual communities where, together with companions, the hard lessons from dark night experiences have been learned.

Both of these elements of the "apophatic way," the *via negativa* and the dark night, testify to a surprising conjunction between instances, human and divine, of apparent absence and intense presence. The experience of absence is not exploited as evidence of God's non-existence, but as a path to greater understanding and acceptance of God's hiddenness; and the necessary experience of solitude in prayer is not to be confused with an inevitable loss of community. Those who pursue the *via negativa*, ideally not in isolation from sympathetic companions, do so precisely whilst exercising passionate faith in one who transcends all possibilities of empirical proof; and the dark night is generally taken, admittedly in retrospect, to overlap with times and places where God is most creatively at work in the contemplative soul. In *Dark Night of the Soul*, attributed to St. John of the Cross, there can be no doubting the awfulness of the experiences to which the author refers:

> For indeed, when this purgative contemplation is most severe, the soul feels very keenly the shadow of death and the lamentations of death and the pains of hell, which consist in its feeling itself to be without God, and chastised and cast out, and unworthy of Him; and it feels that He is wrath with it. All this is felt by the soul in this condition—yea, more, for it believes that it is so for ever.[9]

Over and over again, the text seeks to emphasize the extremity of these experiences, but the purpose of the work as a whole is to commend a way of prayerful discipleship that can lead towards the richest possible encounter with God, and the fashioning of strong communities of prayer. As the writer puts it: " . . . God leads into the dark night those whom He desires

---

9. John of the Cross, *Dark Night of the Soul*, 101.

to purify from all these imperfections so that He may bring them further onward."[10] Indeed, we would be unlikely to have received this extraordinary body of spiritual literature, were it not for an ultimately fruitful outcome from a commitment to the apophatic way in the writers' lives. These authors consistently testify that experience of feelings of intense absence, painful as they might be, are in fact key to building a maturity of spirit capable of withstanding the very worst that life can inflict, on themselves and on their communities. This, they would say, is a road to strength and endurance in the face of adversity, illness, pain, and even martyrdom.

Atheism and a Conversation with Thérèse

Nowhere in this book is the significance of hiddenness focused more sharply than in Brian Haymes' chapter on Thérèse of Lisieux. "Dying in the faith of Christ in no way insures us against any and all of these ways by which our earthly life comes to an end. My purpose in this chapter is to reflect on facing death in the communion of saints, among those who live and face death in God,"[11] he writes in a brief introduction, and then proceeds to illustrate in detail how this reality describes both her life and early death. All that I have been describing in respect to the apophatic way is exemplified in Thérèse's life: the silence of God, the experience of a dark night, a thick darkness, the feeling of forsakenness, trial and doubt, but also the strength that can be found as these are experienced with companions in a loving community. None of the terrors that threaten to overwhelm her finally succeeds in breaking Thérèse's love for God or her conviction that she is loved by God. As Brian Haymes puts it, "She lived with the experience of a wall between herself and God, or being in a dark tunnel, such that she had to live with many doubts, to feel at times what it was to be an atheist in a world without God"[12] but, as Thérèse says in her final conversation with Mother Agnes, "How can I fear the one whom I love?"[13] For Thérèse, it seems, it became possible for her to understand these torments as a creative but painful mode of identification with the experience her many suffering human neighbors have, many experiencing terrible anguish without the benefit of Thérèse's love for God or community in the Carmel. Even more significantly, Thérèse embraces identification with Jesus, who had walked a similar road on his

---

10. John of the Cross, *Dark Night of the Soul*, 32.
11. See chapter 4 above, 78.
12. See chapter 4 above, 89.
13. See chapter 4 above, 87.

own approach to death. Holding fast to these convictions, she is able in the end to die well, ultimately secure in the love of God.

Central to the reflection in his chapter on Thérèse, however, Brian Haymes explores the impact that this extraordinary life had on the creative work of composer, John Tavener, and his librettist, Gerald McLarnon. Overall, I think, we emerge from engaging with the structure and content of this opera with a sense that Tavener's own reading of St. John of the Cross, and probably other contemplative writers too, has enabled him to hold, musically at least, a true and helpful balance between the extremity of Thérèse's dark experiences and the profound and unbroken confidence that the love for God had inspired in her—through to the very end. Brian Haymes helpfully notes the quotation with which Tavener heads to the original musical score of the opera, "Let us not forget, that the way to this superabundant love lies through the depths of hell. We must not be afraid of this descent, since without it, plenitude of knowledge is unobtainable."[14] That, I judge, represents very well the true strength and importance of Thérèse's story.

McLarnon's use of motifs from the poet Arthur Rimbaud, however, introduces an altogether different dimension. The idea of introducing the poet's words into the libretto arose, we gather, when Tavener and McLarnon first visited the Carmel and heard the use of the word *athéiste* on the lips of the sister who greeted them. Its use in the finished opera pushes to one extreme the question whether in Thérèse's experience God was ever finally absent, and whether she was pushed to a point where she actually lost her faith. Rimbaud's words are used so as to upset the delicate balance that is implied in Tavener's choice of quotation at the head of the musical score, seeming to tip it in the direction of an admission of God's radical absence. The insistent cry "atheist" on the lips of her dark assailants and the insistent accusation of childish sentimentalism are delivered with brutal force. In Thérèse's story they symbolize powerfully her willing self-exposure to the desperate cries of the wider human community in the face of extreme suffering; but handled in the way that McLarnon chose through the words of Rimbaud, they probably say more about his own disposition toward contemporary atheistic claims in the context of France in his own day. Her own "atheism," so called, would appear to be of a quite different kind, and in no way evidence of a final collapse of faith.

I find myself encouraged by Brian Haymes' highly creative reflection in his chapter, and it provokes me to try and distill from Thérèse's story how better to live with irremovable elements of hiddenness within which we all must find our own ways of living and dying. I am deeply moved by Thérèse's

---

14. See chapter 4 above, 93.

growing desire to embrace "solidarity in suffering" with the hard experiences of the majority of our human population. In our own time we are confronted daily with the reality of global suffering as never before, given unprecedented powers of global communication; news of genocide, and humanitarian and natural disasters, reach us from every direction. Whether in the case of Thérèse her community's commitment to solidarity justified withholding the morphine to ease pain, I am not convinced; but the aim to take seriously the reality of human suffering, and to be open to find ways to take some shared responsibility in the extreme pain of the world is very challenging. I am also challenged by her growing conviction that the courage of faith can be based on the love of God alone, and not on external signs or personal benefits—however gratifying these might be if and when they arise—and I am impressed that both of these lessons are crucially based on a strong conviction about the love of Jesus, God's Christ.

At the core it would seem, Thérèse's strength to endure a dark night in solidarity with her "ordinary" human companions, known and unknown, was rooted in the example of Christ, especially in his dying; and we must never underestimate the importance of her dying in a Christian community. The famous cry of dereliction, *eli, eli lama sabacthani*,[15] echoed in Tavener's opera—far from exposing to Thérèse an inability in Christ to meet her need, as Rimbaud might have suggested—takes pride of place as the supreme example of the sacrificial love she resolves to imitate.

As Brian Haymes brings out in his chapter, the vision that Thérèse offers to the world is essentially a christological vision; she invites us to follow her in the way of Jesus. It was unfortunate in editing so drastically the original opera to fit the occasion of its 1991 performance at the Trinity College of Music that so much of the christological content was removed. Perhaps in an attempt to make its message more acceptable to a largely secular audience, the power of Christ's presence in Thérèse's is radically reduced; no wonder, you might say, it sometimes seem that Rimbaud wins out. The truth is that for Thérèse the true affirmation of God's real presence, even in the context of radical hiddenness, is essentially inspired by her vision of Christ, without which the devastating possibility of an ultimate divine absence would have been impossible to confront.

Similar themes are present in Brian Haymes' other chapter in this book. In recalling the requiem mass for his friend, Graeme Parfitt, he highlights just how much has been lost in many contemporary Christian responses to a death and to the funeral service that follows. The common choices of our time: not to bring the body in the sanctuary and to avoid some complicating

---

15. Matt 27:46.

issues that might be raised by including the sacrament of bread and wine, result in massive losses for us all. He writes: "The theological significance of our own embodiedness is effectively denied. It is this flesh and blood, the life we call creation that God called into being and shared in Jesus Christ."[16] It is as embodied persons that we find our solidarity with the entire human community, that we best celebrate a holy life in the physical context of the church where that life has been nurtured, where in the sacrament we can renew our solidarity with Jesus of Nazareth, the flesh and blood companion who became the pioneer of salvation.

Hiddenness and the Universal Church: a Baptist Conversation

This book, primarily concerned to explore the communion of saints through the creative arts, is also written by Baptists who continually have an eye to their distinctive Baptist heritage. Here the theme of hiddenness is of particular interest for us in connection with its theological use in connection with the terms "visible" and "invisible" church. There is a long history of religious communities, not just our own, finding themselves incapable of strongly holding to their own convictions about God and God's church and, at the same time, respecting those who hold interpretations significantly different from their own. Claims to be unique guardians of salvation and the only true church have been everywhere. Counter to such claims, with energy and remarkable commitment, work on ecumenical conversation and possible convergence has seen unprecedented changes, from the 1910 World Missionary Conference in Edinburgh through to the present day. Baptists have been significantly involved at every stage of the process, and a major theological building block, a *sine qua non* for enabling greater collaboration between divided communions, concerns the hiddenness of God's presence in the world and church. Whilst separated communions still hold strongly to the conviction that there is a simple equation between "my community" and the "true (visible) church," little progress is likely to be made.

Some inroads in the direction of mutual recognition have been achieved by appeal to the limited conceptual model of an "invisible church," known only to God; we are invited to imagine something like a cosmic Venn diagram, marking out the set of all "true communicants" across the diversity of contemporary Christian communions. Although at first such an approach might look promising, its potential for real advances in wide-scale ecumenical relationships is in fact very limited. What is needed is a much

---

16. See chapter 6 above, 128.

more radical proposal concerning our various uses of the word "church" that can break the deadlock and enable real respect for integrity and authenticity spanning the great diversity of actual "visible" churches, both global and local. One viable theological strategy is to reserve the concept of "invisible church" to describe and embrace the much greater vision for a communion of saints, living and dead, known finally only to God, ultimately held in union only in the mystery of God's unconditional love.

Baptists through their four-hundred-year history have often struggled to find their way through these issues and can be found, even today, with a great variety of understandings. It is interesting, however, that despite this, Baptists have managed to play such a major role in the ecumenical conversations of these last hundred years; clearly some Baptist representatives have felt themselves able to affirm models of church, visible and invisible, that have enabled them to engage, at local and national levels, in ecumenical partnerships. Of particular historical interest is a remarkable moment in the eighteenth-century development of Baptist life in Oxford, one which demonstrates the creative ecumenical possibilities that are open within a coherent Baptist understanding of church, visible and invisible. This has been extensively researched by our co-writer Paul Fiddes, who is a member of the present-day New Road Baptist Church in Bonn Square, Oxford.

Although there had been earlier covenantal agreements between Protestant congregations in the area, the formation of a new congregation of Protestant Dissenters in Oxford in 1780, comprising "Presbyterians, Baptists and a few Methodists", was accompanied by a covenant document that included some new and striking wording. It was largely achieved under the guidance of Daniel Turner, then minister of the Abingdon Baptist Church. It sums up its intention with the words:

> We denominate ourselves a *Protestant Catholic Church* of Christ, desirous to live in peace and love with all men.[17]

The words "Protestant" and "Catholic" in this sentence need some further elaboration. The word "catholic" here simply means universal, not explicitly "Roman Catholic," but although the New Road Covenant was primarily a collaboration between three Protestant denominations, it becomes clear elsewhere that, as Paul Fiddes puts it: "Turner's thought reaches out to a vision of the whole 'Church of Christ' which finally transcends in its universality even its Protestant and Reformed members."[18] For also in the New Road covenant we find the phrase "to hold the communion of Saints with

17. Fiddes, "Daniel Turner," 112.
18. Fiddes, "Daniel Turner," 113.

all Protestant Churches *and* such as love our Lord Jesus Christ in sincerity." The "and" transgresses all formal boundaries.

Turner's vision of the church universal, articulated in his earlier book, *A Compendium of Social Religion,* enabled him to cut through much of the narrow parochialism that has so often accompanied and drastically isolated Baptist life. In a published version of Turner's sermon, *Charity the Bond of Perfection,* preached on the occasion of signing the New Road Covenant, we read:

> We do not mean to set up this little Society in *Opposition* to *any* other Protestant Church in *particular*; nor as a *Separation* from the Church of Christ in *general,* but as an *Addition* to it, connected with it in the *Bonds of Christian* Charity—a small hallowed Porch annexed to that grand common *Temple,* which *is the Habitation of* GOD *through the Spirit . . .* [19]

It is indeed a remarkable statement and its proposal only becomes possible because of clear and rigorous attention to the definition(s) of the word "church." For Turner the term can be used in three related but clearly distinguishable ways:[20] first the universal, invisible church comprising both earthly and heavenly parts; then the universal (catholic) visible church comprising all who make visible profession of faith in God; and finally a particular (local) visible gospel church, of the kind on which historically Baptists have put their greatest emphasis.

This is a far-sighted theological strategy for holding in communion Baptists, with their strong emphasis on the local church, and the wide diversity of actual Christian congregations in the contemporary world. It also offers a great vision of the universal church to which we have here been drawing attention under the title communion of saints. Clearly, as Paul Fiddes notes, this still has much to say to those who today continue to work against the stream towards ecumenical partnerships—global, national, and local—which seek to make a unity of churches "visible." Turner's vision demands much from those who would make it their own. It certainly requires humility, an open generosity towards others, and careful restraint in the exercise of arrogance about exclusive access to truth. All of these require an acknowledgment of limits to human knowledge in matters concerning the mystery of God; in other words, they require an ability to accept and live with "hiddenness" as an essential component in our understanding of God, God's world, and God's people.

---

19. Turner, *Charity the Bond of Perfection,* vii–viii.
20. Turner, *Compendium of Social Religion,* 3–5.

Amongst Baptists at the global level, Turner remains a minority voice, certainly in the Southern United States where huge numbers of today's Baptists are located. Elsewhere it has been possible to find Baptist congregations with a commitment to wide Christian collaboration, beginning with the use of the term "catholic" in some of the English Baptist Confessions of the seventeenth century. In the *Orthodox Creed* of 1679, for example, a production of English General Baptists, a similar distinction is made between "the invisible catholick Church of Christ," "the catholick Church as visible" and "several distinct congregations, which make up that one catholick church."[21] But Turner possessed a singularly prophetic vision, one that is very much in tune with the spirit of this book, anchoring our own stress on hiddenness in the practices of being the church in the world.

Aspects of Hiddenness

What, then, have we learned from our focus on hiddenness, writing as twenty-first-century Baptist Christians on the communion of saints? First, we have found that attention to the concept of hiddenness, the hiddenness of God, and the hiddenness of our neighbors, gives us greater freedom than we would otherwise have in conversation with a wide range of Christian companions who do not necessarily share our particular stance on issues that have become significant for Baptists: these include the local church and the baptism only of believing disciples. Second, we have found freedom to engage with the imaginative work of creative artists, many not confessing religious commitments for themselves, who nonetheless have gifted us with a fund of rich metaphorical resources that enable us to explore aspects of hiddenness, without trapping ourselves into a dead-end obligation to defend our insights by resort to empirical analysis. We have discovered depth and integrity in the works of musicians, poets, and painters, such that they inspire trust that their insights can make a real contribution to our understanding of God and God's world. Third, we have been strengthened in our ability to embrace some important dimensions of an important Christian realism. Thérèse, in particular, has enabled us to face something of the scale of radical suffering in the world and to be challenged by her example and call to deeper incarnational discipleship; we have learned never to underestimate the awfulness of feelings of abandonment, whilst still finding courage to take delight in the adventures of exploration and to remain hopeful within the good news of God. The setting for this empathetic response to the needs of the wider human community is strengthened by our own readiness to live

21. *Orthodox Creed*, 318–19.

at ease with the hiddenness of our neighbors, the full reality of whose lives must remain known to God alone.

It would, I think, be unwise to claim that the metaphor of hiddenness is without its own difficulties but, as I noted above, the tendency of metaphors both to help and to hinder does not come as any surprise. In particular, I am sometimes troubled when the word "hidden" is used to suggest that God inflicts deliberate hurt by intentional hiding; for example, as might be implied by the psalmist who writes, "Do not hide your face from me"[22] or in Isaiah where we find, "Truly, you are a God who hides himself."[23] Much of this chapter has been devoted to exploring the implications of living with the God who is intrinsic mystery and with intrinsic hiddenness, but these verses raise difficult issues. Whatever idea of divine judgment they assume, and which I would want to contest, these words of the psalmist and Isaiah do articulate very well the depth of the human struggle with feelings of abandonment and absence. But it is a common testimony amongst advocates of the apophatic way that there can be a hidden gift even in the darker experiences of apparent absence. It is parallel to something with which we are familiar in experience of parenting, where it is clear that real learning and maturing will only begin when some kind of withdrawal of parental presence takes place. When, as we saw earlier, St. John of the Cross speaks about contemplation as "purgative," it is something like this to which he refers; but he would hasten to affirm that such "hiding," if that is the right way to describe it, should not be confused with the actual absence of God.

The aim of this book has been to explore how the imagination of faith can help us to find our way through our experience of darkness, the hiddenness of God, and the hiddenness of neighbors and still find ourselves emerging strengthened and hopeful into a greater light. Our claim is that it is possible to live with hiddenness in creative ways and not to be overwhelmed if we hear, from others or from within ourselves, the accusation "atheist." God, thankfully, has revealed God's self both in the good news of incarnation and also in the experience and testimony of a great cloud of witness, people of faith, living and dead—although there remains much that will always remain hidden. There is enough, we believe, to live and die well, in sure and certain hope of resurrection and of lasting participation in a communion of saints, concerning which the book of Revelation (7:9) says, ". . . a great multitude that no one could count."

---

22. For example, Ps 27:9.
23. Isa 45:15.

8

Participation

Paul S. Fiddes

Two Aspects of Participation

REFLECTING ON THE CHAPTERS of this book, it seems to me that two aspects of participation in the communion of saints have emerged. I approach the first by observing that in his first two chapters[1] Richard Kidd draws our attention to the "strangeness" of the physical world, and especially its spaces and its places as portrayed in the visual arts. Contemplation of these images can, he urges, draw us into another space, into a deeper reality which exceeds but does not abandon the materiality of the everyday. With the artist Paul Nash, the occasion is a *place*, associated with memories of the past which are sometimes deeply-buried, and sometimes lying more on the surface. With Rothko, what prompts us is a *space*, or spatiality, where an apparent "nothing" alerts us to a "something" which takes us beyond our narrow lives.

As a Christian theologian, Richard Kidd identifies this experience of entering an "other" realm as encountering the God who is hidden in the world. He is describing an experience which might be called, impartially, "the mystery at the end of life," and if we take a word for it from the discourse of Christian doctrine we can name it as "eternity," which is "life beyond life." Places (Nash) and spaces (Rothko) thus offer us intimations of eternity, or rumors of transcendence.

So, as I reflect on Kidd's compelling treatment of this phenomenon, it seems that he mainly brings it into association with talk about involvement in the communion of saints in a way I shall, for convenience, call aspect A. In A we become aware that we are being drawn into a mysterious space,

---

1. Chapters 2–3 above.

or are being brought to confront the mystery at life's end, in company *with* others. Whether we bring them with us in our memory, or travel with them because they are an inseparable part of the community to which we belong, we do not come alone. We have an experience of "connectedness," or "interconnection" which helps to open us up, or make us more sensitive, to the deepest level of what is real. If, with him, we name the mystery at the heart of the universe as God, we are journeying into God in the company of others, and we may name this as "the communion of saints." Because God is always the "God of the living," we are moving further into God in the company of those who have died and yet live, as well as with those who accompany us in the present moment.

There is, however, a second aspect of the communion of saints which emerges from other chapters in the book, including Kidd's immediately preceding chapter to this one, in which he opens up the idea of participating in a "hidden" universal church. In aspect B we move deeper into the community of persons who are present in a hidden way, at the same time as we move deeper into the "other realm." This kind of involvement would follow naturally from the conviction that the God into whom we are being drawn holds community within God's very self. If our companions are the dead as well as those living now, aspect B will include some kind of interaction with them, a mutuality in which each can affect the other and—in some way—assist the other. Journeying into the mystery of the hidden God in company with others (aspect A) means also an active participation in a community of the living and the dead (aspect B). The first aspect is essentially about companionship, reaching across time and space. The second adds an interaction, or mutual activity.

The second aspect of involvement may be hinted at in Kidd's sentence about a Rothko abstract painting, that "this is a potential place for meeting not only with a hidden God but with hidden friends, hidden in God, too." All depends on the nature of the meeting. But the emphasis of both chapters is on the first aspect of engagement. As he writes in his chapter on Nash, "As a Christian pilgrim I live my life out of the shared memory of fellow travellers," moving towards the mystery perceived dimly here and now in the material world, and which we hope to know more fully at the end of life. For a clearer example of aspect B we can turn to Brian Haymes' account of John Tavener's opera based on the life and death of St. Thérèse of Lisieux.[2]

This is "a death observed," not "God observed," and half the chapter is about the way that an artist has observed it too. We are reflecting on the way that members of the communion of living and dead interact with each

2. See chapter 4 above.

other—though of course, because they are all held in God. We see the way that Thérèse came to believe that she had been given the grace to pray for others. These might be brother priests, like the missionary priest for whom she was given a special responsibility to pray, or they might be those usually regarded as "sinners." Indeed, it appears that she came to understand the "dark-night moments" in which she felt deserted by God, and in which belief was supplanted by doubt, as empathetic identification in prayer with those who lived in unbelief and the darkness of life. She wished to join sinners in hell out of love;[3] in Taverner's opera she exclaims quite early on that "I shall sit with sinners now and dark souls for whom God is dead." This is exemplified in her prayers for Pranzini, condemned to death for murder, and her presumed prayers after her death for soldiers in the First World War, who are reported to have seen visions of her; in Tavener's opera they cry out to her, "we do not know how to die." The relationship of mutual prayer in the communion of saints is summed up in Theresa's reported wish, "I want to spend my time in heaven doing good on earth", a phrase highlighted in Tavener's opera. Such prayers "lift the world" until "the end of time."

I am prompted to wonder why this work by Tavener apparently failed as an opera. Was it that there was too much religion and spirituality in general in the work, or was it that the portrayal of intercession in the communion of saints was, in particular, too dogmatic? This raises the question of whether aspect B can ever be satisfactorily represented in works of art, an issue to which I intend to return by the end of this chapter—which will also be the end of our book. Kidd's first two chapters alone show us that there is no problem in portraying or evoking aspect A.

I want to make clear that by speaking of two "aspects" I am not advancing another duality or polarization. We have been aiming throughout this book to avoid dualisms. I could perhaps have called A and B two "emphases" within one reality, or two modulations of one melody. The point of this can be seen by returning to the convergence between the communion of saints and the tradition of "covenant" which we have been urging throughout this book, and in our first one.[4] Covenant has two vectors that we may call "vertical"—relating to God—and "horizontal"—relating to each other, though the directions must not be taken literally. Depth images, with God as the "ground of being," are just as appropriate as height-images ("vertical"). Writing on the nature of the church in 1582, the Separatist Robert Browne set a pattern for those who were to develop such a "covenant ecclesiology" in the following century, including Baptists.

3. Thérèse, *Story of a Soul*, 120.
4. Fiddes et al., *Baptists and the Communion of Saints*, 127–42.

> How must the church be first planted and gathered under one kind of government? First, by a covenant and condition, made on God's behalf. Secondly by a covenant and condition made on our behalf... The covenant on God's behalf is his agreement or partaking of conditions with us that if we keep his laws, not forsaking his government, he will take us for his people, & bless us accordingly . . . What is the covenant or condition on our behalf? We must offer and give up our selves to be of the church and people of God.[5]

Though formative, his thinking however was to be improved by the early Baptist John Smyth, who perceived that there were not two covenants, as Browne appears to imply, but two directions within one covenant. Writing in England two years before he was to adopt the baptism of believing disciples as the baptismal practice for himself and his congregation in Amsterdam, Smyth affirmed two "parts" of one covenant: "A visible communion of Saints is of two, three or more Saints joined together by covenant with God & themselves," so that "the outward part of the true form of the true visible church is a vow, promise, oath, or covenant betwixt God and the Saints . . . This covenant hath 2 parts. 1. Respecting God and the faithful. 2. Respecting the faithful mutually."[6] Smyth then went on to integrate the two directions within this covenant even more closely by a bold and innovative step; he realized that the intersection of the horizontal and the vertical dimensions of covenant must mean that the covenant-making of a local congregation in one time and space is actually fused with God's eternal covenant of grace for the salvation of created beings.[7] By the time of his residence in Amsterdam he was writing: "We say the Church or two or three faithful people Seperated from the world and joyned together in a true covenant, have both Christ, the covenant, & promises. . ."[8] Clearly, "the" covenant referred to here, in contrast to "a" covenant, is the eternal covenant of gracious salvation, containing all God's promises. When people are joined in "a" covenant, they have *the* covenant itself. In modern times, the Reformed theologian Karl Barth has based a magisterial dogmatics on the conviction that God has eternally made covenant with all human beings in the one historic man Jesus Christ, that this primal decision cannot be separated from God's inner communion as Trinity, and that this covenant is

---

5. Browne, *Booke which sheweth*, 254–56. Spelling modernized.
6. Smyth, *Principles and Inference*, 1:252, 254. Spelling modernized.
7. So White, *English Separatist Tradition*, 128.
8. Smyth, *Paralleles, Censures, Observations*, 403. See also 389.

the very ground of creation;[9] but he failed to carry this insight through into ecclesiology, or the structure of the church.

In the developed tradition of covenant ecclesiology, the two dimensions are always integrated as covenant *with God and with each other*, both faithfulness to Christ and faithfulness in "walking together," but they may *combine* with different emphases. What I am identifying as two "aspects" are not then the two covenant directions themselves, but ways of blending them. The horizontal may tend to assist the vertical, so that human relationship with each other deepens relation with God; persons travel further into God as covenant companions. It is this kind of combination of two dimensions that I am calling aspect A. On the other hand, any exploration of being in God is going to deepen human relationship with each other and assist a journeying into the lives of each other. This combination is what I am calling aspect B, and extending to relations with those who have died.

While the covenantal principle can be seen most clearly in the shape of the Christian church, and it is in that context that the doctrine of the communion of saints has its immediate location, the idea of two intersecting vectors can be extended beyond the walls of the church if we understand the relation of God to the world to be generally covenantal.[10] The Hebrew Bible (the church's Old Testament) witnesses to covenants that are made beyond the boundaries of the "chosen people" of Israel. God is portrayed as establishing with their ancestor Noah an "everlasting covenant between God and every living creature of all flesh that is upon the earth" (Gen 9: 16) and the same cosmic breadth of covenant is contained in a promise given to the prophet Hosea of a covenant "with the wild animals, the birds of the air and the creeping things of the ground" (Hos 2: 18). Baptist Old Testament scholar Mark Brett has proposed that we can find a "Priestly imaginary" in the universalism of the Noachian covenant, a vision of God's relation to all creation in the Priestly school of theology which is setting itself over against a restrictive view of a merely national covenant and national sovereignty.[11] Through the prophets, God constantly reminds Israel that—while his relationship with them is a particular covenant—God still has a relation with other peoples. While the actual word "covenant" is not

---

9. Barth, *CD* 4/1: 199–205; 4/2: 99–102. See Fiddes, *Creative Suffering of God*, 68–71, 119–22; later, McCormack, *Karl Barth's Critically Realistic Dialectical Theology*, 350–67.

10. For this idea among Baptist scholars, see Haymes, "Covenant and the Church's Mission," 63–75; Fiddes, *Tracks and Traces*, 45–47; Fiddes, "Covenant and Participation," 119–37.

11. Brett, "Permutations of Sovereignty," 383–92; see also Brett, *Political Trauma and Healing*, 91–109.

used, the ideas are certainly covenantal. Amos in the eighth century BCE refers to God's having played a similar part in the salvation-history of the Philistines and the Aramaeans as of Israel (Amos 9:7), while two centuries or so later, Isaiah of Babylon hails the Persian King Cyrus with the same kind of words that had been spoken in making the covenant between God and King David (Isa 45:1-4). It may be that Luke in the book of Acts is taking up this Hebraic tradition as well as Greek philosophers and poets when he presents Paul as declaring in Athens that "From one ancestor God made all nations to inhabit the whole earth . . ." For "In him we live and move and have our being" (Acts 17:26-28).[12]

The participation of all created things and people in God alluded to in these texts will lead us to envisage a *diversity* of covenants between God and creation, not leveling all these relations out by one common denominator. The church offers the context for a *particular* covenant, living under the word of God through Scripture and exercising the covenant signs of baptism and the Lord's Supper, thus playing an indispensable part in the mission of God. But others outside the community of the church will, like Cyrus, be living in another covenant. This perspective makes it possible to apply the covenantal model to prayer with, and for, the saints of all religions. The *particular* covenant in the Christian church offers a way of thinking of the mutual relations of the living and the dead which is wider than the church, and to find insights into this reality through art generally, just as the particular sacraments in the life of the church make it possible to find sacramentality in the whole world, and a distinctive sacramentality in the materials of the creative arts.[13] Michael Perham is surely right that any doctrine of the communion of saints will be unsatisfactory if it fails to include non-Christians.[14]

In a Christian perspective, the two vectors of covenant are integrated by the idea of a God whose being is relational: as we journey into the community which is held in God—or the communion of saints—we are bound to be developing relations, expressed in mutual love and also in mutual prayer. In actuality, the two movements exist together, but in different contexts the stress may be different. When we review the accounts of various works of art (including liturgy) in this volume we can thus find at least three different ways in which they may contribute to the idea of the communion of saints.

---

12. For the "nearness" of God, see Haenchen, *Acts of the Apostles*, 523-25.
13. For this claim to sacramentality in art, see Brown, *God and Grace of Body*, 42-46.
14. Perham, *Communion of Saints*, 112.

Interpreting Aspect A

In one kind of Christian response to creative art, we may find only aspect A in the artifact itself, bringing to it a Christian understanding of what is going on in the work, while taking care not to distort its meaning, or to impute motives to the artist that are not in his or her intention. The interpretation, though Christian, will not explicitly include aspect B, but will be open to it. In Nash's paintings, for instance, we become aware of the company with which we journey (aspect A). The community is to be found in the place itself, as an "absent presence." In Nash's developed style there are no overt figures, but Richard Kidd suggests that the place is populated for several reasons: it has been inhabited from ancient times, people have shaped the landscape into the appearance we see now, and there is an analogy of pattern between natural and human forms so that we feel the presence of a multitude of human beings through the natural forms themselves. This last claim seems close to the personification of—especially—trees that the wall-labels and catalogue[15] of a recent retrospective exhibition of Nash insist upon, and Kidd himself writes of the human cries of agony that seem to be uttered by the body-like stumps of trees on the devastated landscape of war. But Kidd does not confine absent-presence to these examples; we become aware of a company of people who move unseen *among* the circles of trees, or we notice the invisible tracks of persons who are making their way into dark, tunnel-like entrances in the forest. So the image of a journey merges with the image of place: we are moving towards the mystery in a company of pilgrims who belong, like us, in a place which is both disturbing and secure.

In Rothko, the company of pilgrims is brought into the "empty" space by the viewer, rather than already haunting it as the genius of place. The viewer is coming as part of a community which has been shaped by the dead as well as the living, carrying memories of others with him or her. If the paintings are being viewed by a number of people at once, then those people themselves form a company with their own traditions and memories. In Rothko's mature style, as with Nash, figures have disappeared from the portrayal itself, and here they are replaced by the viewing figure who is looking with attention at the doorways or windows which take indeterminate shape in the space to which Rothko is courageously committing himself, breaking with the assumptions of "common sense" as Kirkegaard's Abraham did. Rothko is creating an environment in which the mind and spirit of the observer is encouraged to journey on, drawn through the portals to ever deeper levels of reality, to a "transcendent ground," to an "eternity" that can be found

---

15. Chambers, "Life of the Inanimate Object," 35–38.

in the face of death which also confronts us in the doorways. And even when there are no others visibly present in the same viewing space, this is never an individualistic experience but an entering a space beyond space with others.

Bringing the interpretation of a Christian theologian to his observations, Kidd names the transcendent space as God who is disclosing God's self through these windows on eternity; it is God who is the final goal of the desire we feel, and he names the company on the journey as the communion of saints. As in his reception of place in Nash, Kidd finds Rothko's space to be the opportunity for journey into God; both artists offer us an absent-presence, where apparent emptiness alerts us to fullness, and in which we find that what we thought was absence is in fact hiddenness. Following the rejection of dualism which ran through our earlier book, this hidden presence, of God and other human companions, is mediated by, and inseparable from, physical objects, since represented place or abstract space is embodied in solid masses of paint and canvas.

Kidd's perception of communion in art, an interconnectedness with others, as opening us to the divine Mystery and accompanying us into it fits with the biblical picture of the heavenly worship. What we may call in non-religious language a corporate focus on ultimate reality accords with the symbol of a great multitude gathered round the throne of God, offering worship and praise to God and to the Christ who has redeemed them (Rev 5:11–14). All this is what I am identifying as aspect A of involvement in the communion of saints, and it is an understanding of the role of prayer in eternity with which, I suspect, churches of the Reformation such as Baptists will feel most comfortable. Any element of involvement with others who may be praising God in their own way is minimized, in contrast with medieval Catholicism; all the focus here is on God who is the goal of prayer as adoration.

Thomas Hardy's poetry of loss and regret, which I consider in my opening chapter, also seems to exemplify this first aspect of engagement in the communion of saints. The places which he celebrates testify to the *absence* of those who were once loved and have passed into oblivion. They are no longer here, and yet the very place with which they were associated will not—it seems—let them go; the place preserves their presence. Despite Hardy's agnosticism about a personal God and his opinion that death is the end of everything, his poetry tells us that there is presence in absence, indeed communion in absence, an experience that defies rationalization: "Woman much missed, how you call to me, call to me . . . ". In the light of Nash's use of place, Rothko's use of space, and Brian Haymes' experience of a requiem funeral, we can see more clearly how the sense of communion with the dead is enabling an entry into a deeper reality within the materiality of life, prompting the poet to stumble onwards on his journey:

> Thus I; faltering forward,
>
> Leaves around me falling . . .
>
> And the woman calling.[16]

In shorthand, Hardy's poetry offers us aspect A of involvement with the communion of saints, though it is only Christian theological interpretation that names the consequently transfigured world as of God, or new creation in God. In my chapter I dare to say that when we understand the many forms that the covenant between God and human persons can take, it is not illegitimate to read Hardy's own emotions and convictions from this Christian perspective. Reading my chapter in light of the others clarifies the underlying pattern and awakens us, as readers, to transcendence.

The artform of a liturgy would seem better adapted for both aspects A and B, but in his very moving account of sharing in a requiem funeral (in chapter 6), Haymes focuses again on aspect A. I do not mean for one moment that aspect B is unimportant for Haymes; his writing on Taverner's *Thérèse* shows this. But I am intrigued that in commenting on the artform of a public liturgy, it is the first aspect of involvement in the communion of saints that, in effect, he thinks is well expressed. We might sum up his whole account with the observation that worship can make a journeying together into God visible, especially in the Eucharist. In a requiem funeral, much of the communion of saints will be invisible (an "absent presence" or at least a "hidden presence," to use terms from Kidd's discussion), but some of that communion will be visible, including both the living (the worshipers) and the dead (represented in the body of the deceased). Celebration of the Eucharist together in the context of a funeral makes manifest in a more vivid way than perhaps no other form of liturgy can do the corporate journey into God. As Haymes writes, "Here we were with the living, the body in the coffin, Mary, the saints, martyrs, angels and archangels, all united in God, Father, Son and Holy Spirit." This, he underlines, was "covenant love."

Thus, much of Haymes' theological reflection on his experience warns against giving too much attention to the human companion, the deceased, in funerals and instead urges a focus upon God and God's mighty works. He deprecates the growing habit of using symbols and objects connected with the deceased, as turning the attention towards him or her instead of God; the key symbols must be the bread and wine which prompt us to give primary attention to God, inviting a sharing of our life in God. Together

---

16. "The Voice," in Hardy, *Complete Poems*, 346.

with his fellow-authors, Haymes rejects dualism of body and spirit, and makes the insightful point that there is a parallel between a dualism about the afterlife where a soul is separated from the body, and a dualism in worship when word is separated from sacrament. The one dualism encourages the other. But the very materiality of the sacrament prompts us to give attention to it, and so to encounter with Christ, and to the hope of new creation rather than some bodiless ascent to heaven. Again, the stress here is on aspect A, on the way that communion with all the saints enables us to glorify God. The otherness of God means living, he urges, in the biblical ethos of waiting for and on God.

Haymes does not treat here the possibility of mutual prayers of intercession between the living and the dead, although in our previous book we had all commended a praying with and for—but not to—the saints in light. Here, reflecting on a moving and precious funeral experience, the stress is on the "with" (aspect A) with no mention of the "for" (aspect B), although he does expressly rule out one *excess* of intercession for the dead: "It was no 'requiem mass', as understood in the Roman Catholic tradition, offered for the soul in purgatory. It was a gathering of the church offering worship to God . . . " Thus he shows full awareness of the horizontal dimension of the covenant, recalling the intention: "to pray, in full funeral recognition of the deceased and the grief of mourners." Yet he continues, "The focus however was firmly on the triune God and our participation in the life of God by grace."

It is in order to avoid the dangers of a human-centered commemoration that Haymes stresses the aspect I am calling "A." Yet exploration of this aspect is inevitably open—for a Christian interpreter—to the second aspect, as in Kidd's impression of a "meeting" with hidden friends in viewing Rothko's art. So Haymes stresses that when we come to pray, held within the praying of Christ, we do so bodily, and it is in the body that "With all the saints we pray for the coming of the Kingdom." As soon as we envisage the saints who have left this life as still praying "your kingdom come"—surely implied in the cry "how long will it be?" in Rev 6:10—such a prayer must involve an empathetic entering into the lives of others who are still alive. We have argued that the saints who have died share in the embodiment of God in the world, and Kidd shows in his discussion of Merleau-Ponty that the body is precisely the point of contact with others, not a boundary of individuality but the area where the life of one flows into the life of another, and where community makes its impression on the individual person.

Discerning a Movement From Aspect A to Aspect B

Christian interpretation of a work of art may go one step beyond *openness* to aspect B, and find a movement from A to B in the artifact itself. This is likely to be the case when the work is explicitly dealing with issues of hope for life beyond death, whether or not it has been written out of religious convictions held by the artist. In Brian Haymes' exploration of St. Thérèse of Lisieux's own account of her short life and death, together with his reflection on an operatic version, *Thérèse*, by John Tavener, the movement becomes evident. Here, appropriately, Haymes deliberately invokes the parallel between the "communion" of saints and the Baptist idea of covenant. The opera first illuminates aspect A of engagement in the communion of saints, as Haymes shows how the story of Thérèse typifies the way that all the living and the dead in Christ can be drawn together deeper into the love of God. Thérèse's conviction that "my vocation is love," prioritizing acts of love above the Rule of her enclosure, enabled her to carry others with her in her prayers into the eternal love of Christ, to see the hidden face of Christ. She herself seems to be aware of being part of a community that exceeded the narrow confines of the Carmel and its often petty concerns. In this way the horizontal or lateral dimension of covenant interacts with the "vertical axis" and enables us to participate in the Godward movement. Haymes tells us further that it is the intention of his piece to enable *us* to face death, and face the One whom we meet in a new way beyond death, in community with others, in the communion of saints.

Thérèse herself finds a phrase and an image from the Song of Songs which seems to her to express the point of her praying: "Draw me; we shall run after you in the odour of your ointments." She was being drawn into the love of Christ, but she realized that this never happened in isolation to those who love: "I have no other treasures than the souls it has pleased you to unite to mine." So she is aware of being drawn deeper into God *with* others, and being drawn deeper *into* them at the same time, an intertwining of the two aspects of communion I have identified. Tavener takes this phrase, "draw me after," and builds upon it three journeys taken by Thérèse in the company of her father and her ironic tormentor, the poet Rimbaud. On these journeys she enters empathetically into the experience of the convicted murderer Pranzini and the dead soldiers of the First World War, as Christ sings "come" and she replies "love", both key words from the Song of Songs. The abbreviated performance remains faithful to this empathetic engagement, but misses its grounding in the Christian experience of "dying" daily with Christ.

As soon as we locate this journey into God in a new creation beyond death there thus emerges aspect B, a deeper journey into the *community* which is being held in the communion of the triune God. If, in the "horizontal" vector of covenant we are noticing each other, giving attention to each other, and being concerned for each other, then prayer must include intercession. The living and the dead will be praying for each other and for the coming of the kingdom in the world.

In my own chapter exploring music by Elgar and Brahms,[17] I aimed to make my point of departure the aspect I have been naming as B. I began the chapter with the suggestion that these two pieces of music might offer us images to express, imaginatively rather than rationally, a fellowship of reciprocal and mutual prayer between all those who are "in God" through Christ, whether living or dead. The images are those of a journey and a dwelling, which we may now notice are the same images that arise from our studies of Nash, Rothko, and Tavener. Their powerful effect prompts us in turn, I suggested, to do some theology in asking, "How do the saints live on?", or to think about what kind of existence would make credible the notion of this kind of fellowship of prayer if we adopt an anti-dualist stance and discount the survival of disembodied souls.

Nevertheless, listeners to the drama, *The Dream of Gerontius*, by Elgar and Newman, will find themselves first engaged with aspect A. They are invited to share in a journey, expressed through various musical techniques, although theologically, I suggested, we will want to extend the journey after death beyond the purgatory which seems to be the limit of movement for Newman. If it is true that persons made in God's image are always as active and adventurous as God is, then the journey will surely *never* come to an end. The image of Gerontius' journey towards the vision of God expresses a movement towards that mystery in which we are accompanied by other pilgrims. But then aspect B appears, as Gerontius in his journey towards God in judgment is assured by the angel that "Masses on the earth, and prayers in heaven / Shall aid thee at the Throne of the Most High." It is precisely this doctrine that seems to concern Haymes in his rejection of a certain kind of requiem,[18] sensing a danger of slipping from a gift of intercession by the saints and others into the financial abuse of indulgences against which the Reformers protested.[19] For all this, the central point of the work is the *journey* of Gerontius and its outcome, not intercession. By contrast, the prayers of Thérèse for sinners on earth do appear to be a central feature

---

17. See chapter 5 above.
18. See above, chapter 6, 124.
19. Perham, *Communion of Saints*, 36–41.

of Tavener's *Thérèse*. In this sense, Tavener is more dogmatic than Elgar, despite the strong Catholicism of Newman's poem. Yet in both instances the music works to enable us, the listening audience, to make our own journeys into the love of God, accompanied by many pilgrims who include the composers and performers in past and present.

Within the Catholic tradition of pilgrimage and the veneration of relics of the saints we can surely see the same shift of thought from "A" to "B." In the first place, pilgrims wanted to get as close as possible to the material remains, such as the bones, of those who had experienced a closeness of presence to God. In this valuing of the body, rather than a dualistic contempt for it, there was a sense of "belonging to each other, whether in this world or the next."[20] The pilgrimage to a holy place came to its climax with a journey into God in company with the saint(s) who dwelt with God. David McCarthy proposes that longing for nearness to the saints is a "social desire" which discloses a "metaphysical desire," to be connected to God in our time and to human community across time and space. The saints are thus people with whom we share a common life that "embodies the kinship of God."[21] It followed, however, from this companionship with the dead that there could also be a mutual fellowship of intercessory prayer which transcended the barrier of death. As McCarthy puts it, the saints "call us in" to participate in their lives,[22] so that "intercession points to the social miracle: social relations are constituted as a metaphysical communion." The dwellings of saints, for instance in the desert, become "the destination for pilgrims seeking a place to be near God in the world" and this leads to the conviction that living and dead can affect each other through intercession: "the lives of the saints establish gathering places of interaction and interchange."[23]

Developing Aspect A into B

A third way in which the critiques in this volume have approached works of art does not simply leave the first aspect implicitly *open* to the second, while on the other hand it does not go so far as to claim that the work itself presents a movement from one to the other. Rather, in at least one instance the approach has been to *develop* the second aspect out of the first, in the conviction that a Christian exegesis of the artifact demands it (though again taking care not to distort the work itself).

20. Perham, *Communion of Saints*, 11.
21. McCarthy, *Sharing God's Good Company*, 4–5.
22. McCarthy, *Sharing God's Good Company*, 66
23. McCarthy, *Sharing God's Good Company*, 115.

In my account of Brahms' *Requiem*, I have stressed that the musical evocation of the image of "dwelling" (for example, in a heavenly city) leaves open the mystery of exactly how we can go on living after death. What matters is that the dead are "in the Lord," and so the place of dwelling or rest is in God. The disadvantage of this picture of dwelling is that it tends to be static, unmoving. It is associated with the image of "rest" and this can often—wrongly—be understood as non-activity, and even as sleep. So the image needs to be balanced and corrected by the image of a journey. For Brahms, journey and rest interpret each other through the juxtaposition of movements in the requiem. He gives greater prominence to the image of rest than Elgar does, finding it conducive to his reservations about any dogma of life beyond death. Nevertheless, Newman/Elgar while putting the image of the journey to the fore also include allusions to rest. These composers are using imaginative pictures which correspond to the truth, but which cannot be taken as exactly mimetic of reality: the saints "dwell" in God and they are on a "journey" to God's future. They are journeying first towards resurrection and then they will journey on to new quests and new adventures in God's new universe, only because they are held in a dwelling-place within God.

In my chapter I suggest that the overlap of these two images and their mutual modification enable us to think imaginatively about the fellowship of prayer between the living and the dead—aspect B—although it is only *explicitly* invoked in one of the pieces, *The Dream of Gerontius*. The image of dwelling, especially in the Brahms' *Requiem*, is however strongly associated with mutual love, and this enables us to envisage an interweaving of love and concern as the multiple saints indwell one God in Trinity. They dwell in God and each other, and so we can begin to conceive how the prayer of one for another in love has an effect, not because of any direct communication between them, but because God is the transmission of their love and the already-existing divine love is enhanced by theirs. Intercessory prayer depends on having a "place" within God. In prayers of intercession we find that we are dwelling in a zone of inter-connection. This kind of prayer is supremely social as we are being swept into a current in which nothing is separated from anything else, no one from anyone else.[24]

This is also congruent with a particular understanding of survival after death: the image of indwelling is not about the housing of disembodied souls but about God's own retaining of a person's identity in God's self. At the same time, the image of the journey, when applied to intercession, evokes the New Testament image of the journey of Christ as High Priest into the

---

24. Fiddes, *Participating in God*, 124–5.

Holy of Holies of the divine presence (Heb 4:14–16), and so makes clear that all prayer in the communion of saints shares in the praying of the risen and ascended Christ. Looking back on the chapter about Thérèse, we may recall that she tells the readers of her story, in the context of her praying for others, that she wants to be able to pray the high priestly prayer of Jesus.

The Intersection of the Two Aspects in Mystery

The three ways of linking aspects A and B which have been undertaken in this volume all demonstrate that it is easier to represent or discern the first aspect in the creative arts than the second. In theology too the point of intersection between the two is mysterious. One way to solve the issue of the kind of interaction there might be within the communion of saints, or what McCarthy calls a "ceaseless triangulation of one time and space joined to others through the divine life,"[25] is to confine the companionship with the saints to a relationship through texts. What makes an impression on us in that case would be the stories of the saints that we read, so that their continuing existence beyond death is "textual." Edith Wyschogrod, for example, regards the saints as a "a text of flesh,"[26] the solid written text preserving the saints' experience of their bodily life, so that their stories confront us with a moral imperative to notice and respect what is "other" from ourselves in a way that bypasses mere propositions: "Saints' lives are not only communicated *in* texts but *as* texts, so that the character of textuality is pertinent to grasping saintly life and practice." [27] Wyschogrod thus envisages the materiality of texts as "incorporating absence" in a way that exceeds merely inspiring the reader. For David Jasper, the saints "live in their narratives" that embody, textually, the spaces of an interior and exterior desert.[28]

Victoria Burrus seems to take a similar approach in re-writing Christian hagiography in a myriad inventive ways in order to confront us today with the often-ignored erotic loves—for God and other people—of fourth- and fifth-century saints: "Hagiography thus continually generates new worlds of text in which love of God—a sacred eroticism—disrupts subjects and traverses the sex(ed) lives of men and women, disclosing the joy at the heart of existence."[29] That the whole world is a form of text and can be read

25. McCarthy, *Sharing God's Good Company*, 139.
26. Wyschogrod, *Saints and Postmodernism*, 47.
27. Wyschogrod, *Saints and Postmodernism*, 30. For further comment on the position of Wyschogrod, see Fiddes et al., *Baptists and the Communion of Saints*, 143–46.
28. Jasper, *Sacred Desert*, 58–59.
29. Burrus, *Sex Lives of Saints*, 161.

with open-ended interpretations is a significant insight of late-modern thought,[30] and is thoroughly consistent with the Christian tradition that the world is a "book of nature";[31] it draws attention to the way that a *written* text can transmit from generation to generation the experiences of a person's body as a text to be read by others. Thus Burrus portrays the saints as living on as our contemporaries, through the effect of any life on subsequent lives in a historic causation. Our position in this book is that the experience of prayer in the communion of saints nevertheless calls for a kind of existence beyond death that cannot be exhausted into textuality, and although she admits some mystery of "the spirit" in the way the impact of our ancestors is communicated to us, she gives no indication of any further mutuality between generations:[32]

> We inhale the exhalations of other mortal creatures: this is the logic not only of ecosystems but also of history. Our children breathe our own breath in turn. Some of the fumes of the past ... have proved toxic ... Other holier breezes, equally ancient and equally fired by passion, may also blow our way—may, in grace, even blow us away, catch us up in the spirit ... Dare we inhale such dizzying drafts of desire?

By contrast, at the other end of a spectrum of what "companionship" with the saints might mean, McCarthy insists that it involves knowing the saints as "living agents."[33] This means for him that the saints, in answer to our requests, may intercede with God for what we will recognize as miracles, though he stresses that God is "the unifying agent" of history, so that "prayer for a miracle is a prayer for change in the world, that makes God's pure action more immediate to us."[34] Saints, he explains, "are where the world is open to God."[35] An instance he cites is from a narrative written by Beverly Donofrio[36] about a "growing relationship with Mary," such that "Mary becomes an agent of Beverly's pilgrimage and the story of Beverly's life."[37] According to Beverly's own account she receives two signs from Mary, the "Blessed Mother," which McCarthy emphasizes have their meaning as media of communication between Beverly and Mary. Saints, McCarthy constantly repeats, are not

30. Derrida, "Afterword," 148.
31. Augustine, *Contra Faustum Manichaeum* 32.20.
32. Burrus, *Sex Lives of Saints*, 161.
33. McCarthy, *Sharing God's Good Company*, 45.
34. McCarthy, *Sharing God's Good Company*, 6.
35. McCarthy, *Sharing God's Good Company*, 114.
36. Donofrio, *Looking for Mary*.
37. McCarthy, *Sharing God's Good Company*, 33.

moral ideals, but "are defined by their kinship," by their capacity to open up a web of relations across time and space.[38] But the point of the story, which McCarthy accepts as authentic, is that saints are "living agents" to the extent at least of offering signs of their presence and care.[39]

From this perspective, McCarthy is critical of Elizabeth Johnson's account of the communion of saints. While Johnson presents the saints as "friends . . . [who] open avenues of relationship to God,"[40] McCarthy judges that "these friends of God are texts and not living friends," and so he assigns Johnson to the postmodern affirmations of the textuality of the saints, like Wyschogrod and Burrus.[41] In the end, he thinks, for Johnson the saints offer "lessons of encouragement" and "encouragement to hope" as we read and remember their stories. Certainly, while Johnson affirms the pattern of relationship between the living and the dead as being a "companionship in grace" (our aspect A) she thinks that there are problems with the idea of a fellowship of mutual prayer (our aspect B). Modern or late-modern Christian reflection is "intensely aware of the unknown character of what lies beyond death" and realizes that "there can be no direct communication between the living and the dead."[42] Moreover, there is a modern, and especially feminist, resistance to the idea that relationship between the living and the dead embraced in God's love should be structured along the lines of "patronage,"[43] which tends to be both hierarchical (a "pyramid of power") and patriarchal; the picture should rather be of saints joined with their companions on earth in one community of grace, which also includes the non-human creation.[44] Asking saints in heaven to "pray for us" is thus in reality one limited expression of "solidarity in the Spirit" through the ages and across various modes of human existence. The request, Johnson thus explains, is "symbolic" rather than literal, "by which we join our lives with the prayer of all who have gone before in a common yearning for God."[45] McCarthy, by contrast, precisely wants a "patronage" model, in which the saints become both our friends and our benefactors, and understands Johnson's term "symbolic" as meaning that for her the saints are merely "tropes rather than people, figures of

---

38. McCarthy, *Sharing God's Good Company*, 37.

39. One claimed sign seems outside natural explanation—the disappearance of a ceramic tear from a statue: McCarthy, *Sharing God's Good Company*, 35–6.

40. Johnson, *Friends of God and Prophets*, 20.

41. McCarthy, *Sharing God's Good Company*, 22.

42. Johnson, *Friends of God and Prophets*, 131–32.

43. Johnson, *Friends of God and Prophets*, 27–29.

44. Johnson, *Friends of God and Prophets*, 137–38. Johnson has developed the idea of a community of all creation in Johnson, *Ask the Beasts*, 260–68.

45. Johnson, *Friends of God and Prophets*, 135.

speech that we use to refer to ourselves as well as inanimate things . . . rather than living agents in our lives."[46]

In this assessment, McCarthy appears to have at least partly misread Johnson. She is not actually denying any continued existence of the saints, but being apophatic about the *manner* of their state, preferring silence to speculation.[47] McCarthy seems to work with a polarization of either a "living agent" or a "text," when in fact Johnson occupies a place on a spectrum of "companionship with the saints" somewhere between Burrus and Wyschogrod at one end, and McCarthy at the other. This becomes clear when Johnson finds inadequate Rosemary Radford Ruether's total reduction of eschatology to the historical plane of responsibility to the world and others;[48] she observes that the experience of poor women articulated in third world liberation theologians suggests that hope for life after death actually sustains justice.[49] When Johnson notes the difficulty of explaining how "persons continue in some fashion as themselves after death, finding definitive fulfilment in God" in the face of contemporary philosophical and scientific insights "that undercut the dualistic body-soul model of the person,"[50] it seems that she might be open to some resolution of the problem, but for herself she prefers to affirm simply that "We do not know, in the literal sense, but we hope. In the end everything depends on the character of God."[51]

In this and our preceding volume on the communion of saints, I and my fellow authors have not presumed to "know in the literal sense," but we have proposed a set of metaphors that fill out the hope that Johnson has, and which we think do justice to a rejection of dualism. The sustaining of the personalities of created beings in the triune God, prior to resurrection of the body—another metaphor of new creation—does allow us to say more about the fellowship of prayer with the dead (aspect B) and their impact on the life of living disciples than does Johnson in perceiving a "strengthening bonds of persons today with the whole holy people of God."[52] McCarthy finds God's agency in responding to prayers as being a "unifying" of the work of the saints who are individual "living agents." Our approach, by contrast, is to find God as the *sole* agency in answering prayer—in the sense of

---

46. McCarthy, *Sharing God's Good Company*, 18–19, referring to Johnson, *Friends of God and Prophets*, 1–2.

47. Johnson, *Friends of God and Prophets*, 132.

48. Ruether, *Gaia and God*, 253.

49. Johnson, *Friends of God and Prophets*, 197.

50. Johnson, *Friends of God and Prophets*, 192.

51. Johnson, *Friends of God and Prophets*, 201.

52. Johnson, *Friends of God and Prophets*, 134.

offering persuasive love which changes personalities and situations—while this activity incorporates within it the love, the personal characteristics, and the concern of the saints for the world, which may therefore make their own impression upon recipients. Prayers may be addressed to the saints, but they participate in the currents of loving communication between the relations in God that we may call symbolically the prayer of the Son to the Father,[53] and so the action is God's. We may invoke the saints, but we get the response of God. Johnson is right here to think that the tradition of the Catholic church distinguishes between the prayers of the saints and the direct giving of "blessings of any sort,"[54] a distinction which Michael Perham also finds to be established by Aquinas and Anselm.[55]

Our understanding of the fusion between aspects A and B thus takes up the proper concerns of Johnson about a supposed "pyramid of power," and sits somewhere between Johnson and McCarthy on the spectrum of "companionship with the saints." Surprisingly, McCarthy makes no effort to face the challenge of dualism, as identified by Johnson. He offers no explanation for the mode of existence of saints who are—according to him—patrons, benefactors, and agents. Implicitly he seems to diverge from the traditional concept of disembodied souls, since he affirms that agents of God's action in all times are embodied, participating in the embodiment of Christ as a human being; throughout the contingencies of history they are all connected "typologically" to the incarnate Christ.[56] But unless McCarthy can offer some account of how saints who have died *remain* embodied, he does not seem to have advanced far beyond the insights of Wyschogrod and Burrus that they have corporeal form in the material of the text. Our own suggestion in this book is that the characteristics and attributes of the dead are taken into the triune being of God, who is continually embodied in the world. This has some affinity to the early thought of Rahner, that the soul has a relation through the body to the whole material universe of which the body is a part and that in death the soul, separated from an individual body, becomes pan-cosmic, more deeply and intimately connected to the ground of the world.[57] Consummation in God thus, for Rahner, brings a person into the flow of God's own love which is always directed towards the material world, so that a person's soul can become the ground of the personal life of

---

53. So Johnson, *Friends of God and Prophets*, 132.
54. Johnson, *Friends of God and Prophets*, 133, citing Brownson, *Saint Worship*, 28.
55. Perham, *Communion of Saints*, 35–37.
56. McCarthy, *Sharing God's Good Company*, 136–39.
57. Rahner, *On the Theology of Death*, 26–27.

other spiritual-corporal beings.[58] There seems to us, however, to be no need to maintain any dualism of soul and body, or "separation" between them at death, if God sustains our identity by assuming into God's being everything that we are as persons, preparatory to re-making us as whole embodied beings in resurrection from the dead.

An unnecessary dualism also seems to linger on in the thought of John Zizioulas in his idea of a "hypostasis of ecclesial existence" which survives death. He affirms that the life of God is eternal because it is personal, which is to say that "it is realized as an expression of free communion, as love." God survives eternally, not because of a divine substance but because of a "trinitarian existence" in relationships of love. The reality (*hypostasis*) of the human person likewise endures, not because of a substance ("soul") but because it is relational: "because it is loved and loves"—especially within the church (hence, it is an "ecclesial hypostasis," transformed from a merely biological hypostasis by baptism). Since a person is constituted by relation to God, then Zizioulas affirms that even in the shattering of death one is held in communion by this relation of love, which everywhere creates new being.[59] This account is close to the position we are adopting in this book; but a question still hovers as to the relation between the hypostasis as "an ontological principle" and the physical body. We are suggesting rather that the relational *structure* of the person (or of the *hypostasis*)—that is, all its capacity for relations and its partial fulfillment of this potential—is mapped on to the relations of the triune God. Only the divine hypostases in God can be pure relations,[60] and so can assume this relational quality and experience of the human person into themselves; the human hypostasis must "have" relations, however relational it is, or—as Zizioulas puts it—there is an "it" which is the subject and the object of love ("it is loved and loves").[61] Thus, *pace* Zizioulas, it must die with the body, and yet the relations it has developed and the personal characteristics that inhere within these relations, can be immersed into God's relational life, ready for new creation.

McCarthy in his discussion of the communion of saints is critical of Johnson for not being sufficiently trinitarian.[62] He himself, we notice, only develops any relation of saints to the Trinity in the final pages of his book, writing that: "The saints are important because they connect us to a

---

58. Rahner, *On the Theology of Death*, 31.

59. Zizioulas, *Being as Communion*, 48.

60. See above, chapter 1, 19–20.

61. Of course, Zizioulas insists that the ontological principle of the person can never degenerate into a "thing": *Being as Communion*, 49n44.

62. McCarthy, *Sharing God's Good Company*, 18.

metaphysical landscape of relationships . . . the communion of saints comes to us through the inner life and outward movement of God's Trinity . . . Giving account of holy people requires appeal to the activity of the Spirit who gathers and joins and draws up into the love of Father and Son."[63] However, he relates the saints to God, not as dwelling within those relations, but as being agents which share in the distinctive agencies of each divine person, which he identifies as "loving, knowing and ruling".[64] But neither the saints who have died, nor the three "persons" in God, can be individual "agents"; rather the "agency" of God is in taking the whole of creation into God's threefold relations and so shaping and influencing it with the creative currents of love. Talk about divine persons as "relations" is not objectifying, as if God could be an object of our knowledge. It is a way of speaking that is only possible through participating in these relations, and so is a form of language that is both apophatic (non-objectifying) and kataphatic (metaphorical) at the same time. To speak of saints as having their personal identity sustained by God and their prayers as making their own contribution to God's loving action is likewise both apophatic and kataphatic. What I have been naming aspects A and B—companionship and mutual prayer with the saints—intersect in mystery.

Conclusion: The Interplay Between Community and Communication in the Arts

We have observed that the creative arts are especially suitable for expressing or intimating aspect A of the communion of saints, a shared journey in human community towards the final mystery of God. We have also detected in some works a movement towards what I am calling aspect B, an engagement in mutual, though indirect, communication and intercession, so giving a more total picture of a covenant relationship. The oscillation from one aspect to the other is always going to be a playful one, and cannot be dogmatic. This is exemplified in my opening chapter about three literary versions of communion with the dead. All three concern a kind of "absent-presence" (or more accurately, a hidden presence) in a place, variously Boscastle, Little Gidding, and Dublin, and each also includes a journey on which the writer sets out in imagination.

In the second and third of these pieces both aspects of engagement in the communion of saints appear in the text, and the *way* the second (B) is presented may offer us a clue about the possibilities as well as the limits of art

---

63. McCarthy, *Sharing God's Good Company*, 166–67.
64. McCarthy, *Sharing God's Good Company*, 168.

for expressing the communion between living and dead. The predominant mood of both pieces is the first aspect, an openness to the mystery at the heart of life which is assisted by some mysterious communion with others. Making his journey to Little Gidding in midwinter spring, evoking the journey of life towards death and the promise of life in death, the poet is accompanied by other invisible pilgrims who have found that this is a place where "prayer has been valid." The poet exclaims "we are born with the dead;/ See they return and bring us with them." The place offers a "timeless moment," not in the sense of a loss of all time, but as a redemption of past and present in hope of the future. In my chapter I focus on the words:

> And what the dead had no speech for, when living,
> They can tell you, being dead: the communication
> Of the dead is tongued with fire beyond the language of the living.

Two possible readings of this text do not take us beyond the first aspect of involvement in the communion of saints. It might mean that the words of those who are now dead can, in their textuality, purify the language and culture of the living when we recall them in new ways, or that when someone has died we can more fully understand the direction—and gain from—the journey of his or her experience. We can now see how these two meanings fit into a communion of saints which assists us on our journey to contemplate the love which is the "unfamilar name" behind the sufferings of life (aspect A). Yet the meaning spills over, with its excess, into something else. As I point out, literature uses images playfully where doctrine tries to use them analytically. Indirectly, with ambiguity and ambivalence, the phrase about the "communication of the dead . . . tongued with fire beyond the language of the living" opens the possibility that the relation between past, present, and future can be experienced in a new and liberating way through prayer in the communion of saints. With their intercession for us the saints who come from the past, even our recent past, may help us to untangle our *confusions* about the past. Their prayer may even help the poet to sort out his bafflement about the passing of time, and redeem it.

We find the same kind of playful leap between the two aspects of involvement in the communion of saints in James Joyce's short story. Allowing the absent-presence of Michael Furey in his "flickering existence" to impinge on his life rather than trying to shut it out in jealousy enables Gabriel to understand his own lack of love, and so better make his journey forwards (aspect A); Gabriel decides in the wake of this experience that "the time had come for him to set out on his journey westwards. Yes, the newspapers were right: snow was general all over Ireland." The journey is literally to recover a familiarity with his country in its westward parts that he has lost, but the phrase "journey westwards" is freighted with the symbolic weight of a journey towards the horizon of death where the sun finally sets. Yet this effect of communion with the dead reaches out towards something more mysterious: we feel that Gabriel needs also to enter more deeply in sympathy into the realm of the dead (aspect B), for the snow "was falling, too, upon every part of the lonely churchyard on the hill where Michael Furey lay buried."

Joyce's story makes clear that there must be some means of mutual relation and interaction to join the emotions of Gabriel with Michael, so that Michael is not felt as a hostile force intervening between husband and wife but can be simply accepted as one who loves. The narrative hints that there can be some mysterious housing of people's emotions towards others, and this takes form in the symbol of the snow "falling faintly through the universe on all the living and the dead." I argue that the theological assertion that this covering mantle is God is not just allegorizing the snow, since the material element of the falling of snow is an occasion when God can be encountered. The intercession of, and intercession for, the dead is not explicitly mentioned; but prayer is only a verbal form which the mutual love of living and dead, held in God, can take.

In the art of both Eliot and Joyce, one a committed Anglican and the other nurtured in early years as a Catholic, we are able to explore the variety of intersections between vertical and horizontal dimensions of covenantal love. What I have been calling the expression of aspect "A" involvement with the communion of saints is sufficiently open to draw in readers of all faiths and none; it resonates with a very wide range of experience and is a phenomenon easily recognized, for which Richard Kidd has very helpfully offered the terms "strangeness" and "interconnection." But we see that it is possible for art to hint, indirectly, at the idea of mutual intercession between living and dead (aspect B) such as catches Haymes' imagination in the story of Thérèse; there is a moving boundary between the two. The second is, of course, not superior to the first and cannot exist without it; the first also prompts us to realize that anything said about the second must be provisional, and cannot be a literal description of what is mystery. From a Christian theological perspective, art has the capacity to open up these dimensions of the ultimate mystery which is God only because mystery is taking the initiative and opening itself to us as a gift.[65]

Works of art, whether in the visual arts, music, literature, or liturgy thus enable us to move forwards towards the horizon of death in companionship with a great (though often hidden and mysterious) community of

---

65. See chapter 1 above, 17.

living beings and living things. Whenever we interpret this as a journey towards the God who is the source and final goal of all life, we will also experience our companions on the way as the communion of saints. The history of the church and the stories of our own lives will help us to identify this company that spans time and space. In turn, the witness of art will help shape and even make theology, insisting by its very materiality that the communion of saints cannot be understood in a dualistic way as an assembly of disembodied souls. Some artworks will then prompt us to discover an interaction and interchange in this communion, so that we find ourselves sharing in a rhythm of personal and reciprocal relations that are universal, faithful, and enduring. From worshiping in church and receiving its sacraments we can identify this mutual communication as "praying with the saints," and creative art can help us engage more deeply in it and understand its patterns better.

From attention to art we will thus learn to engage in two major aspects of the communion of saints—companionship and prayer. The three authors of this book are glad to witness that they have shared in such a journey of discovery over several years, through reading texts together, visiting art galleries together and listening to music in each other's company. They have found their theology of the communion of saints to be decisively confirmed, shaped, and enriched by this experience. They are prompted to affirm that, assisted by both art and theology we can be drawn into the space of a covenant with God and each other, in "ways known and ways that are yet to be made known."[66]

---

66. Traditional words of the covenant pledge among Nonformist churches: see the Gainsborough Covenant in the Introduction above, and for other examples see Burrage, *Church Covenant Idea*, 79, 88, 131, 133.

Bibliography

Anfam, David. *Abstract Expressionism*. London: Royal Academy of Arts, 2016.
———. "The World in a Frame." In *Rothko*, edited by Achim Borchardt-Hume, 45–57. London: Tate, 2008.
Armstrong, Tim. *Haunted Hardy: Poetry, History, Memory*. Basingstoke, UK: Palgrave, 2000.
Augustine. *Confessions*. Translated by R. S. Pine-Coffin. London: Penguin, 1961.
———. *The Trinity*. In *The Fathers of the Church, a New Translation*. Translated by S. McKenna. Washington, DC: Catholic University of America Press, 1963.
Balthasar, Hans Urs von. *Theo-Drama. Theological Dramatic Theory*: Vol. V, *The Last Act*. Translated by Graham Harrison. San Francisco: Ignatius, 1998.
Barth, Karl. *Church Dogmatics*. 14 vols. Translated and edited by G. W. Bromiley and T. F. Torrance. Edinburgh: T. & T. Clark, 1936–1977.
Begbie, Jeremy. *Theology, Music and Time*. Cambridge: Cambridge University Press, 2000.
Berger, John. *Ways of Seeing*. London: BBC & Penguin, 1972.
Bonhoeffer, Dietrich. *Letters and Papers from Prison: The Enlarged Edition*. Edited by Eberhard Bethge. London: SCM, 1971.
Borchardt-Hume, Achim. *Rothko*. London: Tate, 2008.
Bradford, William. *History of Plymouth Plantation, 1620–1647*. 2 vols. Edited by W. C. Ford. Boston: Massachusetts Historical Society, 1912.
Breslin, James. *Mark Rothko: a Biography*. Chicago: University of Chicago Press, 1993.
Brett, Mark. "Permutations of Sovereignty in the Priestly Tradition." *Vetus Testamentum* 63 (2013) 383–92.
———. *Political Trauma and Healing. Biblical Ethics for a Post-Colonial World*. Grand Rapids: Eerdmans, 2016.
Brown, David. *God and Grace of Body*. Oxford: Oxford University Press, 2007.
Browne, Robert. *A Booke which sheweth the life and manners of all true Christians*. In *The Writings of Robert Harrison and Robert Browne*, edited by A. Peel and L. Carlson, 221–395. London: Allen and Unwin, 1953.
Brownson, Orestes. *Saint Worship. The Worship of Mary*. Edited by Thomas Ryan. Paterson, NJ: St Anthony Guild, 1963.
Bullen, J. B. *Thomas Hardy: The World of His Novels*. London: Frances Lincoln, 2013.
Bunyan, John. *Grace Abounding to the Chief of Sinners*. Edited by Roger Sharrock. Oxford: Clarendon, 2012.

Burrage, Champlin. *The Church Covenant Idea: Its Origin and Its Development*. Philadelphia: American Baptist Publication Society, 1904.

Burrus, Virginia. *The Sex Lives of Saints: An Erotics of Ancient Hagiography*. Philadelphia: University of Pennsylvania Press, 2004.

Carballo, Robert. "Towards a Non-Dialectic Poetry of Dogma. Newman as Librettist." In *The Best of Me: A Gerontius Centenary Companion*, edited by Geoffrey Hodgkins, 56–64. Rickmansworth, UK: Elgar, 1999.

Casti, John L., and Werner dePauli. *Gödel: a Life of Logic*. Cambridge, MA: Perseus, 2000.

Causey, Andrew. *Paul Nash*. Oxford: Clarendon, 1980.

Chambers, Emma. "The Life of the Inanimate Object." In *Paul Nash*, edited by Emma Chambers, 35–79. London: Tate, 2016.

Chambers, Emma, ed. *Paul Nash*. London: Tate, 2016.

Compton, Michael. *Mark Rothko: the Seagram Mural Project*. Liverpool: Tate Gallery Liverpool, 1988.

Cross, Anthony R., and Philip E. Thompson, eds. *Baptist Sacramentalism*. Carlisle, UK: Paternoster, 2003.

Davis, Stephen T. "The Resurrection of the Dead." In *Death and Afterlife*, edited by Stephen T. Davis, 119–44. London: Macmillan, 1989.

Dawkins, Richard. *The God Delusion*. London: Bantam, 2006.

Dean, Winton, "Music in London." *The Musical Times* 120 (1979) 929–34.

Derrida, Jacques. "Afterword." In *Limited Inc* by Jacques Derrida, 111–54. Translated by Samuel Weber and Jeffrey Mehlman. Evanston: Northwestern University Press, 1988.

Donofrio, Beverly. *Looking for Mary: or, The Blessed Mother and Me*. New York: Viking Compass, 2000.

Dreyer, Elizabeth A. *Accidental Theologians*. Cincinnati: Franciscan Media, 2014.

Dudgeon, Piers, *Lifting the Veil: The Biography of Sir John Tavener*. London: Portrait, 2003.

Einstein, A. *Ideas and Opinions*. Translated by Sonja Bargmann. New York: Bonanza, 1954.

Eliot, T. S. *The Poems of T. S. Eliot, Volume I: Collected and Uncollected Poems*, edited by Christopher Ricks and Jim McCue. London: Faber & Faber, 2015.

Ellmann, Richard. "The Backgrounds of 'The Dead.'" In *Joyce. A Collection of Critical Essays*. Twentieth Century Views, edited by William H. Chace, 18–28. Englewood Cliffs, NJ: Prentice-Hall, 1974.

Fiddes, Paul S. "The Church Local and Universal: Catholic and Baptist Perspectives on *Koinonia* Ecclesiology." In *Revisioning, Renewing, and Rediscovering the Triune Center. Essays in Honor of Stanley J. Grenz*, edited by Derek J. Tidball, Brian S. Harris and Jason S. Sexton, 97–120. Eugene, OR: Cascade, 2014.

———. "Concept, Image and Story in Systematic Theology." *International Journal of Systematic Theology* 11 (2009) 3–23.

———. "Covenant and Participation." *Perspectives in Religious Studies* 44 (2017) 119–37.

———. *The Creative Suffering of God*. Oxford: Oxford University Press, 1988.

———. "Daniel Turner and a Theology of the Church Universal." In *Pulpit and People: Studies in Eighteenth-Century Baptist Life and Thought*, edited by John Briggs, 112–27. Carlisle, UK: Paternoster, 2009.

———. *The Fourth Strand of the Reformation: The Covenant Ecclesiology of Anabaptists, English Separatists and Early General Baptists*. Oxford: Centre for Baptist History and Heritage, 2018.

———. *Freedom and Limit. A Dialogue between Literature and Christian Doctrine*. London: Macmillan, 1993.

———. *Participating in God. A Pastoral Doctrine of the Trinity*. London: Darton, Longman and Todd, 2000.

———. *The Promised End: Eschatology in Theology and Literature*. Oxford: Blackwell, 2000.

———. *Seeing the World and Knowing God: Hebrew Wisdom and Christian Doctrine in a Late-Modern Context*. Oxford: Oxford University Press, 2013.

———. *Tracks and Traces: Baptist Identity in Church and Theology*. Carlisle: Paternoster, 2005.

Fiddes, Paul S., et al. *Baptists and the Communion of Saints: A Theology of Covenanted Disciples*. Waco, TX: Baylor University Press, 2014.

Fowler, Stanley K. *More than a Symbol: The British Baptist Recovery of Baptismal Sacramentalism*. Carlisle, UK: Paternoster, 2002.

Freeman, Curtis W. *Undomesticated Dissent: Democracy and the Public Virtue of Religious Nonconformity*. Waco, TX: Baylor University Press, 2017.

Furlong, Monica, *Thérèse of Lisieux*. Rev. ed. London: Darton, Longman & Todd, 2001.

Gaucher, Guy. *The Passion of Thérèse of Lisieux*. Translated by Anne-Marie Brennan. New York: Crossroad, 1990.

———. *The Story of a Life: St Thérèse of Lisieux*. Translated by Anne-Marie Brennan. San Francisco: Harper & Row, 1987.

Geach, Peter. *God and the Soul*. London: Routledge & Kegan Paul, 1969.

Ghéon, Henri. *The Secret of the Little Flower*. Translated by Donald Attwater. London: Sheed and Ward, 1934.

———. *The Truth about Thérèse*. Translated by Donald Attwater. Manchester, NH: Sophia Institute, 2011.

Gough, Paul. *Brothers in Arms: John and Paul Nash and the Aftermath of the Great War*. Bristol: Sansom, 2014.

Griffiths, Paul, "Thérèse: A Saint in Hell." *The Musical Times* 120 (1979) 814–16.

Guite, Malcolm. *Faith, Hope and Poetry. Theology and the Poetic Imagination*. Farnham, UK: Ashgate, 2012.

Haenchen, Ernst. *The Acts of the Apostles*. Translated by Bernard Boble, Gerald Shinn, and R. McL. Wilson. Oxford: Blackwell, 1971.

Hahn, Scott W. *Covenant and Communion. The Biblical Theology of Pope Benedict XVI*. London: Darton, Longman & Todd, 2009.

Harding, D. W. "Little Gidding." In *T.S. Eliot. A Collection of Critical Essays*, edited by Hugh Kenner, 125–28. Englewood Cliffs, NJ: Prentice-Hall, 1962.

Hardy, Thomas. *Collected Poems*. London: Macmillan, 1919.

———. *The Complete Poems. The New Wessex Edition*. Edited by James Gibson. London: Macmillan, 1967.

———. *Satires of Circumstance: Lyrics and Reveries*. London: Macmillan, 1914.

Hartshorne, Charles. *The Logic of Perfection*. LaSalle, IL: Open Court, 1962.

Hawking, Stephen. *A Brief History of Time*. London: Transworld, 1988.

Haydon, Geoffrey. *John Tavener: Glimpses of Paradise*. London: Victor Gollancz, 1995.

Haymes, Brian. "The Communion of Saints." *Baptist Quarterly* 49 (2018) 50–60.

———. "Covenant and the Church's Mission." In *Bound to Love: The Covenant Basis of Baptist Life ansd Mission*, by Paul S. Fiddes et al., 63–75. London: Baptist Publications, 1985.

Haymes, Brian, et al. *On Being the Church. Revisioning Baptist Identity*. Carlisle, UK: Paternoster, 2008.

Heidegger, Martin. *Being and Time*. Translated by John Macquarrie and Edward Robinson. Oxford: Basil Blackwell, 1978.

Hinton, J. H. *Memoir of William Knibb*. London: Houlston and Stoneman, 1849.

Jaeger, A. J. *The Dream of Gerontius. John Henry Newman and Edward Elgar. Analytical and Descriptive Notes*. London: Novello, 1974.

Jasper, David. *The Sacred Desert: Religion, Literature, Art and Culture*. Oxford: Blackwell, 2004.

Jenkins, David Fraser. *Paul Nash: the Elements*. London: Scala, 2010.

John of the Cross, Saint. *Dark Night of the Soul*. Translated by E. Allison Peers. New York: Dover, 2003.

Johnson, Elizabeth A. *Ask the Beasts. Darwin and the God of Love*. London: Bloomsbury, 2014.

———. *Friends of God and Prophets. A Feminist Theological Reading of the Communion of Saints*. London: SCM, 1998.

Joyce, James. *Ulysses*. London: The Bodley Head, 1969.

Kandinsky, Wassily. *Concerning the Spiritual in Art*. Translated by M. T. H. Sadler. New York: Dover, 1914.

Kapolyo, Joe. "An Inheritance Kept in Heaven." Sermon on 1 Peter 1:1-3, delivered at the Baptist Assembly, Brighton, May 4, 2008. London: Baptist Union of Great Britain, 2008.

Kasper, Cardinal Walter. *Harvesting the Fruits: Basic Aspects of Christian Faith in Ecumenical Dialogue*. London: Continuum, 2009.

Kidd, Richard, ed. *Something to Declare: A Study of the Declaration of Principle*. Oxford: Whitley Publications, 1996.

Kidd, Richard, and Graham Sparkes. *God and the Art of Seeing: Visual Resources for a Journey of Faith*. Oxford: Regent's Park College; Macon, GA: Smyth & Helwys, 2003.

Kierkegaard, Søren. *Fear and Trembling and Repetition*. Edited and translated by Howard V. Hong and Edna H. Hong. Princeton: Princeton University Press, 1983.

King, James. *Interior Landscapes: a Life of Paul Nash*. London: Weidenfeld & Nicolson, 1987.

Levin, Harry, ed. *The Essential James Joyce*. London: Jonathan Cape, 1969.

Limouris, Gennadios. *Icons: Windows on Eternity*. Faith and Order Paper 147. Geneva: WCC, 1990.

Lothe, Jakob. "Authority, Reliability and the Challenge of Reading." In *Narrative Ethics*, edited by Jakob Lothe and Jeremy Hawthorn, 104–9. Amsterdam: Rodopi, 2013.

———. *Narrative in Fiction and Film. An Introduction*. Oxford: Oxford University Press, 2000.

Macquarrie, John. *In Search of Humanity*. London: SCM, 1982.

McCarthy, David Matzko. *Sharing God's Good Company. A Theology of the Communion of Saints*. Grand Rapids: Eerdmans, 2012.

McCormack, Bruce L. *Karl Barth's Critically Realistic Dialectical Theology. Its Genius and Development 1909–1936*. Oxford: Oxford University Press, 1995.

McDermott, Pamela. "The Requiem Reinvented: Brahms's *Ein Deutsches Requiem* and the Transformation from Literal to Symbolic." Doctor of Musical Arts diss., University of North Carolina at Greensboro, 2010.

McGilchrist, Ian. *The Master and His Emissary: the Divided Brain and Making of the Western World*. New Haven, CT: Yale University Press, 2009.

McGuire, Charles E. "One Story, Two Visions. Textual Differences between Elgar's and Newman's *The Dream of Gerontius*." In *The Best of Me: A Centenary Gerontius Companion*, edited by Geoffrey Hodgkins, 84–101. Rickmansworth: Elgar, 1999.

McLarnon, Gerald. *Thérèse, An Opera in One Act*. Music by John Tavener. London: Chester Music, 1979.

McVeagh, Diana. "The Making of Gerontius." *Words on Music: Essays in Honor of Andrew Porter on the Occasion of his 75th Birthday*, edited by David Rosen and Claire Brook, 207–24. Hillsdale, NY: Pendragon, 2003.

Meester, Conrad de, OCD. *With Empty Hands; The Message of St. Thérèse of Lisieux*. New rev. ed. London: Burns and Oates, 2002.

Merleau-Ponty, Maurice. *Phenomenology of Perception*. Translated by Donald A. Landes. London: Routledge, 2012.

Minear, Paul. *Death Set to Music: Masterworks by Bach, Brahms, Pendericki, Bernstein*. Atlanta: John Knox, 1987.

Moltmann, Jürgen. *The Spirit of Life. A Universal Affirmation*. Translated by Margaret Kohl. London: SCM, 1992.

———. *The Way of Jesus Christ. Christology in Messianic Dimensions*. Translated by Margaret Kohl. London: SCM, 1990.

Mott, Michael, *The Seven Mountains of Thomas Merton*. Boston: Houghton Mifflin, 1984.

Müller, Max. *Physical Religion*. Gifford Lectures 2. London: Longman, Green & Co., 1891.

Musgrave, Michael. *Brahms: A German Requiem*. Cambridge Music Handbooks. Cambridge: Cambridge University Press, 1996.

Nash, Paul. *Outline: an Autobiography*. London: Lund Humphries, 2016.

Nevin, Thomas R. *The Last Years of Saint Thérèse: Doubt and Darkness, 1895-1897*. Oxford: Oxford University Press, 2013.

———. *Thérèse of Lisieux; God's Gentle Warrior*. Oxford: Oxford University Press, 2006.

Nuttall, Geoffrey F. *Visible Saints: The Congregational Way, 1640–1660*. Oxford: Basil Blackwell, 1957.

Orthodox Creed, Or A Protestant Confession of Faith, Being an Essay to Unite and Confirm all True Protestants in the Fundamental Articles of the Christian Religion, Against the Errors and Heresies of Rome, An. In *Baptist Confessions of Faith*, edited by William L. Lumpkin, 297–334. Chicago: Judson, 1959.

Otto, Rudolph. *The Idea of the Holy*. Translated by John W. Harvey. London: Oxford University Press, 1928.

Pannenberg, Wolfhart. *Systematic Theology, Volume 2*. Translated by G. W. Bromiley. Edinburgh: T. & T. Clark, 1994.

Perham, Michael. *The Communion of Saints: An examination of the place of The Christian dead in the belief, worship, and calendars of the Church*. London: Alcuin Club/SPCK, 1983.

Phillips, Glenn, and Thomas Crow. *Seeing Rothko*. Los Angeles: Getty, 2005.

Piaget, Jean. *The Construction of Reality in the Child*. New York: International University Press, 1954.
Pinnock, Clark, *Flame of Love: A Theology of the Holy Spirit*. Downers Grove, IL: InterVarsity, 1996.
Polanyi, Michael. *Personal Knowledge: Towards a Post-Critical Philosophy*. New ed. London: Routledge, 1998.
Rahner, Karl. *Foundations of Christian Faith: An Introduction to the Idea of Christianity*. Translated by W. V. Dych. London: Darton, Longman and Todd, 1978.
———. "The Hiddenness of God." In *Theological Investigations, Volume 16, Experience of the Spirit: Source of Theology*, by Karl Rainer, 227–43. London: Darton, Longman and Todd, 1979.
———. *On The Theology of Death*. Freiburg: Herder; London: Burns and Oates, 1964.
Ratzinger, Joseph Cardinal. *Called to Communion. Understanding the Church Today*. Translated by Adrian Walker. San Francisco: Ignatius, 1996.
———. *Many Religions, One Covenant: Israel, the Church and the World*. Translated by Graham Harrison. San Francisco: Ignatius, 1999.
———. *Pilgrim Fellowship of Faith: The Church as Communion*. Edited by Stephan Otto Horn and Vinzenz Pfnür. Translated by Henry Taylor. San Francisco: Ignatius, 2005.
———. "Revelation and Tradition." In *Revelation and Tradition*, by Karl Rahner and Joseph Ratzinger, 26–49. New York: Herder and Herder, 1966.
Robinson, Henry Wheeler. *Life and Faith of the Baptists*. London: Methuen, 1927.
Robinson, Marilynne. *The Givenness of Things*. London: Virago, 2015.
Rothko, Mark. *Writings on Art*. New Haven, CT: Yale University Press, 2006.
Ruether, Rosemary Radford. *Gaia and God: An Ecofeminist Theology of Earth Healing*. San Francisco: HarperCollins, 1992.
Ryle, Gilbert. *The Concept of Mind*. London: Hutchison, 1949.
Sartre, Jean-Paul. *Being and Nothingness*. Translated by Hazel E. Barnes. London: Routledge, 2003.
Scott, Nathan A., Jr. "The Literary Imagination and the Victorian Crisis of Faith: The Example of Thomas Hardy." *Journal of Religion* 40 (1960) 267–81.
Sharrock, Roger. "'When at the first I took my Pen in hand': Bunyan and the Book." In *John Bunyan: Conventicle and Parnassus*, edited by N. H. Keeble, 71–90. Oxford: Clarendon, 1988.
Sinigalia, Tereza and Oliviu Boldura. *Medieval Monuments of Bukovina*. Translated by Diaba Corina Paris. Romania: ACS, 2015.
Six, Jean-François. *Light of the Night: The Last Eighteen Months in the life of Thérèse of Lisieux*. Translated by John Bowden. London: SCM, 1996.
Smyth, John. *Paralleles, Censures, Observations*. In *The Works of John Smith, Volume 2*, edited by W. T. Whitley, 327–562. Cambridge: Cambridge University Press, 1915.
———. *Principles and Inferences Concerning the Visible Church (1607)*. In *The Works of John Smith, Volume 1*, edited by W. T. Whitley, 249–68. Cambridge: Cambridge University Press, 1915.
Stanley, Brian. *The History of the Baptist Missionary Society 1792–1992*. Edinburgh: T. & T. Clark 1992.
Tavener, John. *The Music of Silence: A Composer's Testament*, edited by Brian Keeble. London: Faber & Faber, 1999.

Thérèse of Lisieux, Saint. *Collected Poems of St Thérèse of Lisieux*. Rev. ed. Translated by Alan Bancroft. Leominster: Gracewing, 2001.
———. *Letters of Thérèse of Lisieux, Volume 2, 1890–1897*. Translated by John Clarke, OCD. Washinton, DC: ICS Publications, 1988.
———. *St Thérèse of Lisieux. Her Last Conversations*. Washington, DC: ICS Publications, 1977.
———. *Thérèse, Story of a Soul: The Autobiography of St.Thérèse of Lisieux*. Translated by John Clarke, OCD. Washington, DC: ICS Publications, 1996.
Thomas, R. S. *Collected Poems: 1945–1990*. London: Phoenix, 1995.
Tillich, Paul. *Systematic Theology. Combined Volume*. London: James Nisbet, 1968.
———. *Theology of Culture*, edited by R.C. Kimball. New York: Oxford University Press, 1959.
Tomalin, Claire. *Thomas Hardy: The Time-Torn Man*. London: Penguin, 2006.
Tovey, Donald Francis. *Essays in Musical Analysis: Volume 5, Vocal Music*. London: Oxford University Press, 1968.
Tuck, Patrick. "Brahm's *Ein Deutsches Requiem*: Dialectic and the Chromatic Middle Ground." PhD diss., Louisiana State University and Agricultural and Mechanical College School of Music, 2007.
Tugwell, Simon. *Human Immortality*. London: Darton, Longman and Todd, 1972.
Turner, Daniel. *A Compendium of Social Religion, or the Nature and Constitution of Christian Churches, with the Respective Qualifications and Duties of their Officers and Members . . . Designed as an Essay towards reviving the primitive Spirit of Evangelical Purity, Liberty, and Charity, in the Churches of the Present Times*. London: John Ward, 1758.
Turner, Denys. "Apophaticism, Idolatry and the Claims of Reason." In *Silence and the Word: Negative Theology and Incarnation*, edited by Oliver Davies and Denys Turner, 11–34. Cambridge: Cambridge University Press, 2002.
———. *Charity the Bond of Perfection: A Sermon, The Substance of which was Preached at Oxford, November 16, 1780*. Oxford: 1780.
Udris, John. *Holy Daring: The Fearless Trust of St Thérèse of Lisieux*. London: Gracewing, 1997.
Ulanov, Ann Belford. "Religious Devotion or Masochism?—A Psychoanalyst looks at Thérèse." In *Carmelite Studies: Experiencing St Thérèse Today*, edited by John Sullivan, 140–56. Washington, DC: ICS Publications, 1990.
Walzl, Florence L. "Gabriel and Michael. The Conclusion of 'The Dead.'" In *Dubliners: Text, Criticism and Notes*, edited by Robert Scholes and A. Walton Litz, 423–44. New York: Viking, 1975.
Weil, Simone. *Gravity and Grace*. Translated by Emma Craufurd. London: Routledge and Kegan Paul, 1952.
Weiss, Jeffrey, ed. *Mark Rothko*. New Haven, CT: Yale University Press, 1998.
White, B. R. *The English Separatist Tradition: From the Marian Martyrs to the Pilgrim Fathers*. Oxford: Oxford University Press, 1971.
Williams, Rowan. *The Edge of Words: God and the Habits of Language*. London: Bloomsbury, 2014.
Wilson, Edward O. *Biophilia*. Cambridge, MA: Harvard University Press, 1984.
The Word of God in the Life of the Church: A Report of International Conversations between The Catholic Church and the Baptist World Alliance 2006-2010. American Baptist Quarterly 31 (2012) 28–122.

Wright, N. T., and James Langton. *The Day the Revolution Began: Rethinking the Meaning of Jesus' Crucifixion*. London: SPCK, 2016.

Wyschogrod, Edith. *Saints and Postmodernism: Revisioning Moral Philosophy*. Chicago: University of Chicago Press, 1990.

Yarnell, Malcolm B., III. "The Covenant Theology of the Early Anabaptists, 1525–1527." In *The Fourth Strand of the Reformation*, edited by Paul S. Fiddes, 19–70. Oxford: Centre for Baptist History and Heritage, 2018.

Young, Percy M. *Elgar, Newman and the Dream of Gerontius: in the Tradition of English Catholicism*. Aldershot, Hants, England: Scolar, 1995.

Zizioulas, John D. *Being as Communion: Studies in Personhood and the Church*. London: Darton, Longman and Todd, 1985.

Index

Abraham and Isaac, 57–58, 73, 177
absence, 2–6, 36, 49, 72–74, 98, 144–49, 150, 151, 156, 171
    absent presence, 3, 15, 19, 35, 50, 76, 148, 164
Acts, Book of, xiii, 133, 162
Addicot, Leonard, 135, 136
Amos, Prophecy of, 162
Anfam, David, 52n3, 66
Anglicanism, 9, 12, 14, 21, 122–24, 179
apophasis, 63, 68, 72, 147–49, 156, 174, 177
Aquinas, Thomas, St, 19, 20n58, 110, 118, 175
Armstrong, Tim, 6n19
Augustine, 15, 19, 21, 32–34, 110, 172n31
authorship, 10, 62, 130
Avebury Ring, 36

Balthasar, Hans Urs von, 118
baptism, x, 18, 77, 128, 155, 160, 162, 176
Baptist Missionary Society, 135–36
Baptists, ix, x, xii–xiii, 2, 18, 64, 77, 122, 124, 125–27, 129n7, 133, 134, 135–36, 138–39, 152–55, 159–61, 164, 167
Barth, Karl, 160, 161n9
beauty, 6, 7, 35, 40, 42–43, 45, 49, 80, 91, 94n66, 112, 113, 131
Begbie, Jeremy, 118n29

Berger, John, 25n7
biophilia, 44–45
Blakeborough, Eric, 135, 136
Boars Hill, 46, 48
body, xi, 2, 30–31, 39, 77–78, 83, 109–10, 113–14, 123, 125–26, 127, 130–31, 136–37, 151, 163, 165–66, 169, 171–72, 174, 175–76
Boldura, Oliviu, ixn1
Bonhoeffer, Dietrich, 100, 101n77
Borchardt-Hume, Achim, 54n7, 67n27, 75n37
Bradford, William, x
Brahms, Johannes, 110–13, 115–20, 141, 145, 168, 170
Breslin, James, 56n11
Brett, Mark, 161
Brown, David, 1, 37, 162
Browne, Robert, 159–60
Brownson, Orestes, 175
Bullen, J.B., 3n5, 4
Bunyan, John, 135
Burrage, Champlin, 180n66
Burrus, Virginia, 171–75

Carballo, Robert, 113n18
Casti, John L., 29n18
Causey, Andrew, 24–25, 36, 40n45, 48
Cézanne, Paul, 49
Chambers, Emma, 24n5, 163n15
chaos, 43, 131

189

church, ix, x, xi–xii, xiii, 6, 12, 18, 19, 36, 70, 77, 78, 83–84, 89, 90, 98, 100–101, 103, 104, 107, 109, 110, 114, 123, 124–25, 127–28, 133–34, 138, 141, 152–55, 158, 159–61, 162, 166, 175, 176, 180
communication, 9, 12–16, 17, 21, 31, 49, 151, 170, 172–73, 175, 177–80
communion, ix, xi–xii, 2–3, 5, 8–9, 15–16, 18, 20–22, 23, 24, 25, 35–36, 37, 40, 41–42, 44, 47, 49, 50, 51, 56, 60, 61, 63, 64, 67, 69, 71–72, 76, 77–78, 98, 101, 103, 108, 122, 123–25, 127–28, 132–39, 141, 143, 145–47, 149, 152–56, 157–62, 164–69, 171–80
companionship, 21, 158, 169, 171, 177, 179
complexity, 18, 23, 53, 61, 65, 75, 141
Compton, Michael, 54–55, 56n10, 65
configuration, 31, 41, 42, 43, 49, 52, 56, 74
Congregationalists, ix, x, 134, 135
connectedness, ix, xi, 8–9, 19, 20, 23–25, 30, 34, 36–37, 41, 42, 44, 45, 47, 48, 50, 118–19, 129–30, 131–32, 134, 136, 138–9, 141, 144, 146, 147, 158, 164, 169, 170, 175, 176, 179
covenant, 11
    and communion of saints, 18–19, 77, 123, 161–62, 167–68, 177, 179, 180
    diversity of, 162, 165
    ecclesiology of, ix–xi, xiii, 2, 101, 128, 134–35, 153–54, 159–61, 166
creation, xi, 18, 101, 113–15, 118, 119, 125, 128–31, 134, 152, 161, 162, 168, 173, 177
    new creation, 110, 115, 126–7, 136–37, 165–66, 168, 174, 176
creativity, xi, xii, xiii, 2, 10, 16, 17, 29, 48–49, 55, 62, 71, 74, 91–92, 109, 128–28, 131–32, 134, 136, 148, 149, 155–56, 162, 163, 171, 177–80.
Cross, Anthony R., 129n7

Crow, Thomas, 74n35
dark night, 81, 83, 147, 148, 149, 151, 159
Davis, Stephen T., 110n11
Dawkins, Richard, 28
De Kooning, Willem, 52
Dean, Winton, 93n60
death, xi, xiii, 2, 4, 6, 7, 12, 14–15, 18, 19, 20, 48, 50, 57, 58, 76, 77–78, 80, 81, 83, 87–90, 91, 93, 98, 99–100, 101, 104, 108–11, 113–15, 117–19, 122–24, 127–29, 133, 136–37, 143, 145, 148, 149–50, 151, 158–59, 164, 167–76, 178–79
DePauli Werner, 29n18
depth of field, 47–48
Derrida, Jacques, 172n30
desire, 7–8, 57, 68, 81, 89, 102, 107, 110, 119, 132, 135, 151, 164, 169, 172,
doctrine, xii, 16–18, 109, 110, 128, 132, 134, 157, 178
Donofrio, Beverly, 172
Dreyer, Elizabeth A., 89
dualism, xi, xii, 25, 26, 28, 55, 60, 61, 113–14, 125–32, 134, 137, 139, 144, 159, 164, 166, 174, 175–76
Dudgeon, Piers, 90n49, 91
dwelling, *see*: God, dwelling in
Dymchurch, 36

ecclesiology, *see*: covenant, ecclesiology of
Einstein, A., 30
Elgar, Edward
    The Dream of Gerontius, 104–10, 111, 114, 117, 120, 141, 145, 168, 169, 170
Eliot, T. S., 18, 21–22, 145, 146, 179
    "Little Gidding", 11–16, 178
    "Burnt Norton", 118
    The Waste Land, 1–2, 11, 21
Ellmann, Richard, 9–10
embodiment, 13, 18, 30, 130–31, 135, 136, 166, 175
empathy, 118, 155–56, 159, 166, 167
eroticism, 69, 171–72

eternity, 15, 65, 92, 157, 163–64
Eucharist, 64, 88, 122–8, 139, 165–66
expressionism, 52–53

Fibonacci, 42
Fiddes, Paul S., ixn2, xin5, xiiin9, 2n3,
    15n45, 16n48, 18n53, 19n56,
    23n1n2, 29n19, 31n28, 34n36,
    44n48, 77n1, 78n2, 114n21,
    119n30, 130, 132, 133n15, 134,
    137–38, 141, 143n4, 145–46,
    153–54, 159n4, 161n9n10,
    170n24, 171n27
figuration, 35, 38, 48–49, 66, 76, 146,
    163
Fontana, Lucio, 58n15
form, xiii, 13, 26–27, 32, 38, 39, 41,
    42–44, 45, 49, 53, 54, 57, 68,
    71, 135, 136, 139, 141, 145, 146,
    163, 175, 177, 179
Four Seasons Restaurant, 54, 55, 56
Fowler, Stanley, 129n7
Frazer, James, 21, 48
freedom, 9, 13, 16, 17, 56, 58n15, 99,
    114, 129, 130, 131, 136, 139, 155
Freeman, Curtis W., 135n17n19
funerals, 84, 91, 95, 122, 123–24, 127–
    28, 151, 164–65, 166
Furlong, Monica, 79n9

Gaucher, Guy, 79, 90
Geach, Peter, 110n9
Ghéon, Henri, 138n26
Gifford, Emma, 4–5
gift, xi, xii, 49, 77, 83, 92, 113, 123, 125,
    128, 133, 134, 139, 141, 142,
    154–56, 179
God, as triune
    dwelling in, xi, 19, 20, 99, 110–17,
        118–21, 145, 168, 170, 177
    mystery of, 16, 17, 20, 113, 117, 143,
        145, 148, 153, 154, 156, 158,
        164, 168, 170, 177, 179
    as relations, xii, 16, 19–20, 115, 119,
        120, 130, 161, 162, 175, 177, 180
Gödel, Kurt, 143
Gottlieb, Adolph, 53
Gough, Paul, 38

Goupil Gallery, 37
Graham, Kenneth, 36
Griffiths, Paul, 92n59
Guite, Malcolm, 6, 7

Haenchen, Ernst, 162n12
Handel, George Frederick, 111, 116n24
Harding, D. W., 12n35, 13, 16
Hartshorne, Charles, 18n54
Hawking, Stephen, 142n2
Haydon, Geoffrey, 90n49, 92n57
Haymes, Brian, 101n78, 139n28, 149–
    51, 158, 161n10
Heaney, Seamus, 6
heaven, xiii, 81, 83, 85, 88, 89, 93, 94, 96,
    98, 99, 101, 108, 109, 112, 120,
    125, 126, 129, 133, 134, 138,
    154, 159, 164, 166, 170, 173
Hebrews, Book of, 108–9, 115, 117, 120,
    170–1
Heidegger, Martin, 164–68, 179
Heisenberg, Werner, 143
Herbert, George, 12
hiddenness, 12, 72, 140–56, 164
Hinton, J.H., 136n21
history, 12, 13, 15, 118, 125, 128, 129,
    132, 134, 142, 152, 153, 162,
    172, 175, 180
hope, xi, 13, 20, 22, 27, 34, 37, 40–41,
    43, 45, 48, 50, 57, 65, 73, 76, 81,
    82, 102, 114, 115, 123, 124, 125,
    138, 143, 145, 146, 155, 156,
    166, 167, 173, 174, 178
Husserl, Edmund, 28
hypostasis, 19, 176

icons, 9, 63, 65, 76, 99
imagination, xii, xiii, 2, 4, 11, 16, 17, 20,
    21, 22, 39, 46, 48–49, 50, 53, 60,
    65, 67, 72, 73, 76, 82, 103, 113,
    118, 129, 132, 140–42, 143, 144,
    145–46, 155, 156, 168, 170, 177,
    179
infinite, the, 16, 17, 47, 143
interconnectedness, see: connectedness
invisible, the, 52, 113, 152–55, 163, 165,
    178

Isaiah, Prophecy of, 87, 95n70, 129, 131, 156, 162

Jaegar, A.J., 104–8, 114
Jasper, David, 171
Jenkins, David Fraser, 24n5
Jesus Christ, 102, 153–54, 164
  body of, 101, 135, 139
  and creation, 134, 152, 166
  crucifixion of, 1, 21, 86, 91, 97
  as high priest, 108–9, 120, 170–71
  humanity of, 100, 129, 175
  living in, 77–8, 89, 98, 103, 121, 123, 128, 136–37, 167–68
  and love, 92, 93, 96, 99, 100, 107, 125, 131, 151, 167
  and new covenant, ix, xii, 160–61
  praying with, xiii, 21, 86, 120–21, 166
  resurrection of, 18, 94
Job, Book of, 87
John, Gospel of, 86, 111, 128, 134
John of the Cross, Saint, 91, 100, 148–50, 156
Johnson, Elizabeth A., 54, 173–76
journey, 1, 4, 9, 15, 24, 56, 69, 93, 94–96, 97, 99, 104–10, 111, 113–17, 118, 120, 121, 135, 145, 148, 158, 161, 162, 163–65, 167–68, 169, 170, 177, 178, 179, 180
Joyce, James, 15, 16, 18, 132, 138, 145
  "The Dead" (*Dubliners*), 7–11, 19–20, 178–79
  Ulysses, 20
judgement, 104, 107, 108, 110

Kandinsky, Wassily, 59
Kant, Emmanuel, 32
Kapolyo, Joe, 137
Kasper, Cardinal Walter, xiin6
kataphasis, 63, 147, 177
Kensington Gardens, 27, 34–35
Kess, Rhonda, 97
Kidd, Richard, 24n3, 47n53, 131–32, 157–59, 163–66, 179
Kierkegaard, Søren, 56–58, 74
King, James, 48n54
Klein, Frank, 52

Knibb, William, 135–36
koinonia, xii, xiii

Langton, James, 126n3
Laurentian Library, 65
Levin, Henry, 7n21, 8n22n, 23n25, 9n26, 11n31
liberation theology, 174
Limouris, Gennadios, 65n22
Lothe, Jakob, 10n30, 11
love, xi, 2, 4, 5, 7, 8–9, 14, 16, 18, 20, 21, 27, 39, 44, 50, 77, 78, 80, 82, 83–4, 85, 87, 88, 98, 101, 113, 119, 120–21, 128, 130, 133, 136, 138, 149–50, 153, 162, 164, 165, 170, 173, 175, 176, 177, 179; *see also* Jesus Christ, and love
Luke, Gospel of, 131
Lynch, Fr. Malarchy, 91

Macleod, George, 25n8
Macquarrie, John, 58n15
Mary of Magdala, 86
Mary, Mother of Jesus, 88, 107, 120, 123, 165, 172
materiality, xi, xii, 25, 41–42, 48, 55, 60–62, 65, 67, 74, 76, 126, 128–30, 131, 132, 134, 136, 147, 157, 158, 162, 165, 166, 169, 171, 175, 179, 180
Maximus the Confessor, 118
McCarthy, David Matzko, 169, 171n25, 172–77
McCormack, Bruce L., 161n9
McDermott, Pamela, 112n16, 115n22, 116n25
McGilchrist, Ian, 28n13
McGuire, Charles E., 108, 114
McLarnon, Ger
McLarnon, Gerald, 150
McVeagh, Diana, 110
Meester, Conrad de, 79n7
memory
  of God, 18n54, 115
  of human beings, xi, 3–4, 7, 8, 23–24, 25, 27, 29–31, 33, 42, 50, 85, 89, 132, 145, 158
Mennonites, ix, xi

Merleau-Ponty, Maurice, 27–35, 41, 48–49, 166
Merton, Thomas, 137–38
metaphor, 16–18, 19, 20, 24, 32, 44, 49, 52, 60, 65, 83, 130, 143–46, 155, 156, 174, 177
Michelangelo, 65
Minear, Paul, 113, 119
minimalism, 51, 54, 58, 62, 63, 71
modernism, 13–14, 15, 28
modernity, 21
Moltmann, Jürgen, 118, 129
Monet, Claude, 59
mortality, 2, 6, 22, 57, 58, 113; *see also* death
Mott, Michael, 137n25
movement, 17, 19, 43, 53n4, 64, 104, 107, 117, 118–20, 162, 167, 168, 169, 177
Müller, Max, 3
Munch, Edward, 59
Musgrave, Michael, 111n14, 119
mutuality, xiii, 9, 15, 44, 103, 119, 147, 158, 159, 160, 162, 166, 168–69, 170, 172–73, 177, 179–80
mystery, 17, 26–27, 28, 29–30, 31, 35, 36, 50, 60, 61, 71n28, 72, 131, 143, 144, 145, 157–58, 163, 172, 178; *also see*: God, as triune, mystery of

narrative, 10, 16–18, 21, 35, 36, 98, 108, 134, 171, 179
Nash, Margaret, 25n6, 26, 40, 50
Nash, Paul, 23–50, 52, 131, 146, 157, 158, 163, 164, 168
Neoplatonism, 70
Nevin, Thomas R., 79n7, 80n11, 87n35, 100n76, 101, 102n81
New Road Baptist Church, Oxford, 153–4
Newman, Barnett, 52
Newman, Cardinal John Henry, 104, 107–10, 113–14, 117, 120, 168, 169, 170
non-being, *see*: nothingness
nothingness, 53, 59, 69–73, 85, 89, 93, 101, 157

meontic being, 70, 72, 73n34
oukontic being, 70, 72, 73
Nuttall, Geoffrey F., 135n16
objectivity, 28, 48
Orthodox Church, ix, xi, 65, 91, 92, 98
Orthodox Creed, 135n16, 155
Otto, Rudolph, 36

Painted monasteries, ix, xiii
Pannenberg, Wolfhart, 118
Parfitt, Graeme and Susan, 122–3, 151
participation, 14, 17, 18–20, 63, 84, 89, 98, 99, 100, 119–20, 124, 127–28, 130, 144, 156, 157–59, 162, 166–67, 169, 175–77
Passchendaele, 38
patronage, 173–4
Paul, the Apostle, 70, 73, 77, 83, 114, 115, 120, 127, 133, 134
Pentecost, 11–12, 14
Perham, Michael, 162, 168, 169n20, 175
Peter, Letters of, 125, 133, 137
phenomenology, 27–31, 32n29, 35, 41–42, 48–49
phi, 41–42
Phillips, Glenn, 74n35
Piaget, Jean, 140n1
Picasso, Pablo, 59
pilgrimage, 4, 19, 25, 169
Pinnock, Clark, 129
place, 62, 65, 68, 72, 84, 89, 100, 127–28, 132, 136, 146, 158, 163, 169, 177
  in Brahms, 112–19, 170
  in Thomas Hardy, 2–7, 19, 164
  in T. S. Eliot, 12, 13, 15, 178
  in Paul Nash, 25–27, 31, 34–41, 44, 50, 157
  genius loci, 5, 25, 34–35, 163
Platonism, 2, 15, 113, 126
Polanyi, Michael, 28n17
Pollock, Jackson, 52, 53, 67
portal, 60, 64, 66–68, 71n28, 76, 146, 163
postmodernism, 173
power, 30, 37, 40, 41, 42, 64, 65, 68, 77, 85, 134, 140, 142, 143, 146, 151, 173–75
Pratt Institute, 51–52, 56–57

prayer, 12, 63, 68, 69, 81, 85, 99, 104, 120, 123, 131n12, 147–48, 178, 180
prayer *(continued)*
    for the saints, 107–8, 109, 111, 162, 166, 168, 179
    of the saints, 15, 86, 100, 121, 159, 166, 168, 173, 175, 177
    with the saints, xi, xiii, 14–15, 16, 21–22, 103, 118–19, 120, 137, 146, 159, 162, 164, 169, 170–72, 174
presence, 1, 3–5, 6, 8, 15, 18–20, 32, 35–36, 38, 39–40, 42, 44, 47, 49, 50, 66, 69, 70–73, 76, 106–7, 108, 109, 120, 125, 131, 146, 147, 148, 151–52, 156, 163, 164–65, 169, 171, 173, 177
Priestly school, 161
Psalms, 69, 70, 112, 117, 132, 134, 156
Psychosomatic unity, 18, 42, 65, 114

quantum, 61

Rahner, Karl, 17, 142, 143n3, 175–76
Ratzinger, Cardinal Joseph, xiiin8n9
reductionism, 28–29
Reid, Norman, 56
Reinthaler, Carl Martin, 111
relationships
    between persons and things, 18, 19, 27, 28, 30, 32, 57, 71, 84, 138, 141, 147–48, 161, 162, 169, 173
    between God and the world, xii, 18, 110, 115, 119, 130, 131, 136, 143, 161, 162, 175
relics, 100, 169
requiem, 91, 92, 109, 110–21, 122–24, 127, 139, 151, 164, 165, 166, 168, 170
resurrection, 11, 18, 21, 101, 109–10, 114–15, 118, 124–25, 126, 131, 136, 137, 156, 170, 174, 176
revelation, 17–18, 20, 71, 114, 129, 130–31, 138, 156
Revelation, Book of, 116, 129, 156
rhythm, 105, 106, 111, 112, 115, 116, 118, 180

Riley, Bridgit, 63n21
Rimbaud, Arthur, 92, 94–96, 97, 99, 150, 157, 167
Robinson, Marilynne, 60–62
Roman catholicism, xi, xii–xiii, 18n3, 91, 92, 98, 104, 111, 114, 127, 153, 166
Rossetti, Dante Gabriel, 49
Rothko, Mark, 51–76, 132, 146, 157, 158, 163, 164, 166, 168
    Rothko Chapel, 67
    Rothko Room, 59, 62–63, 67
Ruether, Rosemary Radford, 174
Ryle, Gilbert, 130n8

sacrament, 20, 123–24, 125, 126–28, 129, 152, 162, 166, 180
sacred, the, 19, 75, 138, 171
saints, see: communion; prayer
Sartre, Jean-Paul, 69–73
Scott, Nathan A., Jr., 3n4
Separatists, x, 159–60
Sharrock, Roger, 135n18
simultaneity, 15, 30, 47, 61, 69, 117, 118
Sinigalia, Tereza, ixn1
Six, Jean-François, 79n5
Smyth, John, x, 160
sociobiology, 44–45
space, 7, 19, 70–71, 70–73, 100, 112, 113, 126, 127, 145, 157–58, 169, 171, 180
    in Rothko, 54, 58–60, 63–65, 69, 74–76, 157, 163–64
Sparkes, Graham, 24n3, 47n53
Spencer, Stanley, 46
Stanley, Brian, 136n21n22
stillness, 118
story, 1, 8–9, 17, 19, 57, 78, 79, 81, 97, 98, 110, 134, 135, 150, 167, 179
strangeness, 23, 24, 25, 27, 29, 34, 35, 36, 37, 40, 43, 47, 49, 50, 60, 61, 65, 69, 131, 146, 157, 179
suffering, 77, 80, 83, 87, 89–90. 98, 99, 101, 102, 108, 109, 111, 114, 116, 130–31, 138, 149, 150–51, 155, 178
symbol, 9–11, 16–18, 19, 20, 22, 25, 35, 36–37, 38, 39–40, 47–48, 50, 64,

67, 69, 71, 74, 93, 113, 128, 150, 165, 173, 175, 179

Tavener, Sir John, 78, 90–99, 101, 150, 157, 158, 159, 167, 168, 169
Teresa of Avila, Saint, 92, 100
text, 17, 62, 111, 113, 116, 119, 130–31, 171–74, 175, 178, 180
Thekla, Mother, 98
Thérèse of Lisieux
 "Conversion", 80
 death of mother, 80
 difficulties in prayer, 81, 85
 doubt, 89, 95, 97, 149, 150, 159
 illness, 78, 80, 83, 87, 88, 95, 138
 life story, 78
 "Little Flower", 92, 137
 "The Little Way", 82, 85, 99
 Story of a Soul, 79, 86, 137
 view of heaven, 83, 89, 98, 101, 138
 vocation to love, 82–85, 167
Thomas, R. S., 72
Thompson, Philip E., 129n7
Tillich, Paul, 17, 18n54, 73n34
time, 5n15, 11, 12–13, 15, 21–22, 29, 31–34, 37, 42–43, 48, 55, 59, 69, 73, 84, 96, 98, 118, 132, 146–47, 159, 169, 171, 173, 178, 180
timelessness, 12, 15–16, 53, 126, 178
Tolkien, J. R. R., 36
Tomalin, Claire, 3n4

Tovey, Donald Francis, 116n23, 117
transcendence, 16, 17, 28, 29–30, 31, 40, 50, 54–55, 63, 65, 68, 69, 74, 76, 143, 146, 157, 163–64, 165
Tuck, Patrick, 111n15
Tugwell, Simon, 110
Turner, Daniel, 153–55
Turner, Denys, 147n8

Udris, John, 82n18, 95n69
Ulanov, Ann Belford, 138n27

Van Gogh, Vincent, 59
visible, the, xiii, 35, 47, 48, 90, 113, 134–35, 152–55, 160, 165

Wagner, Richard, 104
Walzl, Florence L., 8n24
Weil, Simone, 131n12
Weiss, Jeffrey, 73n33
White, B. R., 160n7
Williams, Rowan, 28n13, 52
Wilson, Edward O., 44, 45n50
Wright, N. T., 126
Wyschogrod, Edith, 171, 173–75

Yarnell, Malcolm B., xin4
Young, Percy M., 114n19

Zizioulas, John D., 176

www.ingramcontent.com/pod-product-compliance
Lightning Source LLC
Chambersburg PA
CBHW021731220426
43662CB00008B/798